# Homicide

# Homicide

## *A Sociological Explanation*

Leonard Beeghley

ROWMAN & LITTLEFIELD PUBLISHERS, INC.
*Lanham • Boulder • New York • Oxford*

ROWMAN & LITTLEFIELD PUBLISHERS, INC.

Published in the United States of America
by Rowman & Littlefield Publishers, Inc.
A wholly owned subsidary of The Rowman & Littlefield Publishing Group, Inc.
4501 Forbes Boulevard, Suite 200, Lanham, Maryland 20706
www.rowmanlittlefield.com

Estover Road, Plymouth PL6 7PY, United Kingdom

British Library Cataloguing in Publication Information Available

**Library of Congress Cataloging-in-Publication Data**

Beeghley, Leonard.
   Homicide : a sociological explanation / Leonard Beeghley.
      p.   cm.
   ISBN 0-8476-9472-0 (cloth : alk. paper)—ISBN 0-8476-9473-9 (pbk. :
alk. paper)
      1. Homicide—United States.   I. Title.
HV6529.B44   2003
364.15′2′0973—dc21                                        2002154518

Printed in the United States of America

♾ ™ The paper used in this publication meets the minimum requirements of
American National Standard for Information Sciences—Permanence of Paper
for Printed Library Materials, ANSI/NISO Z39.48-1992.

*For my friends and colleagues*
*in the Center for Studies in Criminology and Law,*
*University of Florida.*
*Many thanks.*

# Contents

# Preface

Homicide occurs much more often in the United States than in other Western nations. It can be said with some justification that we are a homicidal society. This fact goes against the pattern of history, which is for societies to become steadily less violent as economic development occurs. For example, throughout the nineteenth and twentieth centuries, at a time when homicide rates in most Western European nations declined to all-time lows (less than one in 100,000 people), American levels of lethal violence remained very high. And this difference has not changed: In some areas, American homicide rates today are higher than those last seen in Europe during medieval times. Murder occurs so often in this country that it is routine, a normal event. This book offers a sociological explanation for this anomaly.

Such an explanation must be synthetic; it must bring together elements from a variety of academic fields and combine them into a coherent whole. This orientation goes against the grain of contemporary scholarly life, which is exceedingly specialized. Thus, in order to gain a firm sense of what it is that must be explained, it is necessary to understand the historical and cross-national dimensions of the problem. In so doing, of course, a sociologist enters the domain of historical and comparative scholars, specialists who inevitably know a great deal more about a particular period or place. Once the dimensions of the homicide problem are clear, it becomes necessary to identify the explanatory variables. Again, a sociologist impinges on specific areas of inquiry about which one's colleagues (especially in criminology, a cognate discipline) know a great deal more. Thus, as my study of homicide progressed I became an intellectual pilgrim, looking into academic fields and areas of specialization with which I was previously unfamiliar.

These difficulties suggest the risks inherent in crossing intellectual boundaries. First, scholars who have spent their professional lives studying a specific subject can easily point out the naïveté of a newcomer's interpretations. Second, and more seriously, there is the danger of the newcomer simply being wrong, of making an error of interpretation or missing a significant variable. But the risks are worth taking.

They are worth taking because the potential benefits are great. The first is personal: One learns a great deal and that is, after all, one of the great pleasures of academic life. The second is scholarly: In an age of specialization, it is important for scholars as well as concerned citizens to draw connections among diverse findings. But this is not an easy task because the complexity of social life often requires a narrow focus if the findings are to be understood. Here is a simple metaphor that illustrates the difficulty. Although specialists studying the characteristics of the trees, bushes, animals, and streams in a forest can provide fundamental insights about each of these topics, the research results inevitably lie scattered among many disciplines. Yet the forest constitutes an ecosystem, and it is important to understand how it functions as a whole. I have found that this "trees and forest problem" characterizes any attempt at understanding and explaining the homicide rate: Many specialists deal with specific aspects of the issue; few try to understand and explain the whole. This is, by the way, a dilemma in all academic disciplines today. The third potential benefit is political: Synthetic efforts are important because after drawing connections it becomes possible to discuss the implications for change. Just as human beings can now determine the nature and fate of ecosystems, we can also affect how social life is organized. Modernity means that fate no longer holds us hostage.

This fact has important implications. Unlike other nations, in this country thousands of people are murdered every year. In fact, any large American city typically endures far more annual homicides than do most Western nations. No one is safe. Every American's life is hostage to the crazy, the immature, and the violent—whether at home, at school, at work, or on vacation. Is this the kind of society in which we wish to live? We can change the social context that generates so much lethal violence.

# Acknowledgments

My friends and colleagues at the University of Florida have been extraordinarily gracious in guiding me through the complexities of the various literatures relevant to understanding the high rate of homicide in America. The dedication only suggests the extent of my gratitude.

Four people read and responded to each chapter as it was written, critically evaluating it, sharing their expertise, and saving me from many mistakes. Throughout the process, Jeffrey Adler taught me about the history of homicide and gave wise council. "My new best friend," Alex Piquero, steered me to sources and taught me what little criminology I have learned. John Cochran and Terry Danner suggested numerous ways to improve the manuscript.

Several others commented on specific chapters as they were written. They include Jack Levin, Karen Parker, Joanne Savage, Jonathan H. Turner, and Judge Larry Turner.

At the end, four people read through the completed manuscript. My friend Mary Anna Evans helped me smooth out the prose. Joseph Spillane offered valuable suggestions and comments. Randolph Roth provided a detailed critique from a historian's point of view. Finally, Steven Messner graciously commented on the text and, in so doing, revealed why he is so well respected in this field.

As he has before, Dean Birkenkamp, vice-president and editor at Rowman & Littlefield, brought his understanding of the academic marketplace to bear on this project. Finally, Jehanne Schweitzer, production editor at Rowman & Littlefield, helped to improve the manuscript as it went through the production process and, most important, put up with me.

This book is better as a result and probably would be better yet, if I had just had the good sense to take more of the advice offered. The usual caveat applies: Any errors that remain are my responsibility.

# 1

# Homicide as a Routine Event

Shortly after midnight on the first day of the new year, a nineteen-year-old African American youth was shot and killed at a nightclub in Gainesville, Florida, where the University of Florida is located. His name was Delvin Darnell Carey. The suspected assailant was a fifteen-year-old youth, also African American. In the local paper the next day, a brief story about the year's "first homicide" reported the event. At this time, the motive for the killing remained unclear—a disagreement perhaps? A week later, a follow-up article detailed the human tragedy that occurs when the surviving relatives and friends of the victim find their lives turned upside down. The story described the alleged assailant as a lifelong friend and next-door neighbor of Mr. Carey. Mutual friends expressed their surprise and ambivalence, family members their shock and outrage. All mourned.

Mr. Carey had dropped out of high school, while his putative assailant attended an alternative school. Both were poor. Like many African American males, both had had previous scrapes with the law, all minor. Although the assailant faced a second-degree murder charge as an adult, neither the state-wide nor the national media picked up the story. It was, after all, only the first murder of the year in a relatively small southern city of nearly 100,000 people. The success or failure of the university's sports teams generates much more interest. Then nothing more was reported, even locally; the subsequent outcome of the case was ignored. By the end of that particular year, there had been eight homicides in the Gainesville area, a rate above that for the nation as a whole. A local police sergeant remarked, more in sorrow than surprise, that all this lethal violence seems "inexplicable."[1]

But are these deaths, whether in this year or any year, really inexplicable? In this book, I offer a sociological account for the peculiarly high American rate of homicide. By *homicide*, I mean the intentional and illegal killing of another human being. This definition excludes killings that are ruled justifi-

1

able, as in self-defense.[2] I use the terms *homicide, murder,* and *lethal violence* as synonyms.

Homicides are of different types. Some occur as attempts at resolving conflicts when the law cannot be used. In illegal drug markets, for example, individual entrepreneurs and organizations cannot settle disputes over sales territory by appealing to the police or the courts. Some homicides take place as by-products of predatory actions. In a robbery, for example, especially when a gun is present, if either the perpetrator or the victim panics then a lethal result may follow. Some homicides reflect disputes between acquaintances, friends, or spouses, often fueled by alcohol. Mr. Carey's murder may be an example. And some homicides are public-place killings with several victims. Although this last type receives a great deal of publicity, it is actually rare. Most homicides resemble Mr. Carey's: They are banal in motive and tragic in consequence. And they are routine.

## WE HAVE A PROBLEM

The shooting of Delvin Darnell Carey was simply the first of the year. This is why the resolution of the case did not seem particularly noteworthy or newsworthy. Both ordinary citizens and the local paper assumed (correctly) that more homicides would follow. None of them would be especially newsworthy either, because similar episodes occur in every city, large and small, in every year. Unless a public-place killing occurs and many people die, a very young person commits murder, or the case displays some other unique qualities, news reports of homicides are sloughed off as part of the background noise that accompanies life in the United States. But the level of carnage in this country is very high. In order to gain some perspective on how high, consider this comparison: More American citizens have been killed by homicide since 1950 than were killed on the battlefield in all the wars this country has ever participated in, including the Gulf War: 789,000 compared to 651,000.[3] During the last half-century, the three years with the highest homicide rates were 1979–1981: The average was 9.9 killings per 100,000 people during each of these years, more than 67,000 human beings. It seems, then, that homicide is a routine event in America, by which I mean that people respond to it as a normal occurrence, as natural, as something that happens every day.

The homicide rate began declining in the 1990s, reaching "only" 6.1 per 100,000 in 1999. This level constitutes a forty-year low. But even this low level remains very high compared to other Western nations. Another comparison: About 47,400 Americans died in battle during the war in Vietnam. All these deaths sparked massive street protests during that time. The United States became a society in turmoil as people tried to end a war and (what they saw as) the needless deaths of American soldiers. But in just three years, 1997–1999, more Americans suffered a murderous assault—50,700—than were killed during the entire eleven years of American presence in Vietnam.[4] Yet because it seems low compared to the recent past, both criminologists and ordinary observers see this huge loss of life due to murder as a pleasant surprise (as I will note later on, it is viewed as a "success"). Hence, even at their current "low" level, homicides like Mr. Carey's and thousands more like it each year—white and black, poor and middle class, young and old—generate no protests, no turmoil. This is because such events constitute a normal part of the social landscape in the United States. Hence, like the police sergeant, Americans feel a sense of helplessness.

Nonetheless, people do respond in a predictable way when something frightening is routine: They display pervasive fear. Americans are afraid of crime, especially violent crime. Fear of crime and violence (the two are seen as linked) is a national obsession.[5] About 40 percent of whites say they are afraid to walk alone near their homes at night. This assertion merits repeating: Four of every ten white people in this country admit to being afraid (at some level) of opening their doors and going for a walk in their own neighborhoods. This is so even though the odds of being killed are relatively low for whites, especially the middle class. Nonetheless, some nut with a gun can open fire on a neighborhood street, or in a restaurant, an office building, or a school, and put everyone at risk. And everyone knows this. Minority people, like the late Mr. Carey, are even more afraid. About 47 percent, nearly half, of African Americans say they are afraid to walk alone near their homes at night.[6] Since African Americans endure a homicide victimization rate of 20.6 per 100,000, compared to a white rate of "only" 3.5, their fear is much more realistic.[7]

In contrast, when Americans visit Europe they are often surprised at how free from danger they feel, how easy it is to wander about without fear for their physical safety. Charles Barkley, a professional basketball player, reacted with wonder at this phenomenon. Although now retired, he played on the "dream team" during the 1992 Olympics in Barcelona, Spain. While there, he traveled about the city, often acting outrageously. If you followed professional basketball during these years, you know that outrageousness was common with "Sir Charles," as he was called. At one point, he exclaimed, "I miss crime and murder. I haven't heard about any good shootings or stabbings lately. There haven't been any brutal stabbings or anything in the last twenty-four hours. I really miss it."[8] In Philadelphia, where Mr. Barkley was playing at the time, 426 murders occurred in 1992. This figure fell in the years that followed, as in most American cities; there were "only" 292 murders in Philadelphia in 1999. Philadelphia has a population of about 1.4 million. In comparison, 73 murders occurred in all of Sweden in 1999.[9] Sweden's population is about 8.9 million. It is common for large American cities to endure far more homicides in any year than do entire European nations.

Although Mr. Barkley's remark contains some hyperbole, a certain truth underlies it. The American rate of homicide is not only high, it is anomalous compared to that of other Western nations. For example, Franklin Zimring and Gordon Hawkins compare Sydney, Australia, and Los Angeles, cities that are almost identical in population size. They show that Sydney displays about 73 percent as many thefts and 111 percent as many burglaries as does Los Angeles, and conclude that the two cities are roughly similar with regard to these and other nonviolent crimes. Sydney, however, displays much less violence, only 13 percent as many robberies and 5 percent as many homicides. In fact, the 1,094 homicides in Los Angeles in 1993 were more than three times the 329 that occurred in all of Australia in that year.[10] Similarly, Professors Zimring and Hawkins also compare New York City and London, showing that the latter has more theft and burglary but far less robbery and homicide. Thus, during the three-year period 1997–1999, New York City had 2,074 homicides, which constituted a forty-year low, compared to 539 in London.[11] This city-level comparison can be generalized to economically developed nations as a group. Professors Zimring and Hawkins summarize the data by observing that these nations' high (or low) crime rates say nothing about their homicide rates.[12] The two vary independently.

A cross-national look at one specific crime suggests this fact. For example, table 1.1 shows the percentage of households that were victimized by burglaries (including attempts) in seven Western nations in 1999. Note that for Americans the odds of someone trying to break into one's home (or even going into the garage to take a bicycle) fall in the midrange compared to other Western nations.

Data on other crimes reveal a similar pattern. For example, victimization surveys show that England and Wales display higher rates of assault, motor vehicle thefts, and (since 1994) robbery than does the United States.[13] These

**Table 1.1. Percentage of Households Victimized by Burglaries, Seven Countries, 1999**

| Country | Percentage |
|---|---|
| England and Wales | 5.2 |
| Canada | 4.4 |
| United States | 3.8 |
| Netherlands | 3.6 |
| Switzerland | 2.7 |
| France | 2.3 |
| Sweden | 2.3 |

*Source:* Barclay (2001:Table 2).

facts suggest, as Professors Zimring and Hawkins emphasize, that despite the public perception that crime and violence are linked, crime is actually not the American problem, not the source of our fear.

Still other crimes, such as pickpocketing and purse snatching, also occur in every Western European city. Crime of all sorts, then, is fairly common. In response, people in other nations counter with practical measures (such as burglar alarms and auto antitheft bars). So do tourists; Americans are typically advised to take precautions to avoid losing their valuables. But neither locals nor tourists fear for their personal safety. This is because homicide is very rare in Europe. At home, however, Americans are afraid. This is because the odds of being victims of lethal violence are far greater. Thus, as Charles Barkley recognized in his own strange way, Americans who travel in Europe feel safer because they are safer.

By contrast, the problem in this country, the real source of people's fear, is not crime but violence—especially lethal violence. The overall rate of 6.1 per 100,000 people translates into 15,500 deaths by homicide in the United States in 1999.[14] Again, this constitutes a forty-year low. Even so, there are about as many deaths from homicide in the United States as from several other factors normally labeled as public health problems, such as drug over-doses (whether from legal or illegal substances).[15] Each year, the National Center for Health Statistics publishes a list of the top ten causes of death in America. Among young persons aged fifteen to twenty-four, homicide is the second leading cause of death, occurring at a rate of 14.8 per 100,000. There are more intentional killings of adolescents and young adults than from all diseases on the top ten list combined. Although the homicide death rate among whites (3.5 per 100,000) is significantly higher, by itself, than that in any European nation, the carnage among minority groups is staggering. Homicide is the leading cause of death among African American men aged fifteen to twenty-four, a rate of 96.5, and the second leading cause of death among Hispanic men aged fifteen to twenty-four, 41.1 per 100,000.[16] These rates are higher than those in such third-world nations as South Africa, Colombia, Brazil, Mexico, and the Philippines, to name only a few.[17] Thus, even though it has declined recently, our homicide level resembles a third-world phenomenon in a first-world nation.

We have a problem. The fact that homicide constitutes a routine event is fundamental to understanding life in the United States. Homicide is the most serious form of violence against persons. In every society, people want to feel safe from attack and intentional death. They want to feel secure in their homes. They want to feel secure on the street. They want to go to the store, send their children to school, or enjoy a vacation in New York City without fear for their personal safety. But in this country, homicide occurs so often that it has an indelible influence on people's personal lives and public policy. When this fact is placed in context—for example, by understanding variations in homicide over time and across societies—observers gain insight into the stresses people experience and the (sometimes misguided) choices that follow, both interpersonal and political.

On an interpersonal level, for example, the fear associated with a high rate of homicide leads to fear of contact with strangers, especially those who differ by skin color or culture. As a result of this suspicion, people purchase guns for self-defense, which has the paradoxical effect of making both their homes and the streets more dangerous. And the people who become the most dangerous are not strangers but intimates and friends. For example, among young women aged fifteen to twenty-four, murder is the fourth leading cause of death among whites and the second among African Americans and Hispanics. Among adult women aged twenty-five to forty-four, murder is the fifth leading cause of death in all three groups.[18] Many of these homicides are committed with guns by male spouses, companions, or boyfriends.[19] Similarly, the streets and other public places become more dangerous because, as Mr. Carey's demise illustrates, a minor argument among friends or acquaintances can turn deadly, especially when guns are present. Everyone is at risk, not just the poor. This result would not happen in any Western European nation, since guns are so rarely available.

The fear associated with homicide manifests itself on a political level as well, leading to "law and order" policies that also have a paradoxical impact. Over the last thirty years or so, every American president has declared a war on crime, a campaign to make America's streets safe. As a result, more Americans now reside in prison than ever before. In fact, the United States (with a population of about 280 million) incarcerates five times more people than do all the nations in the European Union (with a combined population of about 370 million people). About 1.9 million Americans are in prison, compared to 350,000 in all the EU countries combined.[20] These data translate into an imprisonment rate of 682 per 100,000 in the United States, compared to 87 in countries making up the European Union. The impact of this massive (and very costly) policy experiment is potentially significant. For example, it can be shown that the process of jailing more and more offenders has reduced the homicide rate; the estimates range from trivial to about 15 percent fewer murders each year.[21] Some observers argue that this high number of incarcerated persons constitutes one reason why we now live in a safer society; the violent people are confined in prison.

Such assertions omit important details, of course. One is that, despite a vast increase in the number of people incarcerated, homicide rates in this country remain much higher than in other economically developed nations. California, for example, imprisons four times as many people as does Canada (the two are of similar population size) yet endures five times as many homicides.[22] Another problem is that nonviolent offenders constitute nearly all the increase in the prison population over the past forty years or so. The Federal

Bureau of Investigation (FBI) maintains an index of the most serious crimes people commit. In 1999, 88 percent of these crimes comprised burglary, larceny-theft, and motor vehicle theft—all nonviolent acts.[23] If non-index crimes such as drug sales and possession were included, the proportion of nonviolent crimes would be much higher. So most crimes and most criminals are nonviolent.

Still another problem with the assertion that a high incarceration rate makes this country safer lies in the fact that when violent offenders go to prison, even for long periods, they eventually get out. So, of course, do nonviolent offenders. California, for example, must release about 125,000 prisoners back into the community each year. One can only speculate about the impact of these former inmates on community life, since little is known, but it is reasonable to argue that the combination of their prison and post-prison experiences may lead many of them to commit violent acts.[24] This is because prisons confine large numbers of people with similar characteristics together for long periods of time. Since prisoners have little to do but talk to each other, prisons become somewhat like extended conventions where like-minded people network with and learn from one another. But prisons are threatening and violent places. Inmates rarely emerge ready to integrate into society. To the extent they commit homicides after their release, the result would not only cancel out some of the gains from the high level of incarceration, it may also lead to even more killings.

The dirty little secret of public policy in this country is that wars on crime do not deal with the sources of violence. Thus, searching for the sources of violence in our criminal courts ignores the social context that generates such behavior on a wide scale. Nonetheless, although wars on crime cannot solve the problem of lethal violence in America, they remain politically useful: They divert public attention from other issues, such as tax policy, that increase the level of economic inequality in our society. And inequality does affect the rate of homicide.

These choices, both personal and political, mean that we live with the consequences of a high level of lethal violence. In addition to looking at the extent of homicide, examining its consequences provides another way to understand life in the United States.

## SOME CONSEQUENCES OF HOMICIDE

1. *Lives are lost.* Talent is wasted. The impact of loss of life can be quantified, although the numbers do not carry much emotional impact. Most murder victims (like their assailants) are relatively young. They should be alive and healthy but are struck down. Their median age is twenty-five to twenty-nine, which means that most would have about fifty or so years of life left to live.[25]

Mr. Carey was only nineteen, so he would have had (on average) about fifty-five more years of life. This is plenty of time to mature, earn a living, raise children, worship God (however known), and contribute to the community in ways large and small. In America, much more than in other Western nations, the loss of potential life is great.

Another way to place all these lost lives in perspective is to examine homicide in comparison to auto fatalities, a traumatic event that also claims young and healthy persons by sudden death. In 1960, the death rate from homicide was 5.1 and that from auto accidents was 22.5 per 100,000 people, a total of 27.6 from both causes. So that year's homicide rate constituted 18 percent of the total. In 1998, by comparison, the death rate from homicide was 6.3 and that from auto accidents was 15.9 per 100,000 people, a total of 22.2 from both causes. But the homicide share of the total rose to 28 percent.[26] These data mean that over the last forty years or so Americans have become less subject to the kinds of trauma that take otherwise healthy people's lives, mainly because of a dramatic decline in auto fatalities. But even after nearly a decade of falling murder rates, at a time when they resemble those in the early 1960s, the impact of the trauma associated with this act has increased in comparison to automobile fatalities. No wonder people feel helpless and frightened.

2. *The public's exposure to violence is high.* As I argue in chapter 5, exposure to violence rebounds on the larger society: It leads to more violence, more homicide. Many people witnessed Delvin Darnell Carey's death, which occurred in a nightclub. Observing violence and its results is often traumatic, and one response is to become violent. A high homicide rate means that such trauma occurs frequently in our society. The effect, of course, is greater on children, whether they witness violence on the street or in the home (from spouse or child abuse). As psychologists explain, these types of experiences smash the fundamental assumptions people make about themselves and their world, especially their sense of trust.[27] Most people assume they are decent and competent and that the world is meaningful and relatively benevolent. When these (unconscious) beliefs are shattered at any age, people's inner security crumbles and the world comes to seem malevolent and meaningless. Although most people manage to rebuild their lives, some cannot, especially when exposure to violence is severe or occurs repeatedly. And exposure to violence is widespread. For example, one study estimates that about 45 percent of first and second graders in Washington, D.C., have witnessed a mugging, 31 percent have observed a shooting, and 39 percent have seen a dead body. In some public housing complexes, every child knows a victim of homicide.[28] These children do not make up monsters, and parents need not worry about violence on television; the streets provide the real thing. As I show in chapter 5, these children grow up and a few of them eventually commit violent acts themselves. Adults who are exposed to violence also respond in this

way. It is, after all, how they have learned to respond. One way of quantifying the consequences of all this trauma, then, is to look at the high American rate of homicide. Other responses to trauma occur as well, such as drug abuse and various forms of psychopathology, and this list is not exhaustive. All this violence means that many people's lives become hollow, ruined through no fault of their own.

3. *The economic consequences of homicide are great.* Mr. Carey's assailant was Kareem Robinson.[29] About nine months after the shooting, Mr. Robinson (then sixteen years old) pled "no contest" to the charge of second-degree murder. During the investigation, it came out that Mr. Carey had loaned Mr. Robinson $40 some time prior to the murder. On that evening, the two youths argued over the debt and a fistfight ensued. Mr. Carey, being four years older and physically larger, got the best of Mr. Robinson. A few hours later Mr. Robinson, now armed, tracked Mr. Carey down. Early in the morning on January 1, angry words again occurred and then the fatal shots.

The economic costs of this crime and others like it are more easily tallied than the human impact. Some of these costs are unique to this case; others apply more generally.

One category of expenses is medical. At the first report of the shooting, a police dispatcher sent officers and a team of paramedics to the scene. At this point, taxpayer expenditures began. Delvin Darnell Carey was dead when the paramedics arrived. If alive, he would have been taken to a hospital by ambulance (or perhaps helicopter). This costs more money. Each year, American hospitals treat more than 75,000 gun injuries related to intentional assault. In about one-fourth of those incidents, the victims die of their wounds. Violent crime in general (homicide, assault, robbery, and rape) results in about 14 percent of medical spending on the treatment of injuries.[30] In the case of gunshot wounds (both fatal and nonfatal), the estimated yearly cost is about $2.3 billion, nearly half paid by taxpayers.[31] Pronounced dead at the scene, Mr. Carey was taken for an autopsy, paid for by taxes. These huge outlays continue year after year, not only for the 15,000 or so murder victims but also for the thousands more who are assaulted and recover from their wounds.

In addition to medical costs, another category of expenses involves the legal and criminal justice system as it deals with homicides. Even before Mr. Carey's body was removed from the scene, detectives began an inquiry. It is probable that several police officers began looking for the suspect, Kareem Robinson, who was caught the following day. After his arrest, interviews were conducted, reports written, witnesses consulted. All this work costs money. In addition to police time, it included a prosecutor (called, in various states, a district attorney or state attorney) and staff. This was a simple case, so Mr. Robinson's court-appointed attorney only billed the state for about $2,400, a week's work. Many cases are more complex and cost thousands of dollars.

In this one, however, no depositions (pretrial statements) were taken, no expert witnesses were required, and a jury trial did not occur. During the time between his arrest and court date (about nine months), Mr. Robinson was jailed, fed, supervised, and given medical treatment. Expenses mounted each day.

About 69 percent of all homicides result in an arrest, which means the legal costs described here must be multiplied by about 10,000 (out of 15,500 murders in 1999). About one-third of all homicide prosecutions lead to a jury trial, and nearly all convicted defendants go to prison either as the result of a trial or guilty plea.[32] Mr. Robinson was sentenced to 20.5 years in prison, and he will serve at least seventeen of them at a cost of at least $19,000 per year.[33] Thus, his incarceration will cost the state about $323,000. But hidden costs exist as well (such as prison construction and maintenance, and medical and psychiatric treatment) that make the total for each prisoner much higher. If Mr. Robinson had been guilty of first-degree murder and, perhaps, sentenced to death, the costs would be incomparably higher still.

Still another category of costs accrues to the families involved and to the larger society. For example, the financial impact of Mr. Carey's murder on his family and other relatives must be considered. Ignoring their trauma (for the moment), funeral expenses had to be paid. Moreover, after his death, Mr. Carey's family lost a breadwinner. As of a few years ago, the estimated annual cost to the families of homicide victims was about $184 billion; it is probably more today.[34] But this figure does not take into account what economists call *productivity losses,* which refers (loosely) to the value of what people produce on the job. It is, of course, a strictly monetary measure, and people's noneconomic contributions to the society go well beyond that. It is useful, however, to think about the productivity losses incurred as a result of homicide. Although both Mr. Carey and Mr. Robinson had led imperfect lives, they were adolescents, and most young people (even those who get into trouble) mature into productive citizens. Given the average age of murder victims, the nation lost about fifty to sixty years of productivity from each of more than 15,000 people killed in 1999. But this figure can be doubled if one also considers their killers. Mr. Robinson, for example, had no record of violence prior to the murder. It is reasonable to think that he, too, would have matured into a productive citizen. In a sense, without in any way ignoring their violent acts, and while emphasizing the justness of long-term incarceration, assailants like Mr. Robinson are often victims as well. This is so not only because they have often been subjected to violence as children but also because their imprisonment means they lose a chance at living a normal productive life. As with many economic analyses, this loss of productivity due to homicide leads back to noneconomic concerns: the meaning of lost lives, the talent wasted, and the trauma for survivors.

4. Finally, although it is incalculable, *the human impact of homicide on fam-*

*ilies and other survivors is profound;* indeed, it lasts a lifetime. One estimate is that each homicide victim has seven to ten close relatives, plus significant others, friends, neighbors, and coworkers.[35] They represent grief and mourning multiplied, let us say (conservatively), by a factor of ten. So roughly 150,000 American citizens are touched by homicide each year.

After the murder is discovered, family members and others begin to mourn in some way.[36] Much depends, of course, on the respective ages of the victim and survivors, the nature of their relationship, any prior history of trauma, and the like; but in most cases dealing with the immediate reality of the loss is extremely difficult—the word *heartrending* seems appropriate. For many people, allowing themselves to feel their grief rather than shut down psychologically (at least for the short term) is a major problem. Others, of course, feel inconsolable and find themselves overcome with grief. Regardless of their reaction, however, they must tell their story to the police who (of necessity) invade their privacy. "Did the victim know the assailant?" "What was their relationship?" "Was their relationship volatile?" "Did the victim use drugs?" In addition, family members and friends must sometimes also deal with the media, who ask many of the same questions and more. When a murder becomes a media event, the survivors' lives become an open book for the public. So in addition to being traumatized by the loss of a loved one, the survivors may be revictimized in the immediate aftermath.

Over the long term, people whose loved one or best friend has been murdered often relive the event over and over.[37] They feel helpless, afraid, vulnerable, angry, and guilty. They experience nightmares and flashbacks, along with rage and a desire for revenge. They sometimes become depressed, which is to say that they find it hard to get going each day, whether to work or to take care of their families. They are easily startled, cannot sleep, and develop physical symptoms (headaches, ulcers, and the like). When this pattern persists over time, people display the characteristics of what psychologists call *post-traumatic stress syndrome.* And even after people seem to recover, these feelings can return even years later as spasms of grief. Thus, thousands of walking wounded in this country are created as a result of our high homicide rate.

Because so many people are murdered in America, what inventions are not invented? Because so many people are murdered in America, what sports records are not set? And apart from these kinds of possible greatness, how many ordinary income-earning, tax-paying, and church-going husbands and wives, mothers and fathers, are killed? How many thousands more will continue to be killed as the years go by? And how many survivors must there be?

This sketch of four consequences of homicide (lost lives, exposure to violence, high costs, and human impact) is meant to be suggestive, not definitive. And I have limited the discussion to those consequences resulting from murder. Think about the additional impact of other forms of violence, such as robberies and rapes, both of which are much higher in the United States than in other nations. We bear a terrible burden for all this violence.

## SOCIOLOGY AND HOMICIDE

The task in this book is to provide a sociological explanation for the high homicide rate in the United States. Despite the police sergeant's lament, it is explicable. In order to illustrate what a sociological analysis looks like, I would like to consider again the problem of automobile deaths. In the 1950s, public policy with regard to the causes of highway fatalities focused on drivers. The National Safety Council argued that "the most dangerous part of an automobile is the nut behind the wheel."[38] Thus, so the argument went, the reason for the then high rate of auto deaths (recall that it stood at 22.5 per 100,000 in 1960) was that drivers made mistakes. Whether these mistakes resulted from stupidity, falling asleep, because they became frustrated and angry, or for some other reason, people died—and it was viewed, in effect, as being the driver's own fault.

But a change in orientation began occurring, with increasing emphasis on the context in which driving occurs: auto and roadway design. In his 1965 book, *Unsafe at Any Speed: The Designed-in Dangers of the American Automobile*, Ralph Nader showed that poor automobile design contributed to a significant number of highway deaths. The book constituted a political bombshell, leading Congress to pass the National Traffic and Motor Vehicle Safety Act the following year. This statute subjected the design and manufacture of cars to government regulation, and it provides a symbol of the change in traffic safety orientation.[39] During this same period, the construction of the interstate highway system revolutionized the design of roads, another symbol of change.[40] As a result of these landmark efforts, cars are safer; they now include seat belts, air bags, anti-lock brakes, sidebeam reinforcement bars, improved fuel tanks, and other devices designed to protect the occupants. And roads are safer, too; they are now designed with wider lanes, better drainage, clearer markers, harder shoulders, gentler curves, and the like. These *structural changes* mean that the conditions under which people drive have become safer, which is why auto fatalities have declined over time (to 15.9 per 100,000). This decline refers to thousands of people, especially young people, who would have died over the years since 1960. This benefit will, of course, continue into the future. Thus, although persons at the wheel of automobiles still make mistakes and still become angry, when such events occur they are less likely to pay with their own lives or cause others' deaths. Individuals remain responsible for their behavior, of course; when they drive drunk or recklessly and cause a death or injury, they can go to prison. But changes in cars and roadways have made highway deaths less frequent, regardless of individual motives. The result is fewer lost lives, less exposure to trauma, and lower costs.

Note the italicized phrase *structural changes* above. The concept of *social structure* is a jargon term, of course, peculiar to sociology. In plain language, it refers to how the context affects action. More formally, as I explain in detail in chapter 2, this concern involves shifting the analysis from social psychological explanations of individual acts to social structural explanations of rates of behavior.[41] With regard to driving, then, this new angle of vision means a shift from trying to understand the "nut behind the wheel" to trying to understand—and change—the context in which driving occurs. The goal is for it to become less likely that "nuts" will kill themselves or others while driving. Data show that this goal is being achieved. But notice that shifting the focus from individuals to social structures changes the explanatory variables. For example, when investigating the causes of a specific accident, officers will want to know if the driver had consumed alcohol, been angry, or fallen asleep—all of which are social psychological variables. In contrast, when trying to understand why so many people die in auto accidents, observers look to the context in which driving occurs: the design of cars and roads. These contextual factors constitute what sociologists call structural variables.

In an analogous way, the strategy in this book involves identifying the structural variables affecting the high American homicide rate. Sociology, in short, focuses less on the "nut with a gun" and more on the way the social structure (or context) generates so many murders. One of sociology's most important insights is this: Understanding the social context in which people make choices is as important as (or more important than) understanding the specific choices they make. As will become clear, this shift in orientation means that the motives of individual assailants are less relevant. Mr. Robinson killed Mr. Carey over a disagreement about a small debt and, probably, as an act of revenge for having lost a fistfight. Knowing these banal facts, however, says absolutely nothing about why the American homicide rate is so high. The local newspaper recognized this point, albeit implicitly, in its decision not to report the outcome of the case. It was a typical murder that had little news value beyond the initial story. I will show that to understand the rate of homicide we must, as sociologists would say, shift the level of analysis away from individual motives to rather different explanatory variables. My subject is not why individuals kill, but why so many homicides occur in this country. Like the explanation of auto fatalities, a strategy dealing with this problem must examine the social context in which so many murders occur, a context that includes the huge number of guns in circulation, exposure to violence, and the high level of inequality characteristic of this country, among other factors.

In addition to suggesting (by analogy) a strategy for explanation, the problem of auto fatalities also illustrates a fundamental characteristic of modern life that is often misunderstood: If a phenomenon can be explained, the possibility of change arises.

## MODERNITY AND HOMICIDE

In his lecture, "Science as a Vocation," given in 1919, the great German sociologist Max Weber muses about the "disenchantment of the world" that seems to characterize modern societies.[42] It is an evocative phrase, suggesting that human beings have passed from an enchanted and magical world into one that is colder and more heartless; indeed, some would say we are now without morality. Gertrude Himmelfarb makes this kind of argument in her book, *The De-Moralization of Society*. The book's title has a double meaning, suggesting that modern societies (especially the United States) are disenchanted and demoralized in two senses: We lack moral guidance and we lack morale. The poet William Butler Yeats made a similar argument, more evocatively, when he wrote that "things fall apart; the centre cannot hold; mere anarchy is loosed upon the world."[43] Now Mr. Yeats was writing about a different time and place, to be sure, but his fear of modernity (like that of Professors Himmelfarb and Weber) is palpable. As will become clear in chapter 3, I am much more sanguine about the nature of modern life than these observers, especially regarding moral values. But, as Professor Weber recognized, modernization has indeed meant the passing of old ways of thinking and acting precisely because of the dominance of science and its practical results.

Science is a specific way of understanding the world. It emphasizes that each event has a cause that can be discovered and verified by observation. In order to understand the truth about the world around us, in the form of cause-and-effect relationships, science teaches people to use reason based on knowledge. The growth of scientific knowledge, which leads to technological advances and economic development, provides the basis for modern life.[44] Indeed, it makes little sense to speak of fully modern societies before the latter part of the nineteenth century. This two-hundred-year process constitutes one of the greatest revolutions in history. When historians look back on this period, it may be seen as significant as the emergence of agriculture and the development of the first civilizations. The benefits are immense and the implications perhaps more positive than Professor Weber and others believe.

Think about some of the ways people are better off today as a result of technological advances based on science. More infants live because nutrition, hygiene, and prenatal care have improved. Over time, they mature sooner and become taller. They usually have healthy bodies and (straight!) teeth. Women can determine whether and when to give birth. Most people find that their jobs are less physically demanding than those of their grandparents. Old age has become a phase of life experienced by many as the population distribution has changed. The home has become a place of relative luxury, with running water, electricity, and the accoutrements that follow: stoves, refrigerators, telephones, televisions, VCRs, computers, and bathrooms. Improvements in transportation and communication have made the entire world seem smaller, more accessible. These examples show clearly that social life in the United States is far different today than it was just a short time ago. Human beings have remade the world.

But the changes associated with modernity go beyond lifestyle. Science and scientific ways of thinking have become embedded in Western culture, which now has much less room for "enchantment." The surprising implication is the possibility that Max Weber interpreted the impact of modernity exactly backwards. Perhaps modernity has meant a change from a cold and heartless world into one that is more humane. Perhaps modernity has meant that, instead of lacking moral guidance (and morale), we have a firmer sense of the sanctity of life and the dignity and worthwhile quality of every human individual.

In any case, the reason there exists less room for what Professor Weber called "enchantment" is that the combination of technology-induced changes in lifestyle, economic development, and scientific ways of thinking stimulates in most people a rational, practical approach to the problems of everyday life. As a result, modernity is characterized by a mind-set that is impatient with mystery, which looks for scientific rather than supernatural explanations. If many people are dying on the roadways, we ought to be able to make driving safer. Similarly, if many people are dying in the streets and in their homes, we ought to be able to make these locales safer, too. People today want solutions to problems; they do not want either appeals to magic or an attitude of resignation in the face of harmful conditions that can be improved. Homicide, I submit, like auto fatalities, is one of those conditions.

Finding solutions, of course, means changing the social context (or structure). Such changes usually lead to more control over events. Control, in turn, often allows a wider range of choices for individuals, which can be disconcerting. Some of these new choices reflect trivial, albeit costly, changes in lifestyle. As a youngster, I wore an inexpensive pair of "tennis shoes" and used them for every sport. Today, I go into a store, check out the wall of shoes, and the clerk asks if I walk, jog, play basketball, play racquetball, or play softball. As an erstwhile athlete, I say "yes" and leave with five pairs of shoes and a huge hole in my wallet. This is progress?

Well, yes—if one wants to avoid foot problems. "Progress," an old commercial stated, "is our most important product." This could be the American motto. The idea of progress is a metaphor, of course, a way of describing how social life has changed and improved over time because solutions to problems exist. These solutions, based on the application of scientific knowledge to the

practical dilemmas human beings face, have transformed our world and made
us less subject to the caprice of nature. As a result, individuals have choices
today undreamed of in the past. Indeed, and here is my point, the story of
the last two centuries is one of increasing control over every aspect of human
affairs: social, biological, and environmental. Everything is affected. The
changing rate of auto fatalities simply provides but one example.

Recall the National Safety Council's argument that the problem of auto
fatalities was a problem of drivers driving in unsafe ways. The National Safety
Council was an industry-sponsored group acting to protect the political and
economic interests of auto manufacturers. There is nothing wrong (although
there may be something shortsighted) with their doing so. Politics, at least in
democratic societies, is a competitive process in which participants seek to
influence government, at any level: city, state, or national. The significance of
Ralph Nader's book is that it facilitated a change in orientation. The problem
of auto fatalities was transformed from a private dilemma experienced by individuals into a public issue that merited a variety of governmental solutions.
Thus, passage of the National Traffic and Motor Vehicle Safety Act in 1966
mandated the creation of the National Highway Traffic Safety Administration
(NHTSA), which was given the power to set design standards for cars and
trucks. Among the many changes that were introduced in the years that followed, the NHTSA required that passenger vehicles be constructed so that
passengers could survive a car's impact with an immovable barrier at a speed
of thirty miles per hour. During these same years, soft-shield barriers (those
yellow barrels) and breakaway signs came into increasing use, especially on
major highways.

Admittedly, the changes that have occurred remain imperfect; it is conceiv-
able that the auto fatality rate could be still lower and that more lives could
be saved. They are imperfect because politics in democratic societies is never
about finding the "best" solution to a problem; politics involves figuring out
a solution that can be negotiated and passed by a legislative body. Progress is
achieved through compromise among competing groups. Even so, one result
of the many changes in auto and highway design is that when people get
behind the wheel and pull onto the road, they are less likely to die. And this
is true even when drivers act out their frustration or fall asleep. Thus, one
benefit of the modern "disenchantment of the world" is that problems like
auto fatalities are approached in practical ways that save lives.

In this country, however, people are much more likely to pay with their
lives when they have a disagreement on the street, in a nightclub, or in their
bedroom. Even though American homicide rates are at a forty-year low, they
remain much higher than in other Western nations. Despite this fact, a well-
known criminologist asserts that "we are victims of our own success." Crime
rates, he says, including homicide, are at such a low level that it is difficult
to see how they can continue going down.[45] I take this to be an attitude of

resignation: We must live with a high level of carnage. So each year thousands of people like Delvin Darnell Carey will continue to die. And each year, thousands of people like Kareem Robinson will go to prison for murder—simply because they became (really) angry. Mr. Robinson is in prison for at least seventeen years, partly because he had access to a gun. Now it can be argued that the problem here is that he was a nut with a gun and should be incarcerated. And that assertion is correct, which is why he is in prison and deserves to be. But would it not be better to prevent this problem in the first place? Would it not be smarter to make our public places and homes safer?

We have a problem. Homicide rates in this country, even at their current low levels, are still very high; they are anomalous compared to other Western nations. The question posed in this book is quite simple: How can the level of homicide in the United States be explained and, just possibly, be reduced?

## NOTES

1. Voyles (1999); Martin (1999); Swirko (1999); Federal Bureau of Investigation (2001).

2. I do not consider homicides caused by corporate practices in this book. When companies knowingly sell unsafe products to consumers and deaths result, the courts have sometimes held them legally liable. But this issue would require a separate analysis.

3. World Almanac Books (2000:217); Bureau of Justice Statistics (2000a); Federal Bureau of Investigation (2000). I am excluding deaths from disease and other non-battlefield causes.

4. World Almanac Books (2000:217); Bureau of Justice Statistics (2000a); Federal Bureau of Investigation (2000).

5. Glassner (1999).

6. Bureau of Justice Statistics (2001a:120).

7. Bureau of Justice Statistics (2001).

8. Fainaru (1992).

9. Federal Bureau of Investigation (2000); Barclay (2001).

10. Zimring and Hawkins (1997:5); National Injury Surveillance Unit (1998).

11. Federal Bureau of Investigation (2000); World Health Organization (2000).

12. Zimring and Hawkins (1997:7). The data below are from Barclay et al. (2001:Table 2).

13. Bureau of Justice Statistics (2001c).

14. Federal Bureau of Investigation (2000).

15. National Center for Health Statistics (2000:76).

16. National Center for Health Statistics (2000:26).

17. United Nations (2000).

18. National Center for Health Statistics (2000:26).

19. Bailey et al. (1997); Violence Policy Center (2000).

20. Barclay et al. (2001); Bureau of Justice Statistics (2001b). See also Mauer (1997); Schiraldi et al. (1999).

21. Levitt (1996); Marvell and Moody (1997); Rosenfeld (2000); Spellman (2000).

22. Schiraldi et al. (1999).

23. Federal Bureau of Investigation (2000).

24. Petersilia (2000).

25. National Center for Health Statistics (2001:9 and 19).

26. National Center for Health Statistics (2000a:206–15); Federal Bureau of Investigation (2000).

27. Janoff-Bulman (1997).

28. The percentages are from American Psychological Association (1993). Seeing a dead body is from Garbarino (1992).

29. All information about Kareem Robinson and the events of that evening come from his case file and an interview with the assistant state's attorney who prosecuted the case, Marc Peterson.

30. National Institute of Justice (1996).

31. Cook et al. (1999).

32. Bureau of Justice Statistics (2000a).

33. Florida Department of Corrections (2000; 2000a).

34. National Institute of Justice (1996).

35. Redmond (1989).

36. Worden (1991).

37. Worden (1991); Janoff-Bulman (1992; 1997).

38. Quoted in Zimring and Hawkins (1997:187).

39. Nader (1965); Robertson (1981); United States Department of Transportation (1985); Crandall et al. (2001); Waller (2002).

40. Transportation Research Board (1987); Lay (1992); Lewis (1997); Lamm et al. (1999).

41. Beeghley (1999).

42. Weber (1918:139).

43. Himmelfarb (1995); Yeats (1933).

44. Rosenberg and Birdzell (1990).

45. Quoted in Butterfield (2000).

# 2

# How to Understand Homicide

It is a familiar ritual. This time it occurred just after Christmas in Wakefield, Massachusetts, near Boston. On the morning of December 26, a forty-two-year-old software tester named Michael McDermott went to work, arriving on time as usual. About 11:00 A.M., however, after talking with a colleague about video games, he took out several guns and walked from office to office, shooting people at their desks. A total of seven died, most with multiple gunshot wounds. Among them was Jennifer Bragg Capobianco, who had been married for just two years and had returned to work a few weeks earlier after giving birth to a baby girl. She was only twenty-nine and had, on average, another fifty-three years to live.[1] What would she have accomplished had she not been murdered? For one thing, she would have raised her daughter, who is now growing up motherless. Another victim was Louis Javelle, fifty-eight, the single father of three sons and a daughter. He would have had, on the average, another twenty-two years to live, plenty of time to finish raising his children. These were ordinary people going to work and church, building families and leaving a legacy for the future, enjoying the holiday season. The police found Mr. McDermott sitting silently in the lobby of the company building, surrounded by his loaded weapons. He surrendered without a struggle. The story became front-page news in papers around the country, including the *New York Times*.[2] Although public-place killings with multiple victims constitute only a small proportion of the thousands of homicides that occur each year, they receive a great deal of publicity. In this case, the victims' families, relatives, friends, and surviving coworkers spent the remainder of the holiday season grieving—and talking to reporters—instead of celebrating. Christmas will never be the same for them as they try to reconstruct their lives and, inevitably, relive the events of that day over and over again—often for years.

A few days after the killing, an opinion piece in the *Boston Globe* defended the easy availability of guns in America, arguing that they provide the solution to the homicide problem because armed citizens can shoot back at the criminals. From this point of view, guns make America a safer place. After all, "without letting law-abiding citizens defend themselves, we risk leaving victims as sitting ducks," regardless of location—at their desks, at school, at the store, or in their bedrooms—when criminals start shooting.[3] At about the same time, a *New York Times* columnist made the opposing argument. He recited the recent history of this form of homicide (it occurs several times a year, accompanied by the usual front-page coverage) and argued that Americans are "addicted to guns" with their "hideous consequences."[4] From this point of view, it is precisely the easy availability of guns that causes the homicide problem. After all, Mr. McDermott was not a criminal before December 26. Prior to the shootings, he was a law-abiding citizen with no police record. As such, he obtained his weapons with no trouble, even though some of them were illegal to possess in Massachusetts. These contrasting media responses, of course, were also part of the ritual. The ever-recurring cycle of homicide in its various forms, followed by the defense and condemnation of guns, is self-reinforcing to supporters on each side of this issue and has little practical effect.

This is so, I believe, because homicide is such a routine part of life in the United States and we have become so inured to it that the main response is not to act but to weep and wail (whether literally or in print) and to become afraid. The typical analysis that appears in the media—guns cause or solve the problem of homicide—is too simplistic and, as such, does not contribute much insight. Thus, although it is correct to argue that the pervasiveness of guns and the ease with which they can be obtained in the United States may be pertinent to understanding the high rate of homicide, guns are not the only relevant variable. Single-cause explanations of social phenomena are rarely accurate; other variables exist, and the way they interact needs to be considered. Thus, as already discussed, the impact of guns must be placed in the social context in which their lethal use occurs.

Achieving this goal requires a coherent intellectual strategy, such as that outlined in this chapter. In so doing, I try to accomplish two goals that often seem incompatible but I hope are not in this case.

One goal is to make the strategy used in this book clear to professional sociologists and criminologists and explain its importance. Many eminent scholars, such as Roger Lane in *Murder in America* and Steven Messner and Richard Rosenfeld in *Crime and the American Dream*, offer structural interpretations of the homicide rate.[5] I find Professors Messner and Rosenfeld's analysis to be especially important; not only do they make their explanatory strategy explicit and clear, my argument builds on theirs.

The other goal of this chapter is to present the theoretical and methodological issues in such a way that readers who may not be familiar with them, mainly students but a general audience as well, can follow the argument. For example, the strategy used in this book involves a distinction between social psychological explanations of why individuals act (in this case, commit homicide) and structural explanations of differences in rates of behavior (in this case, the anomalous American homicide rate). In explaining this distinction, I make use of Emile Durkheim's work, analyzing his logic in some detail. This is, of course, familiar ground to most sociologists and criminologists. Some professionals, then, may wish to skim through the argument presented here while other readers may wish to peruse it more carefully.

The strategy used in this book has four components. First, the empirical data on homicide must be assembled. Seymour Martin Lipset has argued, I believe correctly, that the characteristics of societies can best be understood in light of both their past and their similarities to and differences from other societies.[6] Thus, in this book, the data are presented in cross-national and historical terms. Second, the appropriate level of analysis must be specified. Given the question being dealt with here—why the American rate of homicide is so high—that level must be structural. Third, the variables that explain the high homicide rate in the United States must be identified and explained. As Professor Lipset emphasizes, although most structural explanations must be interpretive, they do not need to be vague or imprecise. Thus, I will show that understanding why the homicide rate is so high in this country requires a "logical experiment" in the spirit of Max Weber's inquiries. In so doing, my interpretation is cast in the appearance of a multivariate analysis, albeit in prose rather than mathematical form. In effect, this method provides a logical model that is used as a framework for the argument. Finally, once the reasons for the high American homicide rate are understood, it becomes possible to think about the implications. If Max Weber's interpretation of modernity is correct, for example, then perhaps the American murder rate simply reflects a larger truth: Modern societies are cold and heartless places, and there is not a whole lot we can do about it. Perhaps the loss of so much human life is just not very important, especially in light of other values. But, then, again, he might be wrong, at least in part. Alternatively, if the variables producing the anomalous American situation are clearly stated, then realistic (although politically difficult) possibilities for change can be discussed.

## CROSS-NATIONAL AND HISTORICAL DIMENSIONS OF HOMICIDE

In his presidential address to the American Sociological Association a few years ago, Melvin Kohn also emphasized the importance of examining the cross-national and historical dimensions of social phenomena.[7] He and his colleagues were interested in using survey data to assess the impact of social stratification on the distribution of personality characteristics in a society. In the United States, for example, they showed that people in higher prestige occupations usually have more opportunity for self-direction, display greater intellectual flexibility, and come to value these traits in themselves and their children. Conversely, people in lower prestige occupations often lack opportunity for self-direction, display less intellectual flexibility, and come to value conformity to external authority in themselves and their children. Moreover, the Kohn group also discovered this same relationship in both Poland (a communist nation at that time) and Japan. This consistency indicates a robust finding: The association appears to occur regardless of the nature of the economy (communist or capitalist) or culture (Eastern or Western). Even though these three nations display quite different histories, and even though their unique pasts remain important to understanding the nature of each society, the Kohn group found that the impact of social stratification is similar in all of them.

Although my interests differ, Professor Kohn's argument that cross-national and historical comparisons are especially useful in understanding social life remains valid regardless of topic. *The first step in understanding the high homicide rate in the United States is to assemble the data on homicide, cross-nationally and historically.* The result becomes the phenomenon to be explained, so the process needs to be much more thorough than the illustrations used in chapter 1. Cross-national data indicate the extent to which a social condition in one country occurs at a similar or different rate than in others. In this book, I usually restrict cross-national comparisons of homicide to Western industrial societies. Since these nations share a common cultural heritage and developed advanced economies earlier than other nations, the similarities and differences in their homicide rates can be especially revealing. Historical data reveal how much change has occurred over time within a single society, such as the United States, England, or some other nation. Homicide is a unique topic in that records go back rather far in time, which means the analysis can be extended over several centuries. Thus, even though gaps in the data exist and problems of interpretation remain (both of which will be discussed), long-term historical changes in homicide rates provide a glimpse into the transition to modern life. And this is so in several countries.

This emphasis on beginning the analysis by assembling historical and cross-national data constitutes a relatively uncommon intellectual strategy. In the social sciences, students usually learn that research proceeds by forming a hypothesis and then gathering data to test it. Although the real world does not work that way very often (since scholars often have data and then figure out a hypothesis to test), most research reports published in academic journals display a typical format: (1) introduction, (2) review of the relevant literature and statement of a hypothesis, (3) description of the data and methodological technique to be used, (4) presentation of results, and (5) conclusion. For example, after reviewing the literature, one might hypothesize that racial discrimination in the form of housing segregation is related to homicide among minority groups. The answer, after analyzing the data, is yes, the greater the residential segregation of African Americans from whites, the greater the African American homicide rate.[8] Such findings are valuable. I make use of them in developing the argument in chapter 5 and, in the process, explain the reason for the relationship between segregation and homicide. So this methodological design, in which statistics help observers to explain some topic of interest, is very useful. It represents, in fact, the most common way of reporting research in the social sciences. It limits the questions that can be asked, however, because many interesting issues cannot be studied in this manner. As the great economist Joseph Schumpeter once observed, "we need [data and] statistics not only for explaining things but also in order to know precisely what there is to explain."[9] And with regard to homicide there remains a great deal to explain.

## LEVELS OF ANALYSIS AND HOMICIDE

Knowing how homicide rates vary historically and cross-nationally leads to productive questions, the key to understanding. Science, it seems to me, is simply the art of asking questions. The idea is that there are no secrets. The characteristics of nature, social life, even people's unconscious motives, can be discovered if one asks the right questions and seeks appropriate data to answer them. Thus, understanding homicide, or any other social phenomenon for that matter, depends on the questions asked. For example, one can ask why Michael McDermott killed his coworkers or why Kareem Robinson killed Delvin Darnell Carey. In either case, the answer will be social psychological. Alternatively, one can ask, as I do in this book, why the American rate of homicide is anomalous compared to those of other nations. In this case, the answer will be structural. In sociology, this difference between social psychological and structural questions is referred to as the level of analysis. Each provides different, albeit complementary, insights.

To illustrate the importance of the level of analysis and why it reflects the different questions observers might ask, consider one of the most famous paintings of the impressionist era, *The Café Terrace at Night,* completed in 1888 by the Dutch master, Vincent Van Gogh. As you may (or may not) recall, in this work Van Gogh depicts the exterior courtyard of a modest café, where tables are placed. Light coming from the interior shines on the customers as they eat, drink, and converse. Other patrons are arriving, seeming to emerge out of the surrounding darkened street. The cobblestones on which they walk are very uneven and buildings loom above them. Although some of the buildings feature lighted windows and the stars above are unusually large, the result has little effect on the ground. All the light on the street seems to come from the café, a fact that is important to understanding the painting (as I will suggest later). Here I would only note that, like much great art, this piece can be understood on several levels, depending on the questions asked.

An observer might wonder, for example, about the chemical composition of the paint. This question is important because the painting (like much of Van Gogh's work) is characterized by contrasting bright and dark colors. One way to deal with this issue would be to use a spectroscope to analyze the pigment making up the paint. Another question might be about the artist's brush technique. A magnifying glass would reveal that Van Gogh used heavy, slashing strokes. Still another question might be how the images fit together when viewed from varying distances. So one might stand, say, five, ten, and twenty feet away to see how the significance of each part of the painting changes as the observer moves away from it. These different questions correspond to three levels of analysis. Note that the answer at each level provides a different kind of information. Yet each is valid, and each contributes to an understanding of the painting. By analogy, then, the key to understanding homicide is to recognize that the explanatory variables at the social psychological and structural levels differ because the questions being asked differ.

## Social Psychological Explanations of Homicide

Why do individuals kill? Although this question is not the focus of this book, it is useful to consider it briefly for comparative purposes. By way of anticipation, my point is that although the answer to this question is important, it cannot—even in principle—help observers understand why the American rate of homicide is so high.

If one asks killers, their stated motives are often painfully banal. Nearly all homicides involve arguments over dinner or sex, drug deals gone awry, barroom scrapes fueled by alcohol, or differences between two people (over money, for example). Kareem Robinson killed Delvin Darnell Carey for what seem, to an outside observer, to be drearily trite reasons. In some cases, killers appear to display mental illness or they may be expressing free-floating anger. Michael McDermott, for example, appears to have been angry that most of his wages were going to be seized by the Internal Revenue Service to pay back taxes; he apparently blamed people at work for cooperating with a governmental agency. The week prior to his rampage (just before Christmas), he had asked for a cash advance on his salary, which had been denied. So this was a very angry man. Some homicides seem to be instrumental (such as slaying a robbery victim or witness), and they may be so, but they often have an emotional component as well: venting hostility toward others.

In thinking about these motives, the easy answer to the question "Why do individuals kill?" is that most homicides are irrational, impulsive acts, crimes of passion in which killers' emotions run amok and override reason. Yet Mr. Robinson and Mr. McDermott, like virtually all killers, can say clearly why they killed. Because their stated reasons seem foolish or nonsensical to observers, however, they are dismissed. This dismissal can be seen in the verdict of some scholars that nearly all homicides are "passion crimes" that are "unplanned, explosive, determined by sudden motivational outbursts."[10] It seems to me, however, that this response avoids explanation; it does not lead to understanding. It denies the fact that people make choices in every aspect of their lives, sometimes with grave consequences, sometimes when there is an emotional overlay involved. For example, both athletes and emergency room doctors must sometimes make split-second decisions that not only involve rather complex judgments but whose consequences also are financially and emotionally significant. No one denies that they make choices, the logic of which can be understood. The choices murderers make ought to be amenable to understanding, too.

Research shows that in order to figure out why individuals kill, observers need to examine the differences between killers and nonkillers in some fashion. In so doing, it becomes necessary to develop a theory, an abstract statement that shows the characteristics of killers in ways that take into account their disparate reasons for the crime. If one extrapolates loosely from the extant literature, a highly simplified and illustrative answer to the question can be phrased something like this: *The greater a person's frustration and the more one has been socialized to violence, the more likely one is to commit murder.*[11] The phrase "more likely" is hugely significant, of course, because very few people commit murder, even in the United States.

A case of road rage provides one way of thinking about the nature and consequences of frustration: It is nighttime after a long day and you are in your car and in a hurry. Alas, the person in front of you is driving slowly for no apparent reason in an area where it is hard to pass. The inability to do what one wants when one wants to do it is the essence of frustration. More formally, *frustration* occurs when people find their goals blocked, especially when this blockage appears to be intentional, unjustified, and unexpected.[12] One result of these conditions can be aggression. Do you, for example, honk your horn, flash your headlights, scream, make an obscene gesture, or even pass recklessly? All are aggressive acts. Or do you wait patiently because your mother is with you? But aggression sometimes goes beyond angry gestures. Motorists have been known, in fact, to shoot at (and kill) other drivers in such situations.[13] This response is rare, however; it usually takes more than goal blockage to trigger violence, especially lethal violence.

Violence as a means of problem solving is learned behavior. The author Thomas Wolfe summarized how such learning occurs when he described the characters in his autobiographical novel *Look Homeward, Angel*: "Each moment of their lives was conditioned not only by what they experienced at that moment, but by all that they experienced up to that moment."[14] He is referring to what sociologists (less evocatively) call *socialization:* the process by which individuals understand values, develop internal (often unconscious) motives, acquire social skills, and act on what they have learned.[15] This process begins in childhood in primary groups (such as one's family) and continues over the course of people's lives as they interact with others who are emotionally significant and with whom they have long-term contact (in their neighborhoods, for example). In a way, then, socialization describes how people grow up—with the addendum that it continues throughout life—and learn the norms and values of their community.

So when people act violently, their behavior must reflect, in some way, "all that they experienced up to that moment," all that they have learned about the kinds of behavior expected in certain situations. One illustration of what these experiences might be is found in Lonnie Athens's *The Creation of Dangerous Violent Criminals.*[16] He interviewed and obtained life histories from fifty imprisoned people who had committed exceedingly violent acts. Based on these data, Professor Athens argues that people learn to use violence based on events in their lives that are "consequential and unforgettable." Thus, he found that individuals who are especially violent have been treated especially brutally, usually in childhood. Their life histories also display a pattern: First, authority figures (whether in family, gang, or clique) use violence to force individuals to submit to their authority. Individuals respond with a sense of humiliation and rage. Second, individuals witness others being violently beaten down. The psychological impact, an uneasy combination of fear and rage, is especially great when those others are emotionally significant (such as one's mother). Third, individuals are coached to use violence to solve problems, often as a point of honor. Given such experiences, Professor Athens argues, individuals begin resorting to violence. If successful, this violence develops into a normal part of their behavioral repertoire. Such individuals become truly dangerous. In the language social psychologists use, they have been reinforced for violence and, hence, use it.[17] The people Professor Athens interviewed displayed extreme behavior, of course, but their descriptions of their lives and their motives for their actions are useful for precisely that reason. Even if most killers have not been brutalized to the degree that his subjects were, their life histories suggest the conditions under which people who become frustrated might resort to violence—and murder. Professionals in the field will recognize, of course, that this simple frustration-socialization hypothesis (deliberately) cuts across some of the typical social psychological theories in criminology—especially social learning, differential association, and strain theory—with which some students and general readers may be unfamiliar.[18] My goal in this hypothesis is only to illustrate the kinds of variables that must be used to explain why individuals kill.

As such, I want to return to the murder of Delvin Darnell Carey and speculate about what happened that evening. Recall that he and Kareem Robinson had a fistfight over a $40 debt. Why would they do this? Although some people find this behavior odd, perhaps it seemed reasonable at the time, especially to Mr. Carey, who had not been paid. Moreover, perhaps both of them had learned as children that interpersonal violence is a legitimate means to use in settling disputes. In *The Code of the Street,* Elijah Anderson describes the lives of young African American males residing in areas plagued with housing discrimination, poverty, illegal drug markets, and violence.[19] In contexts like this, the police do not protect, they abuse; the courts do not resolve disputes, they punish disputants. As Professor Anderson shows, the "lesson of the streets" is that "survival itself, let alone respect, cannot be taken for granted; you have to [literally] fight for your place in the world." In neighborhoods like these, some people prey on others and the appearance of weakness in public raises the danger of being victimized oneself. In such environs, people learn that they must protect themselves and they develop norms (codes) of behavior about when and how to do this. Thus, a small sign of public disrespect, such as nonpayment of a loan, can trigger great frustration. After all, people without psychological and social resources to maintain the respect of others have few options and know that the threat and occasional use of violence are powerful sources of control and personal safety. This background, one might speculate, provides the context in which Mr. Carey and Mr. Robinson argued over the debt and a fistfight ensued. Mr. Carey won, saved face, and the parties went their separate ways. But that did not end the matter. Given this situation, perhaps Kareem Robinson was not simply a "nut with a gun." Perhaps he was an adolescent who had lost a lot: the respect of others. I suggest that his murder of Mr. Carey now seems explicable, that it cannot be explained away as a crime of passion. It is impossible to know, of course, if this speculation about what happened on the evening Delvin Darnell Carey died is correct; the case file is unrevealing. Such guesswork is plausible for my purpose, however, since it indicates how the impact of frustration can lead individuals to act in different ways depending on how they define their situations.

A famous aphorism in sociology states that if individuals define their situations as real, then they are real in their consequences.[20] In the situation described here, it appears that the consequence of frustration became homicide. Although there are other ways of interpreting and understanding why individuals kill, and the simple frustration-socialization hypothesis phrased above is too incomplete to serve as a general theory of why some people commit homicide, it illustrates a fundamental point: The answer to the question of why individuals kill must be social psychological. Hence, even if a more general explanatory theory includes additional variables (and it must), such variables will deal with an individual's actions and interactions with others;

they will focus on how groups affect individuals and individuals affect groups. There is no other way to answer the question.

## Structural Explanations of Homicide

But the question posed in this book differs from that above and, hence, the explanatory variables must differ as well. *The second step in understanding the high homicide rate in the United States is to specify a structural level of analysis.* As defined in chapter 1, a structural analysis refers to how the social context affects action. In this case, the variable to be explained (the dependent variable) will always be a rate of behavior. So observers want to explain the high (or low) rate of, say, abortion or divorce or—as in this book— homicide.

In sociology, doing a structural analysis, whether of homicide or any other topic, is a little like examining how a house sets the context for action rather than worrying about the motives of individuals who enter and leave it. Thus, every house displays a specific arrangement of rooms, doors, and windows. These characteristics mean, for example, that most people will go in and out through the doors. In fact, most will use the front door, fewer the back. Note, however, that the combination of the footprint of the house and the shape of the lot sometimes means that most people go in and out the back door. But doors need not always be used; it is simply easier to do so. Thus, although it is harder, some people (a teenager seeking to evade parents, a burglar) will use a window as a means of entry and exit. And, although harder still, it is possible to imagine using a sledgehammer to force an opening through a wall. Thus, the characteristics of the house (the social context) determine rates of behavior, making some acts relatively easy and others more difficult. Without knowing which individuals go through doors and which go through windows, or their motives, it remains useful to study the way the house influences how people enter and exit, as well as other behaviors. But people can and do remodel the houses in which they live: a door is moved, rooms and doors are added, a pool is built. These changes, of course, alter rates of behavior. Moreover, houses vary from one neighborhood to another—in size, for example—and this difference influences rates of behavior as well. Just as we build houses and sometimes remodel them, human beings increasingly control the social structure in which we live. We pass laws, for example, or invent new technology, or transform the workplace. Recall, for example, the many changes in lifestyle that have accompanied modernity. These changes mean that our "social house" has changed, and so, consequently, have the choices people face.

The house metaphor suggests two characteristics of social structures that should be made explicit. Both are associated with the great French sociologist

Emile Durkheim, and I want to dwell on his work even though it is familiar to most professionals in the field.

The first characteristic of social structures is that they exist externally to individuals and influence their range of choices. By "external," I mean that people are born into a certain time and place, with its set of values and norms and its ongoing way of life. In *Rules of Sociological Method*, published in 1895, Professor Durkheim summarized this situation when he said: "Social facts are things."[21] The aphorism means that, like houses, social structures have an objective existence. They are real. A person cannot make them disappear through an act of imagination. Alas, the language Professor Durkheim used is unfortunate. He argued that social "things" display "a compelling and coercive power" over individuals. I advise, however, against taking this notion of "coercive power" too literally, as if this is the only way social structures affect people.

This advice is important because the second characteristic of social structures is that they can be changed, and in a controlled and deliberate way. Just as a house can be remodeled, so can social structures. As I pointed out in chapter 1, human beings are increasingly able to control our physical and social environment. And Professor Durkheim, like all the classical theorists, was trying to understand this phenomenon. What happens, he pointed out, is that after human beings create or change the social structures in which we live, these changed "social facts" become, in turn, social structures that are external to their creators. As such, they comprise a separate (the jargon term is emergent) class of objects that must be explained in their own terms, at their own level, separately from the social psychological variables associated with individual behavior.

The problem of abortion illustrates these two characteristics. For nearly all of human history, pregnancy meant that a woman had little choice but to give birth (or die trying). But advances in medical technology during the latter part of the nineteenth century made abortion a relatively safe procedure.[22] As one result of this new choice (along with other changes), an increase in the abortion rate occurred, especially among women in the nascent middle class. So a change in this "thing" (medical technology) encouraged a new behavior. Put metaphorically, a door was installed and opened. In response, however, most states passed laws making abortion illegal, which made it more difficult to terminate pregnancy.[23] Thus, a choice that had been briefly available became far more difficult because a "thing" (the law) changed. A door was, quite deliberately, closed. Now it is not possible to tell, with this information, which individuals obtained an abortion and which gave birth; these facts are based on people's personal experiences. But it is possible to state that the rate of abortion at any particular point in time and place reflects the impact of advances in medical technology and legal changes, along with other structural factors.

Gun technology provides another illustration. In the second half of the nineteenth century, technological improvements in the way guns were manufactured made them smaller and easier to conceal.[24] A new choice became available (like a door being installed), and the number of gun-related homicides increased, at least in the United States. In this case, as above, "things" that are real sometimes have an enabling effect, at least in this country. In contrast, Western European nations legally regulated possession of handguns, thus keeping them out of most people's hands, and so this choice remained less easily available (the door, although accessible, was kept closed). Levels of gun-related homicide did not increase. In this case, laws discouraged behavior. Once again, "things" sometimes limit rates of behavior by restricting people's choices.

Divorce offers a third example. Even though marriages broke down in the nineteenth century, probably as often as they do today, divorce was very difficult because laws were so restrictive. There was at least one alternative, however: A few couples dissolved their marriages informally by one partner either moving to another place or even fleeing to the frontier. But this choice was difficult (since people often had economic, familial, and other ties to their local residences) and occurred rarely. Most spouses remained together in their pain (and sometimes abuse). Today, of course, the social context differs a great deal. Communication has improved and, hence, keeping track of people's movements is easier; moreover, the frontier no longer exists because people have filled it up, so these options are closed. But changes people made in the economy and law have opened other doors. And it turns out that a worldwide pattern exists: As economic development occurs, most nations change their laws, and the divorce rate goes up.[25] In the United States, this process has meant that couples who have developed irreconcilable differences can now divorce. My point is paradoxical: On the one hand, individual men and women do not decide their range of choices for themselves; it is given by the fact of living in a particular place at a particular point in history. Thus, the average couple in an unhappy marriage does not determine what its options are. Rather, the social structure does. On the other hand, people changed the options available to themselves, leading to new rates of behavior. Thus, as communication improvements, territorial expansion, economic development, and legal changes occurred—all of which people initiated—the rate of some behaviors declined: staying in broken marriages, moving to another location. And the rate of another behavior rose: divorce. People today have choices undreamed of in the past.

Economic development has implications for the homicide rate, as well as other forms of deviance. Economic development means that governments (which is to say legislators, economic regulators such as the Federal Reserve Board, and executive branch officials, all of whom presumably represent the people) can increasingly control what goods are produced and who benefits;

they thereby determine how much inequality exists and what forms it takes (extremes of poverty, for example). In the United States, the level of inequality is much higher than in any Western European nation, as is the extreme of poverty. This fact is important because, for reasons that will be explained later, the rate of inequality in a society affects the rate of homicide. These differences in inequality and homicide thus reflect deliberate policy choices. This result may not be intended, however, since many people, including decision-makers, may not recognize the relationship between inequality and homicide.

These four examples illustrate why it is so important to understand the context in which individuals make choices. To use Emile Durkheim's language, while observers can rail against "things," like laws or technological developments, their external existence and influence over individuals cannot be denied. In addition, these diverse illustrations suggest that Professor Durkheim's idea can be applied to many issues.

His own example appeared in *Suicide*, published in 1897.[26] As is well known to sociologists, the "thing" he wanted to account for was variations in the rate of suicide among different nations, as these rates were revealed by statistics available in the 1890s. Thus, he did not concern himself with "the individual as such, his motives and ideas," but rather focused on how the "social environments" (contexts) into which people were born and in which they lived affected the rate of suicide. In part of his analysis, Professor Durkheim found that extremes of attachment to the group, too little or too much, produce high suicide rates. He called the extreme of too little attachment "egoistic suicide." For example, according to his data, nations that were predominantly Protestant displayed higher levels of suicide than predominantly Catholic nations. Protestant faith groups did not encourage suicide, of course; rather, they emphasized each individual's own relationship to God and the importance of free inquiry. But the unintended result of these positive values was that people were less attached to the group and, hence, displayed a higher level of suicide. Professor Durkheim called the extreme of too much attachment "altruistic suicide." For example, during periods of military conflict, the values of honor, loyalty, and obedience lead more soldiers than civilians to engage in suicidal acts. In this case, those who act know the likely result. More generally, then, the nature of the bonds binding people to society lead to high or low suicide rates. And again, these bonds exist externally to individuals, who are born into them or (in the case of the military) learn them upon joining.

As a sidebar, I should mention that Professor Durkheim's analysis displays some problems. The quality of his data was poor. In addition, despite his intent, he did not always succeed in keeping the analysis at a structural level. Finally, some of his key concepts (such as egoism and altruism, but others as well) are not as clearly defined as they should have been. Note also that I have simplified his analysis a great deal. Nonetheless, his findings about suicide have held up rather well over time.[27] And the more general argument is unquestioned: With the study of suicide he demonstrated that social structures constitute independent explanatory variables that decisively influence rates of behavior. This line of reasoning means that the rate of any behavior reflects the organization of a society, not individual experiences, and that its explanation requires a focus on the social structure.

I have belabored the point and used several examples because this emphasis on the fact that social structures exist separately from individuals is not easy for many Americans, including some scholars, to accept. An old story in sociology is that the social structure is like gravity: One knows it is there and affects behavior but cannot see or touch it. Moreover, this seeming lack of substance combines, I believe, with the ethic of individualism to make it hard for some observers to accept how the social structure affects rates of behavior. Although the origins of the value placed on individualism are unclear, one possibility is the transformative impact of the Protestant Reformation, especially Puritanism, with its emphasis on each individual's personal relationship to God.[28] Another is the rugged lifestyle of the frontier, as reality and myth, with its requirement that individuals must be self-reliant to survive.[29]

But regardless of origin, the pervasiveness of individualism in America distorts our view of the world in two ways. First, it leads to an overemphasis on people's freedom of choice. People choose. In sociological jargon, they have agency. But their choices are not unlimited (remember the house metaphor). They can, for example, choose to use a typewriter rather than a word processor. Or, instead of getting a divorce, people can choose to marry a second spouse. But because a typewriter is inefficient and bigamy illegal, only a few persons make such choices. This is precisely the sense in which the social structure exists externally to individuals and sets boundaries on action, which are sometimes wide and sometimes narrow. Second, individualism as a pervasive value leads to an overemphasis on social psychological explanations of social problems, including homicide. As I have suggested, explanations of why individuals kill are valid and useful, both by themselves and as a complement to structural analyses. But the latter cannot be reduced to the former. As Emile Durkheim argued, and as I have tried to show, a structural analysis must be conducted at its own level. To use one of his examples, just as living matter is qualitatively different (emergent)—in touch, taste, smell, and many other characteristics—from its component parts (carbon, proteins, amino acids, etc.), so rates of social events are qualitatively different from their component parts (individual behaviors).[30] From this angle of vision, then, the rate of homicide, and other social phenomena, reflects the social structure: They must be explained in their own terms. The question is: What sort of data should be used to explain the high American homicide rate?

## EXPLAINING THE HOMICIDE RATE

*The third step in understanding why the American rate of homicide is so high is to identify the key variables affecting it.* To a considerable degree, much of this task has been done. Thus, literatures exist on the connection between gun availability and homicide, exposure to violence and homicide, inequality and homicide, illegal drug markets and homicide, and racial discrimination and homicide. In short, extensive work exists on all of the variables that could conceivably affect the homicide rate. Most, although not all, of these analyses are both cross-national and quantitative in form.

The next step, the ideal one anyway, is to show how these variables are interrelated and their combined impact on homicide. To achieve this goal, the usual strategy would be to follow the pattern described earlier: Observers would review the literature, state a hypothesis, assemble a data set (that is historical and cross-national in nature), and measure, in quantitative terms, how all the relevant variables affect the rate of homicide. Emile Durkheim called this strategy the "method of concomitant variation," and in so doing he anticipates modern multivariate analysis.[31] As mentioned at the beginning of this chapter, the Kohn group used this strategy in assessing the impact of stratification on the distribution of personality characteristics in various societies. But as Professor Kohn describes in detail, the difficulties he and his colleagues faced were enormous and their relatively high degree of success uncommon.[32]

The usual strategy, however, is not possible when considering homicide. This is because a single data set such as the one required here cannot be put together. It is enormously difficult to assemble data on only one relationship (say, between residential segregation and homicide), and the results are often imperfect. In practice, as it turns out, cross-national analyses linking gun availability and homicide do not (because they cannot) include the effect of inequality. Similarly, analyses showing a relationship between inequality and homicide do not (because they cannot) include the effect of gun availability. So the findings about each variable's relationship to the homicide rate remain discrete and independent even though these factors are empirically interdependent. It is, surprisingly, one of the paradoxes of sociology (and many other disciplines) that some of the most important issues are not susceptible to precise measurement, even though—as here—their component parts are. This paradox means that if observers wait for a cumulative data set in which variance in homicide rates can be parceled out quantitatively, we will wait forever.

Given this dilemma, a synthetic strategy is required, one that builds on current quantitative findings and takes into account the mutual interdependence of the variables. The analysis, of course, must be multivariate in form, since single-cause explanations of social phenomena are rarely accurate.

One way to pursue this task is to develop a logical experiment similar to that of Max Weber. In *The Protestant Ethic and the Spirit of Capitalism,* he began by observing that the most advanced capitalist nations at the turn of the twentieth century were predominantly Protestant and tried to account for this "social fact."[33] As is well known, his strategy involved the construction of a set of logically interrelated variables, which he called ideal types, and an assessment of how actual cases deviated from a purely logical formulation. Thus, he wanted to understand why capitalism as an economic system arose in Western Europe and ushered in modern life. To answer this question, he systematically compared various Western nations in the seventeenth and eighteenth centuries with India and China at the same time and found that what distinguished Europe and the United States from these other nations was not the level of technology, a free labor force, or a variety of other factors. Rather, the West became unique due to the rise of the culture of capitalism as an unintended consequence of the Protestant Reformation. What appears to have happened is that behaviors that were valued for purely religious reasons, such as individualism and hard work aimed at making money and acquiring wealth, became transformed over time into secular cultural values. These ethical standards, in turn, helped to usher in a new kind of society, one never before seen in history. Professor Weber's work is significant here because his research strategy can be used with other topics, such as homicide.

Note that this strategy does not represent an antiquantitative bias; it is, rather, a practical way of making use of the quantitative data that do exist. The issue, as Thomas McKeown observed on another topic, is not between a correct and an incorrect answer; the issue is, rather, between the best answer that can be given and no answer at all.[34] Thus, the data used in this study consist of the quantitative results from other studies, linked together in a synthetic way so that the findings, in their totality, make sense of the homicide rate in the United States. For example, when researchers find a relationship between inequality and homicide in many nations, this result becomes part of the data used here. This strategy might be called a "synthetic multivariate analysis" because the explanatory variables are related to homicide logically rather than computationally, as with a regression equation. I posit as a counterfactual that if these variables had "lower scores," then the level of lethal violence in the United States today would also be lower.

This strategy is not new or unique. A similar procedure occurs in all scientific disciplines, often with some of the most interesting and important questions, when direct measurement proves difficult or impossible.

Economists call them *gedanken* (thought) experiments. They take certain factors, make a set of assumptions about them, and manipulate the variables logically and artificially, often by means of computer simulations. For example, Robert Mendelsohn and his colleagues examined the impact of global warming on agriculture.[35] The typical approach, they observed, assumes a "dumb farmer scenario" in which farmers continue planting the same crops even though the greenhouse effect (increasing levels of carbon dioxide in the atmosphere) leads to rising temperature and precipitation. As a result, the usual prediction goes, the impact of global warming will be catastrophic. In reality, of course, farmers are like everyone else: They adapt to a new social context by making new choices (they go through a different door). So the Mendelsohn group made a set of simple but realistic assumptions about changes in land use that might occur as farmers adapt to climate change over the next few decades and showed that there may well be overall benefits to American agriculture. These benefits, however, if they happen, will not take place everywhere; there will be winners and losers in different regions of the country. Although this is quantitatively sophisticated work, the numbers are illusions. Using a computer does not make the results scientific. Logic does.

Physicists perform logical experiments as well. Research on the impact of thermonuclear war provides an example. During the Cold War, the United States and the Soviet Union faced one another, each armed with thousands of thermonuclear bombs. Carl Sagan calculated the impact of a small nuclear war in which only 10,400 explosions with a total yield of 5,000 megatons occurred.[36] (These totals represented only about 10 percent of the available thermonuclear arms.) He assumed that 20 percent of the explosions would take place over cities. The result, he found, would produce enough dust and soot in the atmosphere that the average July temperatures in the mid-latitudes (for example, the American Midwest) would decline to $-9$ degrees Fahrenheit within a few weeks. Subsequent work, in which researchers used more sophisticated models of the climate, showed that the average temperature would decline to "only" 60–70 degrees Fahrenheit. In both cases, of course, these rather precise numbers were illusions; they were no more useful than the assumptions made. Nonetheless, Professor Sagan showed that one result of a thermonuclear war might be that the temperature would decline "a lot" as a result of "nuclear winter," while subsequent research showed that it might decline "a little" due to "nuclear fall." No matter what the true effect, climatic (and social) catastrophe would follow, so the policy implications were of vital importance. To say these works constitute imaginative research is to understate the case. They were also logical experiments. Naturally, the effects of one variable on another should be empirically observed whenever possible. In this case, however, the true empirical impact of lots of thermonuclear explosions cannot be tested, short of war and the annihilation of much of the world's population. Of course, the issues sociologists deal with, including homicide, are not nearly so important as the survival of the human species. But the methodological point is generalizable: Sociologists should not let either a fetish for measurement or a shortsighted view of the precision that is supposedly characteristic of scientific research in other fields get in the way of a creative approach to the issues. Answers to questions should be sought in the best way possible, given the available data.

Demographers also perform logical experiments. Thomas McKeown's *The Modern Rise of Population* provides one of the best examples.[37] He began by reviewing the evidence, which shows that the most fundamental cause of the population explosion over the last three centuries is the declining death rate from infectious diseases, such as tuberculosis, cholera, and many others. Until recently, he noted, the standard explanation of this decline focused on advances in medicine. But Professor McKeown demonstrated that this explanation cannot be correct because effective medical treatments (either cures or preventive vaccines) were not available prior to the mid-twentieth century, long after most of the decline in infectious deaths had occurred. For example, tuberculosis was the leading cause of death in this country during the nineteenth century. Death rates from this disease began falling, however, after about 1850. This was so even though the bacillus causing this disease was not even known until 1882. Death rates continued falling in subsequent years—drastically. This process occurred even though an antibiotic treatment for the disease did not become available until 1947. By that time more than 90 percent of the decline in deaths had already occurred. A preventive vaccine was not invented until even later, in 1954. This pattern characterizes the declining death rate from nearly all the infectious diseases that used to kill people. So the only possible explanation is that either the disease-causing organisms declined in virulence or some aspect of the environment improved. Evidence shows, however, that virulence remained unchanged. But the environment (social context) did change: Food supplies increased and the level of nutrition improved (leading to better resistance to disease), and sanitation also improved (leading to less exposure). In fact, then, McKeown revealed that medical treatment had little to do with the modern rise of population; rather, improvements in nutrition and sanitation constituted the main causes.

The problem of the causes of rising population is especially useful here because it demonstrates the paradox referred to earlier: Sometimes the answers to some of the most important questions cannot be measured, even though their component parts can. Thus, Professor McKeown had available measures of rising population over the last few centuries, the reasons for which he tried to explain. He also had quantitative data available on the declining causes of death from the various infectious diseases. And he assembled data on food production with its effect on the nutritional status of the population and sanitation with its effect of reducing exposure to infectious organisms. Thus, he showed logically and conclusively that medical treatment did not make much of a contribution to the modern rise of population (although scientific knowledge did). In so doing, none of the measures was combined into one data set. They cannot be. This strategy means that even though no regression equations or measures of explained variance appear, the analysis is determinedly multivariate—in a logical way. Although I have, of course, simplified Professor McKeown's analysis for presentation here, his overall strategy is generalizable to other topics.

I am arguing that a similar situation exists with regard to the study of homicide rates and, hence, a similar strategy must be used to understand them. As I mentioned before, all the potential variables have been identified and many have been measured (albeit imperfectly) both historically and cross-nationally. The last step, however, has not occurred. Thus, the research strategy presented here reflects a process of identifying, based on theory and observation, the structural variables that affect the choices people have—in this case, for committing murder—linking those variables together, and showing logically how they lead to the high rate of homicide in the United States. As will become apparent, I have profited enormously from the literature in the field. My contribution does not identify new variables; rather, it places them in a coherent context, interprets their impact, and explores the implications of the analysis.

## THE DILEMMA OF CHANGE

In thinking about the implications of the strategy presented here, it is useful to remember that the rituals we engage in carry with them a certain satisfying inertia. Michael McDermott killed Jennifer Bragg Capobianco, Louis Javelle, and five other people because he was very angry and (probably) felt hopeless about his future. He thus deprived their families and friends of their love and devotion, and our society of their contributions. Their children will grow up without a parent, with who knows what consequences. Yet their murders are not odd. Still others will be killed on the day you read this paragraph. Their deaths may or may not be reported in your local newspaper. But if such news stories do appear, it is safe to say that pundits will take sides and continue defending and condemning the easy availability of guns. They, like the public, will continue to weep and wail over the violence in America. These responses occur mainly because it is easier to imagine things going on in the same way than to imagine change.

The dilemma of change has been perennial since the latter years of the nineteenth century. For example, it can be argued that Van Gogh's *The Café Terrace at Night* expresses both his optimism about the future and fear of it. Recall my earlier comment that the light coming from the café dominates the front part of the painting. Maybe it represents an optimistic view of the future of modern societies, especially those in which science and scientific ways of thinking predominate. The powerful artificial lighting symbolizes, perhaps, the potential for human progress, which seemed, at that time, to be limitless. In contrast, perhaps the uneven cobblestones outside the café and the darkened buildings looming across and behind it suggest Van Gogh's fear of the social instability that might characterize modern societies in which science and scientific ways of thinking predominate.[38] Whether this interpretation is correct or not, we do indeed live in an uneasy time, full of disconcerting changes. In seeking solutions to problems based on (inevitably imperfect) knowledge, there is no guarantee that things will get better.[39] In fact, attempts at problem solving sometimes make the situation worse, creating new and different problems.[40] Because of such possibilities, some people flee from change. Alas, the one thing we cannot do in modern societies is choose to be people who do not have choices. Regardless of how one views the future, modernity means that we can do more than weep and wail.

## NOTES

1. National Center for Health Statistics (2001:9 and 11).
2. Goldberg (2000); Labi (2001).
3. Lott (2000).
4. Herbert (2001).
5. Lane (1997); Messner and Rosenfeld (1997).
6. Lipset (1990).
7. Kohn (1989). The address was originally delivered in 1987.
8. Parker and McCall (1999).
9. Schumpeter (1954:14).
10. Wolfgang and Ferracuti (1967:141). See also Lester and Lester (1995:5). Lonnie Athens argues that homicides are never senseless from the murderer's point of view (1997). On his work, see Rhodes (1999).
11. Wolfgang and Ferracuti (1967); Lester and Lester (1995:5); Messner and Rosenfeld (1997).
12. Berkowitz (1963; 1989).
13. James and Nahl (2000). Fumento observes that the extent of this problem is probably overstated (1998).
14. Wolfe (1936:51–52).
15. Brim (1966).
16. Athens (1989:19); see also Rhodes (1999).
17. Bandura (1983).
18. For a review, see Akers (2000). See also Messner and Rosenfeld (1997), who describe how various criminological theories apply to the social psychological and structural levels.
19. Anderson (1999:86).
20. Thomas and Thomas (1928:272).
21. Durkheim (1895:60). On *Rules*, see also Turner, Beeghley and Powers (2002).
22. Mohr (1978). For a secondary source with many other examples, see Beeghley (1999).
23. Reagan (1997).

24. Kennett and Anderson (1975).

25. There are exceptions; see Goode (1963; 1993). On the American situation, see Beeghley (1996).

26. Durkheim (1897). The quotations below come from p. 151. On *Suicide*, see also Turner, Beeghley and Powers (2002:345).

27. Henry and Short (1954); Lester (1994).

28. Weber (1905). This is a reference to Weber's *Protestant Ethic and the Spirit of Capitalism;* see also Turner, Beeghley and Powers (2002).

29. Turner (1920).

30. Durkheim (1895).

31. Durkheim (1895:151).

32. Kohn (1989). On the difficulties of cross-national research, see Goode (1993).

33. Weber (1905, 1913, 1917). For an explanation of ideal types, see Turner, Beeghley and Powers (2002).

34. McKeown (1976:5).

35. Mendelsohn et al. (1994).

36. Sagan (1983). The subsequent work referred to below is Thompson and Schneider (1986).

37. McKeown (1976).

38. On Van Gogh and the problem of modernity, see Welsh-Ovcharov (1974).

39. Rule (1978).

40. Sieber (1981); Tenner (1996).

# 3

# Homicide in Cross-National and Historical Perspective

The servants and townspeople gather in the street, all armed with swords and bucklers (small shields). If everyone is going armed during the course of an ordinary day, violence must be common. And it is. Another brawl is about to occur. The feud is ongoing, although its origins are unknown. The two old men, Capulet and Montague, rush into the street with swords in hand, ready to prove they can still fight. The play, of course, is William Shakespeare's *Romeo and Juliet*. Although the two old men make this opening scene farcical, as heads of the noble houses of Verona they enter the skirmish and thereby sanction it. They reveal themselves as creatures of the feud, which has taken on a life of its own. It demands lives to feed on, and it gets them.

*Romeo and Juliet* is unique among Shakespeare's tragedies, according to the distinguished scholar Northrop Frye, because a clear villain does not produce the play's tragic outcome; there is no Iago as in *Othello*, no Edmund as in *King Lear*.[1] Thus, no member of either the Capulet or Montague family is evil, including Tybalt. But they all live by a code of honor in which one's reputation and sense of manliness are at stake in every social encounter. The feud is fueled by the code, since a perceived insult must be avenged violently. So having taken offense, Tybalt tries to force Romeo into a duel, which he avoids. Mercutio, though, takes up the fight, and Tybalt kills him. Romeo then avenges Mercutio's death by killing Tybalt. By the end of the play, six people have died as a result of what began as a minor affront.

It appears that the motives for homicide have not changed much over the last 500 years; whether because of an insult, a small ($40) debt, wages being seized, or (as shown later) a very angry adolescent, the banal nature of most murders remains much the same. In the final scene of the play, old Capulet and Montague propose building golden statues of the star-crossed lovers, a futile gesture by broken men. The code of honor lives on. More deaths will follow every day.

Just as Shakespeare's fictional city of Verona was an exceedingly violent place, so was England in the sixteenth century and so, indeed, was all of Europe. Widespread violence and homicide were medieval legacies. Describing the history of homicide in Europe, even if the analysis is brief, provides a much needed perspective on the American problem. As will become clear, homicide rates in the United States have sometimes been as high or higher than those in medieval Europe. Moreover, this continues to be so even today in some areas.

## A SHORT HISTORY OF
## HOMICIDE IN EUROPE

Murder occurred frequently in medieval Europe, at least ten or twenty times more often than in today's societies. The available records for England at that time (which are actually rather good, but more on this later) portray a society riven by violence. Several studies suggest an English homicide rate of at least eighteen to twenty-three per 100,000 people in the thirteenth century, and it was probably much higher.[2] As James B. Givens remarks in his *Society and Homicide in Thirteenth-Century England*, "murderous brawls and violent deaths . . . were everyday occurrences."[3] Although the robbers and bandits who roamed the countryside instigated a great deal of violence, most fights occurred because of disputes among friends and neighbors. Many constituted ongoing feuds. Everyone, in all social classes, went about armed with knives (to eat with), swords, cudgels, and other weapons. In this context, he found that the ready willingness of kinsmen to assist each other or to retaliate for an injury (whether physical or verbal) meant that aggressive responses were common whenever a disagreement occurred. Moreover, elites fought and killed as often as, and perhaps more often than, commoners. Professor Givens quotes one observer as noting that in the thirteenth century, "few self-respecting gentlemen passed through the hot season of youth without having perpetrated a homicide or two." Unlike today, then, violence occurred at all class levels. Even allowing for some possible hyperbole, the English were a wild bunch in those days.

They were, moreover, no different than the rest of Europe during medieval times. Norbert Elias observes in his study of the history of manners that "fear reigned everywhere; one had to be on one's guard all the time. . . . The majority of the secular ruling class of the Middle Ages led the life of leaders of armed bands."[4] The pervasive presence of such bands meant that violence was the normal and expected method of settling disputes in cities across Europe, such as Paris and others, in the thirteenth and fourteenth centuries.[5]

Brawls and street fights were everyday events; people anticipated and enjoyed them. I say "enjoyed" because underlying the fighting lay a different (and to modern ways of thinking, foreign) sensibility: What Professor Elias calls a "savagery of feeling" pervaded these societies. Casual violence, cruelty, and delight in the torment, mutilation, and murder of human beings and animals were the norm. He describes in gruesome detail people's amusement at witnessing the torture and killing of prisoners and pets. Thus, as Ted Robert Gurr has concluded, descriptions of daily life at the time indicate that medieval Europe comprised societies in which men (rarely women) were easily and often provoked and unrestrained in the brutality with which they attacked one another. Interpersonal violence was an everyday occurrence.[6] Some of the quantitative estimates are telling: Fourteenth-century London displayed a homicide rate of about thirty-six to fifty-two per 100,000 people. The estimate for Oxford was 110. In Stockholm, the educated guess is about forty-three and for Sweden as a whole between ten and forty-five. The average for all European cities was around fifty.[7] Actually, then, it is not accurate to describe the English and other Europeans as a wild bunch in those days; that is too frivolous. Rather, social life in medieval times was the antithesis of that in modern times. European societies during this period were populated by people who committed and took pleasure in what we would call today cold-blooded killings. It was a callous, heartless—indeed, pathological—world by today's standards. It was a world we would not recognize today.

By the end of the sixteenth century, however, when Shakespeare wrote *Romeo and Juliet*, the homicide rate in England had fallen significantly, possibly to as low as fifteen per 100,000 in the nation as a whole.[8] But even at this level, it remained pervasive, an everyday occurrence. The play was first produced in London, remember, probably at the Old Vic Theatre, in about 1595. The historian Lawrence Stone observes that in that period murderous brawls between rival gangs of aristocrats, such as those depicted in the play, were common:

> In London itself the fields about the city and even the main arterial roads were continued scenes of upper-class violence. Bloody brawls and even pitched battles occurred in Fleet Street and the Strand. . . . It was in Fleet Street that there took place in 1558 the armed affray between Sir John Perrot and William Phelippes, supported by their retainers; in Fleet Street that John Fortescue was beaten up by Lord Grey and his men in 1573; in Fleet Street that Edward Windham and Lord Rich carried on their repeated skirmishes in 1578; in Fleet Street that Lord Cromwell got mixed up in an armed affray in 1596.[9]

The frequency of these affrays, and Professor Stone describes countless others like them, meant that members of Shakespeare's audience knew about the problem of interpersonal violence and death from personal observation:

"Fatal quarrels could originate in almost any context—at work, in a drink, or at play."[10] But by the late sixteenth century, when Shakespeare has Romeo get even for Mercutio's death, the social context that affected behavior had changed. Rather than a pervasive joy in violence, as in the Middle Ages, a code of honor had evolved into a dominant norm. At this time, the code probably applied more to the upper classes than to commoners. As one might expect, however, Shakespeare had a good eye for the direction of history. It is not accidental that he has the Prince trying to impose himself and the rule of law as a means of reducing the level of lethal violence: He banishes Romeo in the aftermath of Tybalt's death. Whether this edict and others like it were going to be effective in Verona is left unclear in the play. The historical trend, however, is clear. The rate of homicide was falling.

This assertion is based, of course, on surviving records.[11] The method for determining the "homicide rate" in a country has become standard around the world. Observers add up the number of intentional and illegal killings that take place in a year and divide that figure into the total population as determined by the census. On this basis, it can be asserted with reasonable confidence that the homicide rate in the United States declined to 6.1 per 100,000 people in 1999. There is an error term here, but it is small. Following this procedure, however, is not always easy as one examines records going farther back in time. Thus, even though homicide victims (in the past as well as today) usually know their assailants, and even though homicide has always been more carefully assessed than other crimes, some slippage occurs between actual events and official records.

This slippage occurs for four reasons. First, the meaning of homicide has changed over the years. For example, English records do not distinguish between murder and manslaughter prior to the sixteenth century.[12] Similarly, the classification of infanticide and abortion as murder has varied by time and place.[13] Second, incorrect diagnoses of cause of death were undoubtedly more common in the past. Only since the twentieth century have coroners and physicians been able to accurately distinguish deaths from natural and unnatural causes. Thus, until recently medical ignorance meant that some homicides went uncounted. Third, no official counts of homicide (or other crimes) exist in any nation prior to the nineteenth century. In every locale, then, all the data prior to that time come from surviving coroner and court records for specific counties and cities. Thus, nationwide estimates always reflect the combined results of several studies of records from varying times and places. Finally, even when the numerator (the number of homicides) can be reasonably estimated, the denominator (the population size) must also be estimated. In England, for example, the first national census did not occur until 1801.

These difficulties, however, are not insurmountable. In fact, the available data on homicide are more complete and of better quality than those to be had on most other issues of interest to historians. Allowing for a reasonable amount of error (which is why rates in the past are presented in a plausible range, such as eighteen to twenty-five), piecing together the long-term record of homicide in Western European nations can be done in a relatively accurate way. Ted Robert Gurr has reviewed all the problems associated with the surviving European records on homicide and come to the following conclusion:

> The general trend that emerges is unmistakable: Rates of violent crime were far higher in medieval England than in the twentieth century—probably ten and possibly twenty or more times higher. . . . The 750-year trend is so pronounced that no amount of quibbling about imprecise population data or incomparability of sources can make it disappear.[14]

In order to think about this trend, imagine a graph showing the homicide rate in Europe over a 750-year period. It began at a very high level, say, at least twenty to thirty per 100,000 people in the thirteenth century and possibly higher. Although the graph would show lots of hills and valleys as the rate rose and fell year by year, the overall trend would clearly be downward. Thus, by the time Shakespeare wrote *Romeo and Juliet*, it had probably fallen to about fifteen. In the seventeenth century it fell to about ten, in the eighteenth century to five, and finally to one in the early years of the nineteenth century, where it stands today in all Western European nations (see figures 3.1 and 3.2 later in this chapter).[15] This trend, Professor Gurr asserts, cannot be explained away by changes in public attitudes or official classifications. Rather, it reflects "a real decline in interpersonal violence."

The usual interpretation of this trend is that three structural changes combined to produce a long-term decline in levels of violence and homicide across Europe over several centuries. First, the emerging monarchies increasingly centralized power in the state and asserted a royal monopoly on violence. As Lawrence Stone comments, this success is one of the greatest triumphs of the English crown.[16] It not only altered the political history of England but also made the quality of everyday life more benign. The political motives were not altruistic, of course; they rarely are. Rather, a decline in violence was seen as necessary to ensure a steady income to the state via taxation. Second, courts of law gradually became effective as venues for settling disputes. Conflict is intrinsic to social life. In general, as Donald Black argues, the use of violence to resolve conflicts indicates the absence of law.[17] Today, we often interpret litigation as a symbol of declining civility; actually, however, it has increased politeness because people who disagree can resolve their disputes in the courts rather than in the streets. Third, the slow spread of formal education contributed to what Norbert Elias calls the "civilizing process."[18] Schooling, then as now, meant more than becoming literate; it meant learning manners in the broad sense of civility and propriety. As schooling has become more widespread, people have learned to restrain their emotions and to be civil with one another. Taken together, these factors can be combined into a formal hypothesis that suggests why the code of honor illustrated in *Romeo and Juliet* gradually disappeared in Western Europe: *The more the use of force is monopolized by the state, the more people have access to the courts to resolve disputes, and the more widespread are formal education and other mechanisms for teaching civility, then the lower the level of interpersonal violence and homicide in a society.* Whether this hypothesis is applicable to violent societies today is unclear. But it is worth considering, especially when combined with the historical events that followed.

It can be hypothesized that the three variables above also contributed to another fundamental structural change. Recall from chapter 2 that Max Weber wanted to understand why capitalism emerged in the West rather than in some other part of the world. He suggested that these same variables—the state monopoly on force, calculable legal mechanisms for dispute resolution, and formal education—combined with other factors, especially the emergence of the culture of capitalism in the seventeenth century, to produce the rise of capitalism as a dominant economic system.[19]

Economic development, in turn, also contributed to the long-term reduction in the homicide rate. In fact, the standard finding is that, with one exception, there is a negative relationship between the two.[20] It really does not matter how economic development is measured, whether in terms of gross domestic product, energy consumption, indexes of level of industrialization, or some other variable. Phrased formally, the finding is: *The greater the economic development, the lower the level of homicide.* The exception, however, is important. The United States departs from the pattern in that it is one of the most economically developed nations in the world but also displays a high level of homicide. And that is the reason for this book.

## CROSS-NATIONAL HOMICIDE RATES TODAY

The American anomaly can be seen in figure 3.1, which presents average homicide rates for six European nations along with those for Canada and the United States for the three-year period 1997–1999. The non-U.S. nations shown in the figure all display a low incidence of lethal violence. Sweden is highest, with an average rate of only 1.94 per 100,000 people, and the others are lower. The non-U.S. mean (for these nations, anyway) is 1.57. Although it is not shown in the figure, the mean for the European Union as a whole is 1.70.[21] In examining the figure, note particularly the case of Switzerland. It displays the lowest average homicide rate of all these nations even though guns are more easily available there than in other Western nations (except the United States, of course). I deal with this and related issues in chapter 5.

The usual interpretation of these low homicide rates, offered by Norbert Elias, is that the social structure of Western nations has changed in fundamental ways. They have undergone a "civilizing process" such that "immediate and uncontrolled [interpersonal] violence appears only in dreams or in isolated outbursts that we account for as pathological."[22] This modern orientation contrasts sharply with the common viciousness that pervaded the Middle Ages, when people lived for violence and took pleasure in it. But over time, Professor Elias argues, the social structure (via the state, the courts, the schools, and with economic development) has produced a context (a social house, to recall the metaphor from chapter 2), that leads people to display more emotional control and, hence, to restrain their violent urges. Today, the joy in violence is gone in most Western countries, or it is expressed indirectly in circumscribed contexts. Consider, for example, the underlying psychological implications of football and boxing, both for participants and spectators. Outside of such controlled contexts, those few who do take pleasure in committing violent acts are defined as deviant. We put them in prison.

In a way, Max Weber and Norbert Elias describe complementary aspects of the same historical process, but draw vastly different implications. As you might recall, Professor Weber portrayed modern societies as becoming disenchanted, since faith (in magic, in religion) seemed to be declining. His word for this process was *rationalization,* which he saw as the leitmotif (dominant theme) of the world today. In a rationalized world, people are less emotional; they are, instead, more methodical and systematic in their approach to problems; they emphasize practical solutions to the troubles they face. Hence, whenever possible, they use scientific ways of accounting for cause and effect relationships. Yet the dominance of these new ways of thinking and acting based on reason seemed to him to result in modern societies that are heartless and cold. Over the long term, he feared, modernity meant that societies would become like an "iron cage" in which reason runs amok and oppresses instead of frees human beings. As I mentioned in chapter 1, intellectuals in a variety of fields, such as poets (Yeats) and artists (Van Gogh), shared this fear. The post-modernist indictment of reason, rationality, and science as means of oppression also reflects this concern.[23]

Professor Elias, however, interprets modernity in a rather different way. He argues that not only have old ways of thinking and acting passed away, old ways of feeling are gone as well, replaced by a certain necessary expressive restraint. Hence, there has been, indeed, a decline in emotional reactions and the need to act on those feelings, especially when the action involves interpersonal violence and homicide. But Professor Elias believes this change is a good thing, since it can lead (under the right circumstances) to a more benign social order. The implication is that Max Weber and others have inter-

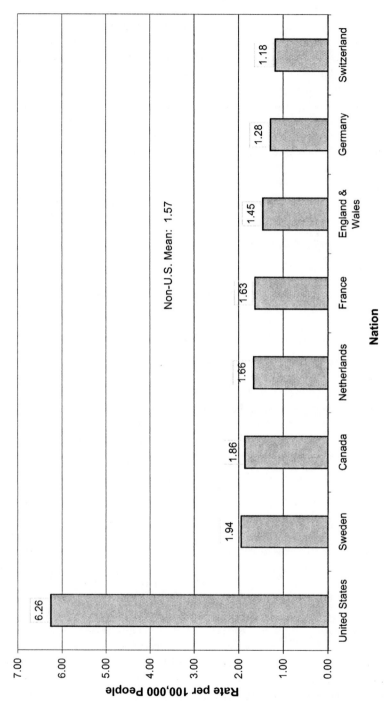

**Figure 3.1. Average Homicide Rates, Selected Nations, 1997–1999**

*Source:* Barclay et al. (2001:9).

*Notes:* Data are averages over three years, 1997–1999.
Canadian data include manslaughter.

preted modernity exactly backwards: We have emerged from a world populated by callous and heartless people who were indifferent to the suffering of others into one in which a dominant cultural value dictates that all human beings have dignity and self-worth. From this point of view every human life is meaningful and ought to be preserved. The pervasiveness of this Western value, which had its origins over two millennia ago, is one reason why I commented in chapter 1 that I am more sanguine than some observers about the nature and consequences of modernity.[24] It is also why the exceedingly high rate of homicide in the United States remains so troubling to many people: It conflicts with the fundamental value placed on human life.

Compared to the European nations shown in figure 3.1, the American average homicide rate of 6.26 for the years 1997–1999 is three to five times higher, depending on the comparison country. Thus, even when the rate in the United States is rather low, as it was from 1940 to 1960 (see figure 3.2), and even when it is declining significantly, as it did throughout the decade of the 1990s (to 6.1 in 1999), the base rate remains very high. The United States is a different kind of society, one that has always displayed interpersonal violence on a more routine basis than do other nations.

## HOMICIDE IN THE UNITED STATES
## FROM COLONIAL TIMES TO 1900

In a way, the American anomaly seems rather odd. The English, whose homicide rates were dropping over time, colonized this country. The English (and the French, of course, in Quebec) also settled Canada, and figure 3.1 shows that Canadian homicide rates resemble those in Western Europe.[25] So without thinking about it, one might predict that the United States ought to display a comparably low level of lethal violence. Yet it does not; the American homicide rate has always been very high. In fact, at certain times and places the level of lethal violence in this country has resembled and sometimes exceeded that in medieval Europe. It still does in some places in America.

Surprisingly, however, historical information on the high American homicide rate is more difficult to obtain than comparable Western European data. Because what became the United States began as an essentially unregulated frontier, records are much more incomplete than those compiled in any European nation. Although it appears that effective judicial systems developed rather quickly in the more settled areas, especially in New England, most colonial governmental entities did not have either the time or the inclination to maintain records of homicide. Even after independence, during the nineteenth century record keeping remained poor, and observers are often forced to rely on indirect evidence of the homicide rate. Nonetheless, it remains possible to see the overall pattern.

In the colonies, one exception to this poor record keeping does exist, and it provides a clue to the level of homicide during these times: executions. A total of 15,174 legal executions have been documented as having taken place in the original thirteen colonies and the fifty states between 1608 and 2000.[26] The actual number is significantly higher. In the past, about 80 percent of those put to death by the government were convicted of murder, with the remainder found guilty of rape and other crimes of violence. (Since the death penalty was reinstated in 1976, all of those executed have been convicted of homicide. My concern here, though, is with the colonial period.) Ted Robert Gurr estimates that executions occurred at a rate of about thirty-five per 100,000 residents of the thirteen colonies in 1640. This figure fell to about twenty in 1690, fifteen in 1740, and ten in 1780, at the time of independence.[27]

Although a few of those legally put to death in the colonies were probably innocent (which remains true today), these records are very imperfect and understate the total number of legal executions during those years. In addition, the use of executions as an indicator of the overall level of homicide is conservative because they represent only individuals who were caught, tried, convicted, and then put to death. Thus, while the number of executions declined over time during the colonial period, as indicated above, this fact only indicates that juries became less prone to impose the death penalty. As Roger Lane comments in his history of murder in America, trials were short, the usual verdict—for whites—not guilty. Even when guilty, many avoided the noose—especially whites.[28] In this context, then, a colonial execution rate of ten per 100,000 in 1780 provides a clue to a much higher total rate of homicide. In comparison, the English homicide rate was only about five per 100,000 over the course of the eighteenth century, in the process of falling to one early in the nineteenth. So the true rate of homicide in the colonies must have been considerably higher than in England or in Western Europe generally.

The reason is not hard to discern, even when the quantitative data are indirect, as here. Roger Lane observes that the American experience was shaped from the beginning by the uneasy entanglement of three peoples from three different continents.[29] Later on, the appearance of millions of immigrants produced a cauldron in which lethal violence occurred at a much higher rate than in other Western nations.

From the beginning, settlement by the English meant displacing the native inhabitants, peacefully when possible, violently when necessary. In 1491, just before their initial contact with whites, the Native American population in what is now the United States probably stood at about 5 million souls, and possibly as much as four times higher. This figure would fall steadily over the next 300 years.[30] Contact between the two peoples sometimes led to accusations of murder. In the more settled areas, Native Americans accused of killing whites were generally referred to white courts, where they were usually found guilty. Whites accused of killing Native Americans, however, were also nearly always referred to white courts, where they were usually found not guilty.

But on the frontier, in both the New England and Southern colonies, the situation was less juridical and more violent. Even apart from individual (usually unknown) episodes, periodic skirmishes and minor wars of great savagery occurred in which both Native Americans and whites committed atrocities, with the other side then retaliating in kind. Roger Lane observes that the level at which these homicides took place is simply unknowable.[31] But it was common, and it was high, in some places very high. In South Carolina, for example, which remained essentially a frontier environment throughout the eighteenth century, social life was vicious between 1760 and the 1780s, with nearly constant fighting, looting, and killing. Whites tried to decimate the Native American population and (as in the other colonies) were largely successful over the long term. In addition, though, South Carolina was unique in that whites fought ceaselessly among themselves: family versus family, neighbor against neighbor, and, during the war, Tories versus Revolutionaries. The whole period left the population with a numbed, casual attitude toward violence, much like that of medieval England.[32]

The institution of slavery was also being established during this period, accompanied by its brand of violence and homicide. The earliest generations, Professor Lane comments, were the most vicious. Since laws and norms were still being established, few limits existed on the brutality of whites as they attempted to subjugate dark-skinned people. Moreover, as the number of enslaved persons rose steadily over the years, so did white fears of revolt. In addition, of course, the need to deal with the daily acts of defiance (sometimes subtle, sometimes not) generated much violence, some of it lethal. In Virginia, the most settled of the Southern colonies, one historian found that about 555 slaves were sentenced to death during an eighty-year period of the eighteenth century. This figure is much higher than in all the Northern colonies at the time. Moreover, it is definitely an undercount, even of formal executions, and does not include random slayings (e.g., of escapees and those deemed incorrigible). The situation for slaves was probably even worse in South Carolina and Georgia during the colonial period, and so the "real," albeit unknown, number of slave killings must have been considerably higher.[33]

Evidence for the nineteenth century is sparse and does not begin until the 1840s. In the North, homicide rates appear to have been rather low by American standards. For example, in 1840 they were about three to four per 100,000 in Philadelphia and about two in Boston.[34] Indictments for murder, which would be much lower than the actual rate of murders committed, were about 3.7 per 100,000 in Philadelphia in 1839–1845, increasing to 4.0 for the years 1853–1859. In New York City, the estimate is about four to five per 100,000 for whites and seven to eight for African Americans in 1852. In the South, homicide rates appear to have been very high. For example, in Edgefield, South Carolina, coroners' reports translate into a homicide rate of about eighteen per 100,000 between 1844 and 1858.[35] The homicide rate in South Carolina during the entire antebellum period was at least four times that in Massachusetts.[36] Indeed, although South Carolina appears to have been an especially violent place, slavery had a corrosive effect on human relationships throughout the South.[37] The practice of continual tyranny meant that whites saw themselves as above the law, free to act out their impulses against those human beings held in bondage. Inevitably, of course, whites were violent among themselves as well; when they took offense, people fought and sometimes killed. Those enslaved also acted violently, but mainly against one another. As Fox Butterfield comments, they were "stripped of all their earthly possessions, even their families and their humanity. For many of the slaves, all that was left was personal honor." This legacy of slavery lives on today.

All these data for the first half of the nineteenth century are limited, that is to say they undercount the number of homicides. For example, they omit infanticides, deaths in urban riots and large-scale street fights, and minor incidents ignored by newspapers and district attorneys (in the case of indictments). These issues are significant. Roger Lane points out, for example, that reports of "dead infants found" (homicides, in other words) reached about one every other day in Philadelphia in the 1850s, and this does not count those inaccurately described as stillborn.[38] There is no reason to believe that Philadelphia was unique in this regard.

Relying on descriptions of daily life at the time, Professor Lane argues that the urban homicide rate in the North was relatively low (for the United States) until the 1840s, then spiked, mainly because of the influx of immigrants, many of whom (such as the Irish) came from violent backgrounds. Their background, combined with their age and sex (most were young males), high levels of unemployment, discrimination (against the Irish and free blacks), the invention of practical (if hard to use) handguns, lots of alcoholic intake, and the lack of trained police forces, created a volatile situation in the streets of every city. This social structure meant that young men without much to do fought one another. And sometimes they killed one another.[39] In addition, of course, the situation on the frontier was undoubtedly just as, if not more, violent. Vigilantes and vigilante organizations increasingly took the law into their own hands, executing many, some of whom may have been guilty of crimes and others not. In Kansas, for example, in 1856, about two hundred people were killed as pro- and antislavery forces committed murder in the name of ideology.[40] Many more homicides went unrecorded as the nation moved inexorably toward the Civil War.

The war's aftermath led to more violence and homicide. Although the issues at the individual level were typical—alcohol, a challenge to one's honor, arguments among friends or lovers, and the like—regional differences reflected varying structural contexts in which homicide occurred. The twin legacies of the slave-owning past and the outcome of the war meant that the South continued to be the most violent section of the country. In the North, the ever-increasing influx of immigrants and the efforts of working people to establish the rights of labor led to widespread urban warfare. On the frontier, now located west of the Mississippi River, the final subjugation of the Native American tribes and the unregulated nature of social life resulted in high levels of homicide.

Almost immediately after the Confederate surrender at Appomattox Court House in April 1865, southern whites began what amounted to a guerrilla war directed at the now free African Americans. Their goal was to reestablish the prewar social order of the South under conditions as near to slavery as possible. Their tool was homicide. In the period immediately following the war, law enforcement was minimal. In this context, murderous race riots occurred in Southern cities, the prewar night watch (designed to capture slaves off their plantations) evolved into the Ku Klux Klan and other secret societies whose members murdered and lynched, ordinary killings apparently occurred often, and various militias practiced their own forms of lethal violence. The murder of individuals (usually men) was thus designed to affect the entire population of African Americans, to cow them into submission. The overall homicide toll among African Americans during this period is unknowable, but surely very high.[41]

One indicator of this toll comes from lynching data, which exist for the years 1880–1930. During these years, the estimates of the number of African Americans murdered in this fashion range from about 2,800 to more than 4,700. The lower estimate translates into a murder rate due only to lynching of about forty-one per 100,000 African American residents of the ten Southern states during this period. The higher estimate, of course, would translate into a much higher rate. By either figure, the frequency of lynching constituted, as Stewart Tolnay and E. M. Beck title their study, a veritable *Festival of Violence*.[42] It is an appropriate title; this rate—just for lynching—is higher than the total homicide rate in Europe during medieval times. And make no mistake, these murders constituted a deliberate reign of terror. The process of lynching often involved sadistic rituals: The victim (or victims) would be tortured, have body parts removed, be hung to death, and then the body would be burned. In their aftermath, coroners typically concluded that "parties unknown" performed these acts, even though prominent members of the community were often present. By their presence, they sanctioned these acts and revealed themselves to be creatures of the campaign of violence. In addition, photographers often took pictures of the lynching process, which were then sold so that all would know about and learn from what had happened.[43]

But lynching did not stand alone; it made up only part of the total rate of African American homicide victimization in the South. It was during this period that, for the first time, guns became the most popular instrument in homicide. In the South, whites were determined to rule "by the pistol and rifle."[44] Some data on homicides other than lynching are available for Louisiana, for example, which became one of the most violent states in the nation. (This remains true today; see figure 3.3.) Excluding New Orleans, the rural areas of this state displayed a homicide rate of about fifty-two per 100,000 for the years 1866–1876, falling to about nineteen between 1877 and 1884. In the northwestern part of Louisiana the rate was 197. In the vast majority of these cases, whites killed African Americans.[45]

Although these rates only refer to one state, they suggest the dimensions of the overall campaign of terror that occurred throughout the Southern United States. Unreported murders of African Americans were common. For example, "whitecapping" occurred as African Americans were driven from their homes or land and sometimes murdered. In addition, of course, race riots, massacres, and day-to-day homicides took place every so often that terrorized all who might resist restoration of white power.[46] Finally, Southern states clearly used legal executions as part of the campaign to control the black population, a form of legal homicide.[47] The "real" total rate of African American victimization, then, is unknowable but must have been incredibly high, well above that recorded at any prior period in Western history, including medieval Europe. It means, even more than in a previous time and place, that "fear reigned everywhere; one had to be on one's guard all the time."[48] In this context, it was not hard for African Americans (especially males) to conclude that they remained alive only at the pleasure of the white community.

During this same period, white-on-white killings also occurred at a high level in the South. Writing in 1880, a newspaper reporter named Horace Redfield looked at South Carolina, Kentucky, and Texas (which was mostly settled by Southerners), using data from statewide newspapers for 1878.[49] Although most of his examples are of white-on-white killings, his data appear to include some interracial incidents. The results, almost surely an undercount because regional newspapers could not report on every lethal event, show a homicide rate of between twelve and twenty-nine per 100,000 residents of the three states. Other data are available for South Carolina, where state prosecutors reported 151 murders in 1891, 210 in 1895, and 280 in 1907, which translate (roughly) into a statewide homicide rate of fifteen to twenty-eight per 100,000 people. In the county of Saluda, South Carolina, the rate was about thirty-five per 100,000.[50] So the level of lethal violence in the South was not confined to terrorizing African Americans; whites killed each other as well, also in numbers comparable to those having occurred in medieval Europe. Fox Butterfield's (implicitly structural) explanation for all this intraracial white violence focuses on the usual variables: The Southern code of honor made people (mainly men) especially sensitive to the opinions of others, widespread and heavy alcohol consumption increased aggression, and guns became more lethal and more pervasive than ever. One might add to these factors the impact of the persistence of frontier conditions in the South, which meant that many people believed they had to solve their own problems without law, and the tradition of extralegal violence directed at African Americans, which redounded to white social relationships.

This overflow effect occurred among African Americans as well, who also appeared to kill one another at increasing rates during the second half of the nineteenth century. In Louisiana, for example, the African American homicide rate was about nine per 100,000 in the years 1866–1876, declining to seven from 1877 to 1884. Virtually all these killings were intraracial, and they probably represent an increase over the pre–Civil War period.[51] In his study of the American tradition of violence, Fox Butterfield offers the impression that the overall African American homicide rate during this period was high.[52] The argument is twofold. First, in a context in which the entire population was being terrorized, a displacement effect occurred in which African Americans (especially men) dared not fight against whites and so fought among themselves. Because they did so in a context in which the law (administrated by whites) was often irrelevant to the daily lives of African Americans, disputes had to be resolved without the police or courts. In fact, this period marked the rise of what came to be called the black "bad man," violent people with few redeeming qualities whose virtue was that they defied whites and what was perceived as white law. To be "bad" became, in the vernacular, to be "good." Second, in this context, the code of honor originally developed among whites grew to be even more powerful, only among blacks the term used was "respect." People, especially men, became extremely sensitive to insult and the opinions of others. When everything else was denied or forbidden—the right to vote, the ability to get an education or a job, the right to a fair trial—respect became vitally important. The consequences were sometimes lethal.

In the North, the situation differed considerably. Some states displayed rather low levels of violence—at least for the United States. For example, Horace Redfield estimated that Massachusetts displayed a rate of about one homicide per 100,000 in 1878. Although the newspapers he used reported no recorded homicides in Vermont or New Hampshire in that year, more recent scholars have found several. These rates are comparable to those in English cities at that time, where levels of homicide were less than one per 100,000. For example, between 1870 and 1900 the average homicide rate in London was only .36, while that in Liverpool was .60.[53] As in the South, however, when homicide did take place, guns were now the weapon of choice.

But lethal violence in other areas of the North occurred at a much higher rate, a great deal of it involving labor strife and much of it apparently unrecorded. As a rule, labor violence did not pit workers against their employers but against one another. Thus, Roger Lane argues, much of the bloodshed described as "labor violence" reflected competition for jobs among immigrant ethnic groups along with cultural differences. For several decades, he concludes, this structural context meant that "sticks and stones and pistol shots took their toll, one, two, three lives at a time, in innumerable skirmishes between strikers and strikebreakers."[54]

Some of these homicides occurred in cities, for which data are available.[55] For example, although the homicide rate for the entire state of Massachusetts may have been relatively low, the city of Boston averaged about three to four per 100,000 residents during the years 1870–1896. In New York City between 1870 and 1900, the average yearly number of white homicide victims was 4.25 per 100,000, and that of African American victims was 8.40. Nearly all these homicides were intraracial. In Philadelphia, murders averaged about 2.8 between 1860 and 1880, falling to 2.1 over the next twenty years. There were only 147 indictments of African Americans in Philadelphia in the entire seventy-two years between 1839 and 1901, but this translates into a homicide rate of about 7.5 per 100,000 within that small community.

Jeffrey Adler has compiled data for Chicago that are more systematic than for any other American city during this period.[56] It became one of the most violent large cities in the United States and saw a steady rise in the level of homicide. Thus, the overall homicide rate rose from 3.19 per 100,000 residents of Chicago in 1875–1877 to 6.86 in 1899–1901. The average for this entire period is 5.03. Because of the huge size of the white compared to African American population at that time, whites committed nearly all of these murders, most of them intraracial. Professor Adler's interpretation of the white homicide rate in Chicago varies by level of analysis and time period. At the individual level, most white murderers during the 1870s and 1880s were men killing other men. They tended to be young, unskilled, Irish, and unmarried. The typical killing occurred in or near a saloon and was fueled by alcohol. Over time, however, the characteristics of murderers changed. By the 1890s, homicides among whites were increasingly committed by married men in their thirties and forties against their spouses and children.

Structurally, it appears that the demographic situation (many young males), their violent background, a high rate of unemployment, and a social life centered around saloons created a context in which many homicides occurred, mostly between strangers. Over the course of the quarter-century, demographic changes took place as these men grew older and married. At the same time, improved law enforcement, the discipline of work, and changing norms about the organization of family life apparently led to greater violence between friends and spouses. The saloons, of course, were still there. The impact of all these factors led to increased homicide rates between 1875 and 1900.

Although the African American population in Chicago remained relatively small, it grew steadily over the last quarter of the nineteenth century, as did its rate of homicide.[57] The African American homicide rate in this city was not only higher than that for whites but also increased from 13.9 per 100,000 in 1875–1879 to 36.5 in 1890–1899. The rate rose still further during the first decade of the twentieth century, to 49.0 per 100,000. In his interpretation of the very high African American homicide rate in Chicago, Professor Adler discounts the idea that a code of honor was transported north (as such, he disagrees with Fox Butterfield). Rather, he argues that the increasing size of the African American population in Chicago led to much greater discrimination in both the workplace and housing. Although I am using the term *discrimination* here rather than *terror* (as occurred in the South), do not underestimate the inherent viciousness of the unequal treatment of African Americans in those days.[58] After two centuries of being confined to the land (in a plantation or a sharecropping system), African Americans moved north and found another trap: the urban ghetto, a context in which people were unable to find work except in menial occupations and were increasingly crowded together in impoverished conditions. This high degree of residential segregation was like a pressure cooker; it had to explode, and it did—often with lethal consequences.

The overall conclusion is clear: Although a few areas in the North did, in fact, display levels of homicide comparable to those found in English cities, this was rare. American cities in the latter part of the nineteenth century were violent. Even at their lowest levels, rates of homicide in Northern American cities were far higher than those occurring in English cities in these same years. And at their highest, American cities were exceedingly dangerous places in which to reside.

So was the American West. During this period, it was the opposite of a pressure cooker, a vast geographical area largely unregulated by law. In this regard, the Canadian frontier differed from the American. In Canada, law and law enforcement (in the form of the Mounted Police) preceded most settlement and, partly as a result, treaties with Native Americans were usually honored. By contrast, in the United States settlers, cattlemen, and corporations moved west on their own—and had to resolve their own disputes.[59] Shown in table 3.1 are estimated homicide rates per 100,000 in selected Western towns and counties during the 1870s and 1880s.

These data show that some parts of the American West were, indeed, very violent places during these years, with homicide rates often exceeding those in medieval Europe. Roger McGrath's structural interpretation of the situa-

**Table 3.1.   Estimated Homicide Rates in Selected Western Towns and Counties, 1870s and 1880s (per 100,000 Residents)**

| Years | Town/County | Rate |
|-------|-------------|------|
| 1870–1872 | Abilene, KS | 76.6 |
| 1873 | Ellsworth, KS | 421.9 |
| 1871–1874 | Wichita, KS | 91.3 |
| 1878 | Dodge City, KS | 160.0 |
| 1879–1885 | Caldwell, KS | 8.9 |
| 1878–1882 | Bodie, CA | 116.0 |
| 1878–1882 | Aurora, NE | 64.0 |
| 1880–1889 | Las Animas County, CO | 21.0 |
| 1880–1889 | Gila County, AZ | 120.5 |

Source: Data for Abilene, Ellsworth, Wichita, Dodge City, and Caldwell calculated by McKanna (1997:8) based on Dykstra (1968). Data for Bodie and Aurora are from McGrath (1989). Data for Las Animas County and Gila County from McKanna (1997:40–41).

tion applies to varying degrees to all of these towns and counties: "The character of the men of Aurora and Bodie and their value system [the Southern code of honor] meant that they would fight. Their consumption of alcohol meant that they would fight often. And their carrying of guns meant that fighting could easily prove fatal." In addition, of course, the fact that little effective law enforcement existed in these less settled places, which were really cattle and mining towns, constitutes another variable. So homicide was not merely routine in some areas of the West, it was a pervasive, everyday affair. Just how pervasive was wryly expressed by the *Bodie Daily Free Press* in June 1881: "Bodie is becoming a quiet summer resort—no one [was] killed here last week." In such contexts, one had to be on one's guard all the time in order to remain alive.[60]

These levels of violence, however, did not exist everywhere in the West. For example, Douglas County, Nebraska, where Omaha is located, was a more settled area and displayed a rather low homicide rate of 3.7 per 100,000 during the years 1880–1889.[61] This level resembled that in Northern cities at that time. Moreover, it is probable (although, so far as I know, no data exist) that the Lutheran émigrés in Minnesota, the Swedish immigrants in Wisconsin, and Mormon settlers in Utah were less violent than those living in other parts of the West. If so, however, it is because the social structure differed: Different values, low alcohol consumption, and fewer guns.

But even in Douglas County, some people had to be on the alert all the time: African Americans. Their situation in the West apparently did not differ much from that in other parts of the nation. The homicide rate among African Americans was about thirty-six per 100,000 in Omaha during the 1880s.

It appears that black migrants out of the South found themselves in much the same trap as existed in Chicago and other Northern cities. Moreover, Douglas County also displayed a significant (how high is unknown) number of lynchings during these years.[62]

Finally, not shown in table 3.1 is a higher homicide rate for Apaches than for other groups in Gila County, Arizona.[63] One tabulation reveals that of all those killed in the wars of conquest between the years 1680 and 1890 in what is now Arizona, about 90 percent were Native American and 10 percent white. Even though whites were the invaders, they nonetheless saw themselves as defending their farms, ranches, and mines; they interpreted their struggle as one between enlightenment and barbarism. As Clare McKanna summarizes the situation, whites believed that "it was necessary to destroy the Apaches [in Arizona] to save civilization."[64] This assertion is generalizable to the nation as a whole: By the turn of the twentieth century, the Native American population had fallen from probably about 5 million people to less than 250,000, primarily due to disease brought by Europeans, starvation, and murder.[65] Although the population has rebounded since then, a 95 percent decline is a good definition of genocide.

This population nadir is peculiarly significant because it occurred just at a time when Americans were celebrating their emergence as a self-consciously modern society. For example, in Chicago, on Monday, May 1, 1893, President Grover Cleveland gave a short speech in which he linked the nation's advanced technology and its democratic values to the rise of American civilization. After expressing the hope that other nations would eventually display similar accomplishments, he turned a key that set in motion a great dynamo that supplied electric power for a world's fair, called the Columbian Exposition.[66] Hundreds of thousands of artificial lights suddenly lit up, revealing the architectural grandeur of the "White City" at night. (It was especially constructed for the Exposition along the city's south lakefront.) Powered by electricity, a Ferris wheel festooned with lights turned for the first time. For many Americans, still unfamiliar with the uses of electrical power, the cacophony of lights and the Ferris wheel's seemingly unfettered motion symbolized the search for scientific knowledge that seemed to epitomize America at the end of the nineteenth century. People were entranced. The attendance on opening day was more than 128,000, and over the next several months more than 27 million people came to see the technological wonders presented in Chicago. With its outrageous extravagance, the Exposition constituted an homage to the modern society coming into being.

And in many ways, the United States was indeed becoming modern. Industrialization meant that economic productivity exploded. Recall, for a moment, the technological advances mentioned in chapter 1; they reflect the current level of economic development, a process that took off in the nineteenth century. During this same period, democracy advanced; by the time of the Exposition, white males had been voting for over a century, ensuring (even if imperfectly) the peaceful transfer of power. Other changes were also occurring, turning back on and reinforcing the changes that had already taken place: Poverty was declining. The infant mortality rate was dropping. Deaths from acute diseases were falling. Discoveries in both pure and applied science seemed to occur every day, providing the basis for modern lifestyles. At the Exposition, for example, the inventor of the light bulb, Thomas Edison, demonstrated an advanced version of his phonograph, the forerunner of the modern compact disc player, and his newly developed kinescope, the forerunner of the modern motion picture. Modernity meant that social life became different, and most people believed it became better.

At the same time, however, the history of the nineteenth century showed that the American anomaly was firmly established. It was (and is) an odd juxtaposition—a tradition of killing one another at a very high rate combined with economic development, scientific progress, and a modern lifestyle—that existed nowhere else in the world. This discordant quality of American society was captured in December 1893, when Antonín Dvořák premiered his Symphony No. 9, subtitled "From the New World." A visitor from Czechoslovakia, he intended the music to record his impressions of the United States. Accordingly, the first movement is dramatic, stormy might be a better word; the famous Largo constituting the second movement is obviously nostalgic and includes a paean to African American spirituals; the third movement is joyous, almost forward looking; but the finale establishes a new theme, one that clashes with that in the first movement. This clash, then, can be taken as a metaphor for the combination of violence and modernity that continues to make American society so unique.[67]

## HOMICIDE IN THE UNITED STATES FROM 1900 TO THE PRESENT

The extraordinary level of homicide that constitutes the American anomaly continued throughout the twentieth century. During this time, aggregate data for the nation as a whole became available. As might be expected, data for the early part of the twentieth century are the most difficult to interpret, especially the first thirty years or so. By way of anticipation, the most plausible conclusion is that the homicide rate for the period 1900–1932 displayed a slight increase. Getting to this conclusion, however, requires an evaluation of the evidence.

Contemporary observers of the American anomaly saw a huge surge in homicide in these years.[68] For example, in 1925 an insurance statistician named Frederick Hoffman compiled data for twenty-eight large American cities that showed a steady increase in the level of lethal violence from about

5.1 per 100,000 in 1900 to 10.3 in 1924. He found that guns were used in 71 percent of homicides, about the same proportion as today. Similarly, arrests for homicide in the twenty largest U.S. cities apparently rose from about seven in 1900 to thirteen or so in 1920. Finally, homicide rates for the newly established "death registration area" for the United States revealed a steady increase during this period, from about 1.2 per 100,000 in 1900 to 9.0 in 1932. In considering these data, Mr. Hoffman concluded that such pervasive violence ought to be considered "the darkest page in an otherwise inspiring history of our American civilization." Although his condemnation reflected a reasonable judgment of the American anomaly, the data on which it is based overestimate the increase in homicide that occurred during this period.

At least four factors contribute to the overestimated increase during the first third of the century.[69] First, advances in medical knowledge meant that coroners and the police became more adept at distinguishing between fatalities due to natural and unnatural causes. They thus identified murders that had previously gone unidentified. Second, police forces became more efficient and the number of officers and detectives devoted to solving violent crime rose. Hence, murders that would have been unknown in the past were now counted. Third, deaths in auto accidents during these years were often defined as murder, thereby raising the count. Such fatalities occurred mainly in large cities, where use of cars was becoming common. Today, of course, virtually all auto-related deaths are classified as involuntary manslaughter. Fourth, and most important, the data for the U.S. "death registration area" displayed artificially low homicide rates at the beginning of the century. This result occurred partly because many homicides were mislabeled as accidents during the first decade. But the low estimate mainly reflects the fact that when the federal government began compiling mortality data by cause, it established an initial "death registration area" in 1900 comprising only ten states, located mostly in the North Atlantic region and the District of Columbia. No more than about one-quarter of the population lived in these states, and most of them had displayed lower homicide rates than did other parts of the nation in the nineteenth century. So it should not be surprising that this pattern continued in the early years of the twentieth. Over the following thirty-three years, however, the "death registration area" expanded steadily to include the entire nation. By 1933, then, the complete data set showed a much higher rate of homicide. But, as noted, this result was misleading.

But an increase did occur. Figure 3.2 presents the aggregate American homicide rate over the entire twentieth century. As shown in the figure, it appears that the American homicide rate began the century at a somewhat higher level than contemporary observers believed and rose in a ragged way from about 6.4 per 100,000 persons to about 9.5 in 1932. Douglas Eckberg, who used econometric forecasting methods to develop these estimates, suggests that while this strategy is subject to error (more for the first decade than later), the results are plausible in light of what is known. For example, he estimates that in the year 1903 the nation's homicide rate was about 7.7 per 100,000, with a plausible range (the error term) between 6.6 and 8.8. Eric Monkkonen has recently argued that the average rate for the nation's ten largest cities in 1903 was probably about 8.8.[70] Thus, Professor Eckberg's estimates for this thirty-two-year period make sense.

Beginning in 1933, the "death registration area" included the entire nation, and by this time the Federal Bureau of Investigation was also compiling nationwide police reports of homicides. All observers agree that the resulting aggregate data are quite accurate.[71] As figure 3.2 shows, they reveal a decline in the U.S. homicide rate during the 1930s, from about 9.7 per 100,000 in 1933 to 5.0 in 1944. Although a spike occurred just after World War II to about 6.4, the rate settled back to less than 5.0 for most years until 1964. The level of lethal violence began a long, spectacular increase during the Vietnam War, reaching 10.2 in 1980. It varied during the ensuing decade in a ragged way, before beginning to fall in 1990. Recall that in 1999 the homicide rate reached a low (for the United States) of 6.1 per 100,000 people. So in a way, the American homicide rate came full circle over the course of the century, beginning in the low sixes in 1900 and returning to them in 1999. Much attention has been paid, in both the mass media and scholarly literature, to explaining why the homicide rate declined at the end of the century.[72] Although there is merit to this task, it seems to me that the recent fall in the American rate of homicide is not the most important story. The plot area of the figure shows that the average murder rate over the twentieth century was about 7.6, assuming Professor Eckberg's estimates are used. This high level suggests that the most important story about lethal violence in the twentieth century is the anomalous American rate. We have a problem. The purpose of this book is to offer a sociological explanation of this fact.

Some perspective on the extent of this problem and, hence, the need for an explanation, can be obtained by comparing the American homicide rate over the course of the twentieth century to that in England and Wales for the same time period. As revealed in the bottom portion of figure 3.2, the English have displayed a homicide level of about one per 100,000 people for the entire century, sometimes slightly below that level, sometimes slightly above it (during the 1990s, for example). As shown in the plot area of the figure, the mean English homicide rate for the last one hundred years is only .9. On average, then, the American rate of lethal violence has been about seven or eight times the English rate. This difference illustrates the American anomaly. Although expressed in quantitative terms that have little emotional impact, these data (along with those in figure 3.1) portray the stark reality that people living in the United States are much more likely to be killed than those living in other Western nations.

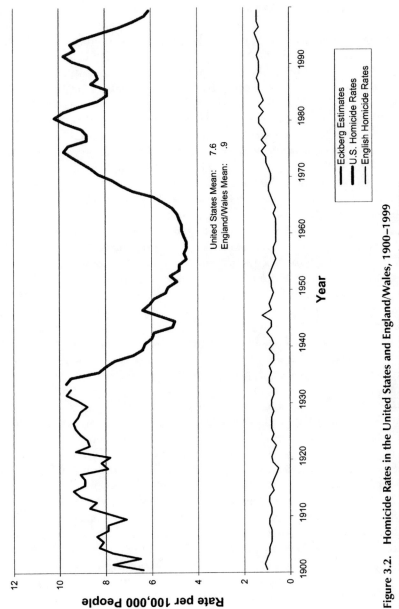

**Figure 3.2. Homicide Rates in the United States and England/Wales, 1900–1999**

*Sources:* U.S. Rates: 1900–1932, Eckberg (1995); 1933–1970, United States Bureau of the Census (1975);
1971–1999, Federal Bureau of Investigation (yearly, most recent 2001).
English Rates: 1900–1945, courtesy of the Home Office (my thanks to Judith Cotton); 1946–1999,
Home Office (2001).

The victims of this extraordinary violence are ordinary citizens of all classes, races, and regions. Here is an example that provides an illustrative way of putting the American problem in perspective.[73] It also suggests once again the banal motives underlying most homicides.

On the last day of the school year in West Palm Beach, Florida, Nathaniel Brazill, a thirteen-year-old honors student in the seventh grade, was sent home by the assistant principal for throwing water balloons. Although young Mr. Brazill had no history of violence (or even acting out), over the years he had witnessed the physical abuse of his mother by various men. His problems had apparently intensified recently, as his grades had begun dropping and he had referred to suicide in a letter to one of his teachers, Barry Grunow. So he was already like a seething pot when the school suspension occurred. He went home, picked up his grandfather's pistol from a drawer, and came back to the school. Once there, he knocked on the door of Mr. Grunow's classroom and asked to speak to a girl, upon whom he apparently had a crush. But Mr. Grunow, who was thirty-five years old and one of the school's most popular and effective teachers, told him to leave. In response, young Mr. Brazill, who himself appeared panicked as the drama unfolded, tried to frighten his teacher with the gun. But the situation deteriorated. Unable to control his emotions, the angry adolescent shot and killed Mr. Grunow. Although young Mr. Brazill is African American and Mr. Grunow is white, there is no indication that race played a role in this crime. In his subsequent testimony, the assailant claimed, plausibly, that he liked and respected the victim; Mr. Grunow was his favorite teacher. But he was boiling with anger and the events of the day marked the overflow point. A year later, a jury found Mr. Brazill, now fourteen years old, guilty of murder.

As a result of a relatively minor prank (water balloons!), a teacher happened to confront a very angry adolescent. Because Barry Grunow was in the wrong place at the wrong time, when a teenager had a gun, his wife and two children have had to endure the incomprehensible grief that comes from having a husband and father's life prematurely snuffed out. They have been forever deprived of his loving presence. They have been forced to completely reorganize their lives because of the lost income and other forms of support he would have provided. In addition, thousands of students will be deprived of his abilities as a teacher. Because he was killed while still a young man, neither the nation nor the community will ever know what else Mr. Grunow would have accomplished in the remainder of his life. Meanwhile, Nathaniel Brazill was sentenced to twenty-eight years in prison, without early parole. He will be forty-one years of age when released. During this time, his incarceration will cost the state of Florida at least $19,000 per year (a total of $532,000) plus medical, psychological, and numerous other expenses. It is doubtful if this honor student will ever realize his potential; prison is not typically a place where one learns to be a productive citizen. It is a place where inmates learn to be violent. I am not arguing about the justness of the penalty Mr. Brazill must pay; he took a human life. I am only recognizing that his incarceration is a pity.

This sad episode is simply an example, of course, and an arbitrary one. But it raises an important question: Would this homicide and thousands more like it happen in England or Wales? One doubts it. Both England and the United States are economically developed nations. In both England and the United States, people (including adolescents) sometimes become angry at one another. In England, they usually get over it without killing anyone. In the United States, however, angry people sometimes commit murder. What if Nathaniel Brazill (and thousands more like him) had not found a gun readily available? Although anecdotes, such as the killing of Barry Grunow, illustrate the problem, the data in figures 3.1 and 3.2 show the degree to which this country is unique in its level of lethal violence. They raise the central questions posed in this book, the story that needs to be explained: Why is the American homicide rate so high? And can we reduce the frequency with which it occurs?

## TWO VARIANTS OF HOMICIDE
## IN THE UNITED STATES

Subsequent chapters consider some answers to these questions. The American data presented in figures 3.1 and 3.2 constitute, as Emile Durkheim would say, a social fact—the "thing" to be explained in this book. Even so, these aggregate data obscure two issues that should also be reported before moving on. The first is regional differences. All the information from colonial times to the turn of the twentieth century revealed that the South and West (in the late nineteenth century) displayed higher rates of homicide than did the rest of the nation. The second issue is racial differences. The historical data also indicated that African Americans exhibited higher levels than did whites. These patterns continued throughout the twentieth century, and they have led some observers to misunderstand the nature and extent of the American anomaly.[74] I argue that the use of these differences to dismiss the high rate of American homicide emphasizes the part instead of the whole. It misses the big story. In the meantime, however, this section presents data on twentieth-century regional and racial variations in the American homicide rate.

### Homicide and Region

The continuing problem of the violent South confronts anyone who would consider the level of homicide in the United States. Every historian of the region, without exception, has had to deal with this vexing issue.[75] And it is not a problem confined to the nineteenth century and earlier. Although the extent of the differences between the South and other parts of the nation has varied over the years (as did the overall level of homicide), the pattern of high Southern homicide rates has been stable throughout the twentieth century. This is so regardless of how the South is defined (more on this later).

Huntington Brearley first presented data for the twentieth century by region in his neglected classic, *Homicide in the United States*, written in 1932.[76] He assembled quantitative data for the decade 1918–1927 showing that fourteen Southern and border states displayed a level of lethal violence two to five times higher than that in other regions of the nation. The following figures show the average rate for these years:

|            |                    |
|------------|--------------------|
| Northeast  | 3.2 per 100,000    |
| Midwest    | 5.4 per 100,000    |
| West       | 7.6 per 100,000    |
| South      | 15.1 per 100,000   |

Referring to the presence of so many guns and the then common habit of carrying them on the person, Professor Brearley, a Southerner, described the South as "that part of the United States lying below the Smith and Wesson line." Although it is a flippant assertion, it identifies a key structural variable.

Similarly, Stuart Lottier showed that in 1938 the eleven former Confederate states displayed homicide rates well over twice that of the rest of the nation.[77] Lyle Shannon provided a mid-century comparison of the South with other regions in a way similar to that of Professor Brearley. Using data for the years 1946–1952, he discovered an average homicide rate for the South that was three to six times greater than that in other parts of the United States:[78]

|            |                    |
|------------|--------------------|
| Northeast  | 1.8 per 100,000    |
| Midwest    | 3.4 per 100,000    |
| West       | 4.5 per 100,000    |
| South      | 12.5 per 100,000   |

Finally, end-of-the-century data reveal the same pattern. Shown below are average homicide rates by region for the twenty-four years 1976–1999. Although differences between the South and other regions declined in the late twentieth century, they remain significant.[79]

|            |                    |
|------------|--------------------|
| Northeast  | 5.7 per 100,000    |
| Midwest    | 6.1 per 100,000    |
| West       | 8.1 per 100,000    |
| South      | 10.4 per 100,000   |

No one, at least so far as I know, disputes the data; the South displays a much higher rate of homicide than does the rest of the nation. It always has. Scholarly disputes occur, however, when observers try to account for this difference. Sometime around the mid-twentieth century, a Southerner was asked by a researcher from the North why the murder rate in the South was so high. He replied "that he reckoned there were just more folks in the South who needed killing."[80] Although this response displays a certain unapologetic purity, it avoids the more fundamental question of why people in this region tend to resolve their disputes violently. The common argument in the literature, at least for twentieth-century Southern homicide, has been that a culture of violence exists in the region that supports the use of aggressive responses to provocation.[81]

Perhaps so. But the argument carries with it three problems along with, for my purposes, a major difficulty.

First, the concept "culture of violence" seems to imply a certain glorification of violence that is misleading. The term is used as a shorthand way of describing the social contexts (or structures) in which aggression and violence seem normal or common. More generally and more accurately, cultural values provide people with a basic toolkit of responses for dealing with the various situations in which they find themselves. In some contexts, then, perhaps the long-term legacy of the nineteenth-century code of honor still leads people to define certain situations as requiring a violent response.[82] In addition, cultural values also lead people to make behavioral choices—such as owning or carrying guns, for example, or drinking lots of alcohol. When these values lead many people to make such choices, it increases the odds of lethal violence occurring when they become angry.

Second, it is fiendishly difficult to isolate and measure the impact of cultural values (Southern or any other kind) in a way that controls for the effects of structural variables.[83] Southern culture may in fact be unique (I think it was and perhaps still is), but these measurement problems make the issue very controversial among scholars. This problem may not have a solution.

Third, it is unclear just what states (or parts of states) the South comprises. It is rare for a research study to provide a rationale for inclusion or exclusion. Most researchers make one of two choices, using either the eleven former Confederate states or the Census Bureau's definition, which includes sixteen states. Both are arbitrary. Figure 3.3 illustrates the problem. As with the data presented previously to contrast the South with other regions, the figure defines the South as the Census Bureau does. But this strategy hides a great deal of variability among the states. Why is Delaware in the South? Why is Kentucky in the West? Why are Missouri and Kansas in the Midwest? Alternatively, if the South were defined as only the eleven Confederate states, then the average difference between it and the rest of the nation would be greater,

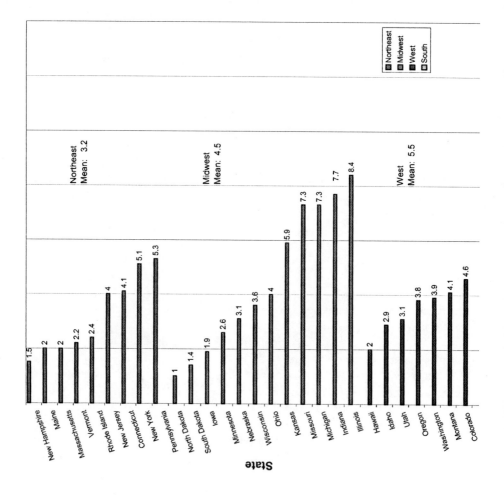

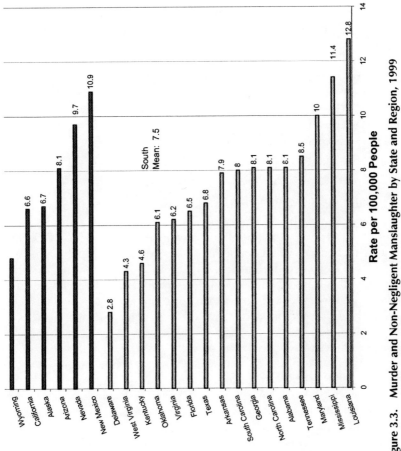

**Figure 3.3. Murder and Non-Negligent Manslaughter by State and Region, 1999**

*Source:* Bureau of Justice Statistics (2001:278).

but one doubts if the South stops there. Ultimately, it is simply unclear where Southern culture begins and ends.

This lack of definitional clarity leads to the major difficulty alluded to previously: Although the Southern rate of homicide is indeed higher than that for the rest of the nation, regardless of the definition of South, nearly every American state displays a higher rate than does any European nation. From the point of view of the argument in this book, this is the issue that needs to be emphasized. When the data in figures 3.1, 3.2, and 3.3 are compared, it becomes clear that only a few American states, such as New Hampshire, Iowa, and North Dakota, exhibit homicide levels similar to those in Western Europe. A few more states, such as Massachusetts, Minnesota, Idaho, and Delaware, reveal levels slightly above the average for Western Europe. All the remainder—North, South, Midwest, and West—display rates significantly higher than those for the European nations shown in figures 3.1 and 3.2. Scholars who try to explain away aggregate American rates as a function of Southern violence miss the big story.

### Homicide and Race

The same point is true regarding race and homicide. Although data are sparse, it appears that by the end of the nineteenth century African American rates of homicide were much higher than those among whites. The pattern continued throughout the twentieth century, as shown in table 3.2, which presents the data by decade. The increase for 1910–1930 reflects, in part, the expansion of the death registration area during these years. But it is the difference between races that is of interest here. Note also that the data in table 3.2 are for homicide victims. My guess is that more interracial homicides were white on black during the first third of the century. More recently, a higher proportion of black-on-white homicides has occurred. The point to remember, however, is that most murders at all times have been intraracial. For example, in 1999, 46 percent of all murders were white on white and 42 percent were black on black—meaning that a total of 88 percent were intraracial.[84] After these qualifications are noted, the pattern is clear: The African American rate of homicide has been much higher than that for whites throughout the twentieth century. In 1999, to take a recent example, about twenty-one of every 100,000 African Americans were victims of murder, compared to about four whites. The table shows that at any given time African Americans have been from seven to ten times more likely to be killed than whites.

One issue posed by these data is why this difference exists and what it means. It appears, at least for the last few years of the twentieth century, that most African American homicides were outcomes of assault and not related to some other offense.[85] This fact suggests that the high murder rate in this community reflects a widespread tendency to resolve conflicts and disputes violently. And this tendency indicates, in my judgment, how pervasive discrimination and other factors have affected African Americans over time. Racial discrimination constitutes one of the variables explaining the high *American homicide rate*. No explanation of the American anomaly can be complete without taking this issue into account.

But note the italicized phrase *American homicide rate* above. It leads to the second issue posed by these data: The level of lethal violence in this country is anomalous regardless of race. Thus, throughout the twentieth century, both African Americans and whites have been victims of murder at a higher rate than have Western Europeans. Compare, for example, the white homicide rates in table 3.2 with the English data presented in figure 3.2. The rates for white Americans were two or three times higher throughout the century. This fact suggests that arguments dismissing the American anomaly as due to racial differences miss the point. Taking part of the nation out and comparing it to other nations is a little like amputating a person's leg, then comparing the mutilated person to another whole person. It does not make sense. For better or worse, we are one nation. And we kill each other often.

## MODERNITY, SOCIAL CLASS, AND HOMICIDE

This propensity of Americans to kill one another is one reason why *Romeo and Juliet* remains so appealing. It is primarily a love story that turns into a tragedy; at least most people seem to see it that way. And Shakespeare does emphasize the peculiar code (or norm) of courtly love that prevailed at that time. Romeo is smitten, with the unseen Rosalind when the play opens and then, more profoundly, with Juliet. One assumes that the reason he initially avoids the fight with Tybalt is because he has fallen in love with Juliet and begun to identify himself with the Capulets. He becomes a tragic figure only after killing Tybalt. More sociologically, however, as Northrop Frye emphasizes, this play (like several others Shakespeare wrote during this period) illustrates the impact of unfettered violence on the social order. By the end of the sixteenth century, when *Romeo and Juliet* was written, Western societies had become less dangerous and lethal compared to the medieval past. Nonetheless, the play offers an account, in miniature, of the disorder and malignant quality of life that exists when feuds among the nobility take on a life of their own.[86] In so doing, it illustrates a characteristic of Europe at that time: Violence still pervaded these societies. It remained an accepted method for resolving disputes, as indicated by the fact that anyone who could went about armed with knives, swords, and other weapons. As a result, gentlemen fought; they and their families and retinues feuded and brawled incessantly.

**Table 3.2.  Homicide Victimization by Race, 1910–1999 (per 100,000 People)**

| Year | African American | White |
|------|------------------|-------|
| 1910 | 22.3 | 4.1 |
| 1920 | 28.8 | 4.8 |
| 1930 | 37.9 | 5.6 |
| 1940 | 33.9 | 3.2 |
| 1950 | NA | NA |
| 1960 | 21.9 | 2.5 |
| 1970 | 35.9 | 4.4 |
| 1980 | 37.7 | 6.3 |
| 1990 | 37.7 | 5.4 |
| 1999 | 20.6 | 3.5 |

*Notes:* Data for 1910–1930 are for the death registration area only. It included twenty-one states in 1910, thirty-six in 1920, and forty-eight in 1930. See Eckberg (1995:7). NA = Not available.

*Sources:* For 1910–1970, United States Bureau of the Census (1980). For 1980–1999, Bureau of Justice Statistics (2001).

More generally, everyone—upper class, lower class, and in between—fought as well. So people killed one another at great rates.

Today, however, the situation differs. The "savagery of feeling" that pervaded medieval societies has disappeared in the West. Modernity, seen as a 750-year process, has meant an increase in civility in interpersonal relations, even when (indeed, especially when) conflicts occur. The result has usually been that daily life is now more benign. One indicator of this change is the data showing that homicide rates in most Western nations have declined and are very low. Norbert Elias called this trend the "civilizing process," and I noted earlier that this insight implied a rather optimistic view of modernity. But a benign social order is not inevitable in modern societies.

In 1904, Max Weber and his wife, Marianne, toured the United States. This country represented, for him, a model of the future. This is because people's behavior revealed certain unique values: Work carries intrinsic worth and is a source of people's identity, immediate pleasure tends to be postponed in favor of long-term goals, people strive to make money as an indicator of virtue, and people organize their lives in methodical ways (not only as a means to an end but as an end in itself). He saw that these values combined with scientific advances, the advent of democracy, and other factors to produce the most economically advanced nation in the world at that time. These observations of America probably helped solidify the argument he would subsequently make in his greatest work, *The Protestant Ethic and the Spirit of Capitalism.*[87] But Professor Weber did not share in the usual American optimism about the future. He was, in fact, rather pessimistic. Although the pervasiveness of values like these have transformed Western societies over the last few centuries and, indeed, made modernity possible, he concluded that social life, not just in the United States but throughout the West, was dominated by coldly rational people whom he described as "specialists without spirit, sensualists without heart." In such a context, he feared that the result would be a self-perpetuating oppressive society. Even though Professor Weber does not explore the implication, he knew that oppression is often buttressed by violence—justified, of course, by ideology. Reason, then, can become a force for evil rather than liberation.

Norbert Elias recognized the same potential; he was not naïve about the nature or future of modernity. After all, he was a German Jew whose family died in Nazi concentration camps. Under certain conditions, what he called "decivilizing" processes can occur, and the twentieth century provides numerous instances of them.[88] Even so, Professor Elias argued that long-term structural changes have led to widespread expressive restraint in the population, with the result that people are more humane than in the past. This orientation reflects the more fundamental Western value mentioned earlier: that human life is sacred, that human beings have worth and dignity. The whole modern conception of human rights, with its implications for war crimes and the rise of international law, follows from this value. I would like to suggest that the historical decline in homicide provides a powerful example of his interpretation of Western history.

This trend began at the top of the class structure and percolated downward. It has meant that the relationship between homicide and social class has changed, and this is so in the United States as well as Western Europe.[89] Here is a thought experiment designed to illustrate this change: The two wealthiest and most socially prominent families in your community have been feuding for years. Someone takes offense, perhaps over a letter to the editor of the local paper, perhaps because they support a different candidate or dispute the outcome of an election, or perhaps because the families back opposing college football teams. So the heads of the two families square off in a duel. Alternatively, they and their best friends gather in the center of town and fight, just like the Capulets and Montagues do in *Romeo and Juliet*. Several people die. Such imagining is, of course, a flight of fancy; neither scenario would happen today in any Western society, including the United States.

Yet conflict has not disappeared. Disputes and disagreements are intrinsic to everyday life; they occur at all times and places. But when a dispute takes place today, the response most people take is simple—sue the bastards— which is a glib way of restating the argument presented earlier: When the state limits the ability of people to use personal force, provides access to a system of law, and ensures that the population is well educated, then nonviolent methods of conflict resolution occur more often. These changes set some of the conditions necessary for the emergence of the middle class, a process that was accelerated by the rise of capitalism and the economic development that followed. Today, then, most people have available nonviolent methods of resolving their conflicts and have learned how to use them. They are civil with one another. So murder takes place much less frequently than in the past, especially among the middle and upper classes. Thus, in the only study of "high status" homicide that I know of, the researchers had a great deal of trouble locating homicides committed by non-poor persons. They found no examples of homicide by elites. Homicides committed by middle- and upper-middle-class people are so rare that no meaningful sample was possible. Even so, the authors found that middle-class men, mostly in the context of domestic disputes, commit less than .5 percent of all homicides, and even this estimate is probably high.[90] The few that do occur become celebrated, as in the O. J. Simpson case a few years ago.

Today, homicide is concentrated at the bottom of the class structure in all Western societies, including the United States. In both Western Europe and this country, the typical murderer is poor, unemployed, and relatively uneducated; and the victim usually resembles the perpetrator.[91] Even so, exceptions exist. Michael McDermott's killing spree, for example, illustrates the fact that killers can come from any class background. As you might recall from chapter 2, he was a software engineer. His status in the community is one (but not the only) reason his violent acts seemed so odd. And as Barry Grunow's death illustrates, a middle-class person who happens to be in the wrong place at the wrong time can easily become a victim. This possibility is one reason why some people move into gated communities. But this strategy is no solution; they have to go out some time. So everyone is vulnerable.

Yet the United States is not a callous and heartless society, nor is it dominated by the joy in violence that characterized medieval societies. But it is a peculiar place. The historical data show that lethal violence was pervasive in many parts of the nation until rather recently. Even today, the cross-national data show that homicide, although actually a rare event, occurs sufficiently often in this country that it is routine. When the problem of homicide is placed in historical and cross-national perspective, the extent to which we are a modern but murderous society becomes clear. This situation is a paradox. How can all this lethal violence be explained? And do we have to live with it?

## NOTES

1. Frye (1986). Details of the play's production presented later on are taken from Gibbons (1980).
2. Sharpe (1996:22).
3. Givens (1977:28 and 34).
4. Elias (1978:195).
5. Cohen (1996).
6. Gurr (1989:29); see also Stone (1983).

7. Johnson and Monkkonen (1996:9 and 22); Gurr (1989:33); Monkkonen (2001:155).

8. Gurr (1989); Sharpe (1996).

9. Stone (1965:231–32).

10. Cockburn (1977:55–56). Quoted in Gurr (1989:29).

11. The next two paragraphs are indebted to Gurr (1989:24).

12. Kaye (1967).

13. Reagan (1997).

14. Gurr (1989:31).

15. Gurr (1989); Sharpe (1996). On variations in the homicide rate in England over time, see Roth (2001).

16. Stone (1965:200).

17. Black (1983).

18. Elias (1978).

19. Weber (1905; 1920). For a more complete analysis of Weber's explanation of the rise of capitalism, see Turner, Beeghley and Powers (2002).

20. LaFree (1999:141).

21. Barclay et al. (2001:9).

22. Elias (1978:192).

23. Lyotard (1984).

24. See Berger (1992).

25. For an analysis of why Canadian culture and social structure more closely resemble that in England than do those of the United States, see Lipset (1990).

26. The data for 1608–1986 were originally compiled by W. Clark Espy. My thanks to Michael Radelet for providing them to me. Ted Robert Gurr's estimates for colonial executions, noted below, came from the Espy data set (see Gurr, 1989:35 and footnote 34). The data for 1986–2000 are from the Death Penalty Information Center at www.deathpenaltyinfo.org.

27. Gurr (1989:36). As an aside, the English also executed people during these years, often for mundane crimes. In a brilliant and very controversial book, Gatrell (1994) argues that the movement against hanging was based less on a moral position and more on a certain squeamishness that reflected projection and emotional repression. McGowen (2000), however, raises important questions about the Gatrell thesis.

28. Lane (1997:57).

29. Lane (1997:33).

30. Thornton (1987; 2001); Mann (2002).

31. Lane (1997).

32. Butterfield (1996). He cites Brown (1975).

33. Lane (1997:61–63).

34. For Philadelphia, see Lane (1979:60); for Boston, see Hindus (1980); for Philadelphia indictments, see Lane (1997:115); for New York City, see Monkkonen (1989:86).

35. Butterfield (1996:8).

36. Hindus (1980:63–65).

37. Butterfield (1996:19–34). The quote below is on p. 32.

38. Lane (1997:119).

39. Lane (1997:92–145); see also Gorn (1987).
40. Lane (1997:130–33).
41. Kennedy (1995); see also Tolnay and Beck (1995:4–13).
42. The lower estimate and the rate of homicide among African Americans come from Tolnay and Beck (1995:38, 271). The higher estimate comes from Zangrando (1980:6).
43. See Vandal on lynching rituals (2000:99). Allen et al. review the lynching photographs (2000). Gatrell provides a chilling description of the process by which one hangs to death (1994:29–99). Brundage examines the various explanations for the Southern reign of terror (1997).
44. Foner (1988:119).
45. Vandal (2000:47–49).
46. On "whitecapping," see Holmes (1969; 1973). On the terror, see Trelease (1971); Foner (1988); Williams (1996).
47. Tolnay et al. (1992).
48. Elias (1978:195).
49. Redfield (1880).
50. Butterfield (1996:51–53).
51. Vandal (2000:164).
52. Butterfield (1996:58–67).
53. Redfield (1880); Monkkonen (1989:86–87; 2001:170–77). For more recent data on New Hampshire and Vermont, see Roth (2002).
54. Lane (1997:156–65). The quotation is on p. 161.
55. For Boston, see Ferdinand (1967:89); for New York City, see Monkkonen (1989:86–87); for Philadelphia, see Lane (1979:71 and 104); for Chicago, see Adler (1999:300).
56. Adler (1997:255).
57. Adler (1999:300; 306–10).
58. Massey and Denton (1993:21).
59. Lipset (1990:90–91).
60. McGrath (1989:136). The quote from the *Bodie Daily Free Press* comes from a website about modern Western ghost towns, at www.smithsonianmag.si.edu/jour neys/01/may01/travel_tips.html.
61. McKanna (1997:40–41).
62. McKanna (1997:45–77).
63. McKanna (1997:40–41).
64. McKanna (1997:130–31).
65. Thornton (1987; 2001); Mann (2002).
66. Muccigrosso (1993:79).
67. My interpretation of Dvořák's musical intent is, let us say, loose. For a comparison, see Machlis (1955).
68. Data for twenty-eight cities are from Hoffman (1925:96). The proportion of gun-related homicides is from p. 4; the quote below is from p. 10. Arrest data are from Monkkonen (1981:77). Professor Monkkonen is aware of the problems with his city-level data, as reviewed in the following text. "Death registration" data are from United States Bureau of the Census (1975:414).

69. Lane (1997); Eckberg (1995).

70. Monkkonen (2001:14).

71. There are actually two nationwide systems for reporting homicide; see Department of Justice (1995). On the relative accuracy of these measures, see Reidel (1999); Zahn and McCall (1999).

72. See Blumstein (1998); LaFree (1999a).

73. Associated Press (2000); Riddle (2001); Canedy (2001).

74. Monkkonen (1989); Messner and Rosenfeld (1997).

75. See Hackney (1969); Reed (1993).

76. Brearley (1932:19).

77. Lottier (1938).

78. Shannon (1954).

79. Bureau of Justice Statistics (2000).

80. Hackney (1969:908).

81. See Hackney (1969) and Gastil (1971).

82. On culture as a toolkit, see Swidler (1986). Among those finding a relationship between Southern culture and violence, see Ellison (1991); Unnithan et al. (1994); and Corzine et al. (1999).

83. Loftin and Hill (1974); Dixon and Lizotte (1987).

84. Bureau of Justice Statistics (2001).

85. Zimring and Hawkins (1997:78). The amputation metaphor in the following paragraph comes from this source.

86. Frye (1986:13).

87. Weber (1905). The quotation below comes from p. 182. On the impact of Weber's visit to the United States, see Collins (1986).

88. Elias outlines the conditions under which "decivilization" occurs in *The Germans* (1989). I am relying on Fletcher (1997).

89. See Cooney (1997; 1998).

90. Green and Wakefield (1979).

91. Cooney (1997; 1998).

# 4

# The American Dream and Homicide: A Critique

The data are now clear: Unlike other Western nations, the United States is a modern yet murderous society. Throughout the nineteenth century, at a time when homicide rates in Western European nations fell to around one per 100,000, the American rate remained (except in a few areas) much higher, often catastrophically higher. Some parts of the South and West resembled war zones in the sense that people, especially African Americans, had to be on guard all the time, knowing that on any day they might die violently. Although the American homicide rate varied a great deal during the twentieth century, this variation occurred above a very high base. Indeed, as shown in chapter 3, a curious symmetry exists in that homicide rates began the century at about six per 100,000 and ended the century at that same level. All this lethal violence is anomalous compared to other economically developed nations.

Some observers, immersed in the problem, either give up trying to explain this peculiar situation or declare victory because the homicide rate has fallen in recent years. You may recall from chapter 1, for example, that a police officer, reacting to a particular murder, lamented that all this violence in America is inexplicable. Also in chapter 1, a scholar was quoted who argued that "we are victims of our own success" at reducing the homicide rate to its current "low" level. He did not add but probably meant that lowering the homicide rate any further would require major (albeit unlikely) structural changes. But neither response provides satisfaction because each implies that Americans, unlike Europeans, must live with carnage all around them and organize our lives based on fear.

Yet in a modern society, problems (not just homicide but other issues as well) should be explicable. Moreover, to describe a homicide rate that has fallen to six per 100,000 as a "success" admits, at least implicitly, that this country is an oddly violent society. Logically, there must be systematic differences—structural differences—between the United States and other Western nations that account for so many Americans killing one another. Hence, the task is to identify the sources of these differences and show their relationship to homicide. This is a tricky process. Much debate is both possible and useful as sociologists and criminologists seek to explain lethal violence in America. And the answers (the plural is deliberate) carry important implications. Although this metaphor may be a stretch, the impact of such answers can be a little like the result of skilled therapy. When neurotic people talk through the issues affecting their lives and develop insight into their unconscious motives, they can (although they may not) change their behavior. Self-knowledge allows them to choose. Admittedly, this is a difficult, painful, often long-term, and usually mistake-prone process for most individuals. By analogy, I would like to suggest that a sociological explanation of the factors leading to the high American homicide rate also opens up the possibility of change—at the structural level. Such change, of course, will not come easily. Entrenched interests, ideological and economic, always exist. But we live in a time of increasing control over the social structure; if the human carnage due to homicide is high in America, it is because Americans choose to live with it.

As described in chapter 2, the sociological goal is to explain why we choose to live with so much lethal violence by identifying the key variables that produce it. Doing so requires, as Steven Messner and Richard Rosenfeld point out, that scholars get out of their academic tower, stop talking to and writing for one another, and "put sociology to work."[1] They begin this task in their book, *Crime and the American Dream*, by arguing that a high level of serious crime—such as homicide—is normal, that it is built into this nation's social structure. They are clearly correct; homicide is a routine part of American life. Indeed, their book, published originally in 1991, in a second edition in 1997, and a third in 2001, has become an important contribution to the literature. It is required reading if one wants to understand the nature of American culture and society.

In attempting to explain the uniquely high level of homicide in the United States, I hope to continue the process of putting sociology to work by building on their analysis. In so doing, however, it is necessary to assess its strengths and weaknesses. In this chapter, I argue that although Professors Messner and Rosenfeld offer a useful way to understand the structural sources of crime and other forms of deviance, their analysis provides only a partial explanation of the high American rate of homicide. The process of evaluating their work and its implications has a larger purpose as well, however, in that it also provides a way of assessing different perspectives on the nature of modernity. For example, from one point of view, the anomic nature of American culture and society (to be explained later) means that it systematically generates deviance. But from the point of view of economic development, modern societies also generate economic opportunity and a radically improved lifestyle for almost everyone, which reduces the level of lethal violence in most nations—except the United States. Each angle of vision is valid, depending on one's purpose. This recognition suggests that the task is to understand how an anomalous phenomenon like a high homicide rate can be generated in a modern society like the United States.

## THE THESIS AND ITS EMPIRICAL BASIS

The authors of *Crime and the American Dream* waste no time; they make their thesis explicit from the very beginning.[2] They ask a "basic question": Why are rates of serious crime "so exceptionally high" in the United States? They answer that the value Americans place on material success, which they call the American Dream, is so great that it encourages the use of illegitimate strategies to obtain it. Moreover, they believe, this cultural emphasis has structural consequences, especially in the United States, as it has led over time to the dominance of the economy coupled with a weakening of the family, government, and education as institutional bulwarks against "criminogenic tendencies." This answer, as professionals know, draws on the work of Robert K. Merton and the rich tradition of theory established by his seminal essay, "Social Structure and Anomie."[3]

In *Crime and the American Dream*, the authors establish the empirical basis for their thesis by assembling cross-national and historical data summarizing the nature and level of "serious crime."[4] Although they do not define "serious crime," they focus on robbery and homicide, using a set of figures similar to those I presented in chapter 3. Cross-nationally, they compare robbery and homicide rates in the United States and various Western European nations and show that the American rate is much higher in both categories. They then present historical data on homicide for 1900–1997, revealing that while a great deal of variation took place during the twentieth century, it occurred at an exceedingly high level. Thus, their concern is identical to mine: The anomalous American rate of homicide constitutes the "social fact" to be explained.

Levels of homicide vary, of course, by race, and Professors Messner and Rosenfeld summarize these data as well, showing the high murder rate in the African American community. They emphasize, moreover, how this variation affects the quality of life experienced by some African Americans. Compared to whites, some African Americans live in what can only be described as war zones, even today. Professors Messner and Rosenfeld use the Englewood section of Chicago as an example, and I want to dwell on it in more detail than they do.[5] There are areas like Englewood in New York City, Philadelphia, and most other large cities, so it serves as an example of the impact of living in

hyper-segregated environments. Moreover, their presentation not only illustrates certain aspects of the data, it also suggests (as will be shown later) some
of the weaknesses of their work.

Englewood lies only ten minutes from the downtown center of Chicago,
where the Art Institute and Aquarium are located. Comprising only 6.5
square miles, it was a crowded but relatively stable residential area during the
early 1980s. According to newspaper reports, it was a place many African
Americans saw as a good neighborhood in which to live and raise children.
This was not, however, a pristine environment. It says a lot about the high
level of residential segregation and the limited housing choices available to
African American families (due to discrimination) that they would take this
view even though Englewood had thirty-two homicides in 1985, which
translates into a rate of thirty per 100,000 people.[6] During the second half of
that decade, however, drug markets expanded in major cities around the
nation, tied to the rise of crack cocaine, and the Englewood section of Chicago proved vulnerable. In just a short time, it became a mecca for people
living in other neighborhoods, and suburbanites as well, who sought the
readily available drugs. They simply exited the Dan Ryan Expressway and
returned to it; the entire process including the purchase took only a few minutes to complete. As in other cities, these illegal drug markets were regulated
by violence as entrepreneurial gangs went to war against one another to control the trade and its profits. Inevitably, of course, bystanders got in the way
and sometimes suffered the consequences. By 1991, police data showed that
Englewood displayed a homicide rate of ninety-three per 100,000. One
newspaper reported the rate for males as 162. The actual number of homicides for the year was ninety-nine, which refers to those people who died
from an estimated total of 1,456 shootings, 729 stabbings, and 1,421 "serious beatings" in that same year.

These figures translate into an average of four shootings, two stabbings,
and four beatings each day, all within a rather small geographical area. The
Chicago police reported that gang members were increasingly using semi-
automatic weapons, some with magazines holding fifty rounds of ammunition
or more. Cook County Hospital indicated that one-fourth of shooting-
trauma patients from Englewood displayed more than one bullet wound. It
should not be surprising, then, that residents of this small district told reporters that gunfire occurred all the time—day and night. No one was safe. The
result was utter desolation in the center of the nation's third largest city,
which Professors Messner and Rosenfeld describe by quoting a local
observer:

> Do you see any hardware stores? Do you see any grocery stores? Do you see
> any restaurants? Any bowling alleys? There is nothing here. . . . Nothing is worth
> anything in the area because you open up and you get knocked off, and you get

knocked off, and you get knocked off until you give up. . . . In the last few months, three of the last gas stations closed up. The Church's Fried Chicken at Madison and Sacramento finally gave up after being robbed nine days in a row by nine different people. . . . You don't see any newspaper vending machines. Everything we take for granted—a laundromat, a cleaner's, anything. It's not here. The school dropout rate is 70 percent. What do these kids have to do? Nothing.[7]

Englewood is a place where hope died, at least for awhile. But its homicide rate declined in the years following publication of the first edition of *Crime and the American Dream,* as it did around the nation. By 2000, it had fallen to "only" fifty-seven per 100,000 residents.[8] Admittedly, the violence in this district has been incredibly high over the past two decades, even by today's American standards. As mentioned previously, however, many large cities have areas similar to Englewood. They constitute America's self-inflicted curse. But not everyone endures this curse equally. It is meted out mainly to people of color, mostly African Americans and Hispanic Americans, due to discrimination—and to only a few of them.

Most people of all races and ethnicity live in areas characterized by far less lethality. For example, there are police districts within six miles of Englewood that display less than one murder per month (and some far less than this). This difference allows residents who live in relatively nonviolent enclaves to adopt a stance of determined innocence about the miasmic environment just a short distance away. But such naïveté is hard to maintain as people go out and about. The existence of very violent neighborhoods redounds to other areas of the community, regardless of residence, and everyone knows this. At some level, all Americans understand that their lives might be at stake if they happen to be in the wrong place at the wrong time—whether at school, at work, at leisure, or on vacation. Just as the murder of Delvin Darnell Carey was not an aberration (described in chapter 1; killed while at a nightclub), neither were the murders of Jennifer Bragg Capobianco and Louis Javelle (described in chapter 2; killed while sitting at their desks at work), and neither was the murder of Barry Grunow (described in chapter 3; killed outside his classroom). Although the odds are low, it is not farfetched to think that one might be murdered while going to or from the Art Institute in Chicago. One would never worry about that possibility when preparing to tour the Louvre in Paris.

Professors Messner and Rosenfeld observe that all this violence makes Americans fearful, regardless of race or ethnicity, regardless of residential location. They note that fear of crime is a distinctly American phenomenon. The political response, they point out, has been punitive, and as a result the United States has one of the highest levels of incarceration in the world, much higher than that in any other Western nation. But, like other observers, they report that this "law and order" strategy is ineffective; it fails to deter either crime or violence. Moreover, it has a paradoxical impact: It diverts attention away from other variables that do affect homicide rates.

As a result, and remember that Englewood serves as an (admittedly extreme) example of the larger truth presented by the cross-national and historical data, the authors of *Crime and the American Dream* assert that America is a "society organized for crime." The key word is "organized," because this problem, they argue, cannot be explained at the individual level. It does not reflect individual pathology or moral failing. Rather, in order to understand why so much "serious crime" occurs in the United States they suggest that observers must focus on the "socio-cultural environments" in which people find themselves. Thus, as good sociologists, they shift the level of analysis away from individuals and assert that high rates of such crimes as robbery and homicide "are intrinsic to the basic cultural commitments and institutional arrangements of American society."[9] How is this possible?

## AN INSTITUTIONAL-ANOMIE
## EXPLANATION OF SERIOUS CRIME

After presenting the data, Professors Messner and Rosenfeld emphasize that the question they are asking can only be answered at the structural level. They begin their explanation by describing a set of interrelated cultural values characteristic of Western societies, which they call the *American Dream*. By the term they mean an ethos accepted by everyone in the society dictating that all citizens should be committed to the goal of material success under conditions of open competition.[10] They believe that while this cultural orientation occurs in all Western nations, it has been taken to an extreme in this country—perhaps because capitalism developed here in more pristine form, without confronting entrenched religious, political, economic, and other structural impediments.

The authors argue that the American Dream consists of six mutually reinforcing cultural values. (1) *Achievement:* People want to get ahead, to achieve occupational success. Failure to work hard to achieve (or at least strive for) occupational success implies that one does not make a contribution to society. (2) *Individualism:* People want to "make it" on their own, as individuals. Americans are deeply committed to, perhaps obsessed with, notions of individual rights and individual autonomy. This emphasis distorts our view of the world because it implies that individuals make their own decisions without regard to social context. Even so, this value stimulates people to compete with one another, emphasize personal self-reliance and self-protection (as with guns), and interpret government attempts at regulating their lives skeptically. (3) *Universalism:* In the quest for success, people want to be evaluated based on merit, on objective standards applied equally to all. This stress on universalism may be one reason why democracy and capitalism are so closely linked. (4) *Wealth:* Above all, people want to make lots of money. A "fetishism of money," the authors argue, characterizes American society, not only because wealth constitutes the standard by which each individual's level of achievement is evaluated but also because it has become a value in itself. The authors mention these four elements of the American Dream explicitly, but as will become clear below, they refer implicitly to two others. (5) *Activism:* People want to master the situations in which they find themselves, ideally in the most efficient way possible. (6) *Rationality:* In the process of "making it" on their own Americans want to deal with problems they face methodically, ideally using science and technology to produce solutions.

These six values have been extremely important historically. As you may recall from chapter 1, what Professors Messner and Rosenfeld label the American Dream constitutes a restatement of what Max Weber described as the modern culture of capitalism. As suggested in chapters 2 and 3, these values are connected to economic development, increasing opportunity for individuals, and other aspects of the rise of modernity. I shall return to this issue.

Yet the American Dream carries with it an inherent irony, due mainly to the existence of great economic inequality. In sociology, this irony is captured by the term *anomie,* which refers to a lack of connection between cultural values and the legitimate means to achieve them. Anomic societies—which is to say all modern societies—are organized based on an internal contradiction: Everyone is supposed to keep striving for success, yet built-in restrictions limit the legally approved means for achieving this goal. As a result, the competition is not really open or equal. Nonetheless, in this context, Americans who become less successful are told and usually agree that they should just try harder; everyone believes that the only real failure consists in giving up. But the pressure to succeed is great and leads to negative consequences. Ironically, then, in Robert K. Merton's words, this "cardinal American virtue, 'ambition,' promotes a cardinal American vice, 'deviant behavior'" because, inevitably, some people try to get around the structurally based restrictions inherent to an anomic society.[11] Crime, then, has a structural source—as does homicide.

In a way, an anomic society is a little like a baseball game, albeit one that is perversely organized. In this game, there are many bases with no real end point, and people's scores (occupationally and economically) depend on how far they advance. The farther they move ahead, the more money they make, which is the mark of achievement in America. The dominance of the American Dream refers to the desire, shared by everyone, to go on to subsequent occupational and economic bases, making loads of money along the way.

The accident of birth, however, means that not everyone begins the baseball game at the same point. Some people, for example, start from the batter's box. They believe that if they are smart and work hard they will get a hit and, because of their great speed, progress to subsequent bases. In playing the game, all they ask is that they be allowed to make it on their own and be evaluated fairly. In this game, however, other people clog the bases ahead of them and so the ability of those who begin the game in the batter's box to advance very far is, in fact, restricted. This is especially so because the base paths become steadily narrower as one advances—one more restriction. The competition, then, cannot be fair or equal; it cannot be based only on achievement. Some of those who begin at home plate recognize this inequality and become angry. Sometimes they turn this anger inward, blaming themselves for their lack of success. And sometimes, they act angrily toward one another, even though such behavior will not get them anywhere.

Others have a better chance at succeeding because they begin the baseball game at first base. They also believe fervently that with hard work they will move on as well, making money as they go. Again, all they want is to be fairly evaluated. In reality, however, even their level of success does not come easily because still others (but fewer) start the game ahead of them—at second and even third base. The dominance of the American Dream is so pervasive, though, that many of these people assume they got there by hitting doubles and triples (by achievement instead of by birth). Although their cumulative wealth is almost automatically higher, and advancing to ever-greater riches is easier for them, they believe intensely in the six values of achievement, individualism, universalism, wealth, activism, and rationality. They tell themselves and everyone behind them that the American Dream is real for everyone; anyone can advance. And nearly everyone playing the game believes them. This metaphor illustrates what Professor Merton means by an anomic society.

As a sidebar on the metaphor, recall that major league baseball prevented African Americans from participating for many years. This prohibition symbolizes the larger historical fact that many people have been arbitrarily excluded from trying to achieve the American Dream until recently. They were unable to run the occupational base paths at all. These were not just African Americans but people of color more generally, along with women, immigrants, and others. Yet, despite the anomic character of the game, with its built-in restrictions, members of these groups have wanted into it rather than to overthrow it. This desire suggests that the anomic nature of American social structure only provides part of the story of modernity. Perhaps increased opportunity and a better life do exist. Again, I shall come back to this issue.

People respond to an anomic social structure in a variety of ways. Nearly everyone simply works hard, resigned to keep striving and do the best they can—including those at the bottom of the class structure. In "Social Structure and Anomie," Professor Merton calls this response "conformity," with the caveat that some people reject success goals but continue going through the motions (called "ritualism"). Others, however, a few really, react differently. For example, they might find solace in drugs or descend into psychopathology (called "retreatism"). This is one way in which people turn their anger inward.[12]

Alternatively, some people strive to succeed in different ways by taking illegal shortcuts. In his charming way, Professor Merton calls this response "innovation." To continue with the metaphor, they try to cut across the field and go right to second or third base, thus increasing their score in the game—albeit in deviant ways. In Professors Messner and Rosenfeld's words, people strive for success "by any means necessary." If this requires selling drugs, robbery, or even murder, so be it. From this perverse but sociologically sound point of view, those individuals and organizations (gangs) trying to operate drug markets in the Englewood section of Chicago and other cities are simply entrepreneurs striving to realize the American Dream. They have gone bad, perhaps, but are entrepreneurs nonetheless. And when they use guns and other methods of violence to control markets and work out disputes, they are simply mimicking what the price fixer or inside trader does. The use of violent methods, the authors of *Crime and the American Dream* point out, "receives strong, if indirect, cultural support in our society. High rates of gun-related violence, in particular result in part from a cultural ethos that encourages the rapid deployment of technically efficient methods to solve interpersonal problems."[13] This stress on an active strategy for dealing with a problem is typical. The United States is unlike other nations, it is said, because the first answer to a medical problem is often surgery, the first answer to a psychological problem is often Prozac, and the first answer to an interpersonal problem is often violence—sometimes with a gun. Although I am being a little glib here, these are quintessentially American orientations. Whether they are wise or whether we must live with them, especially the last one, are matters to be discussed.

The last response to an anomic situation described by Professor Merton is rebellion, which means "efforts to change the existing cultural and social structure rather than to accommodate efforts *within* this structure."[14] Yet, for reasons to be indicated later on, rebellion occurs rather rarely, and never in capitalist societies. What happens instead is that people at the bottom of the class structure express their free-floating alienation and anger in inchoate ways: against one another. In psychological terms, it is not much of a leap to suggest that when impoverished people denied opportunity shoot one another, they are shooting into a mirror. The result, at least in the United States, is a high rate of homicide.

Professors Messner and Rosenfeld extend Robert K. Merton's analysis of anomie by arguing that social institutions in the United States do not restrain the "criminogenic tendencies" inherent to the American Dream. By the term *social institutions*, they mean "relatively stable sets of norms and values,

statuses and roles, and groups and organizations that regulate human conduct to meet the basic needs of society."[15] As professionals know, this is a
standard definition, similar to one that would be found in any introductory
sociology textbook. Institutions function, sociologists argue, to meet basic
challenges that every society confronts: how to adapt to the environment,
allocate resources, and socialize people to accept dominant values and norms.
The economy refers to those activities centered on producing goods and services from the environment. The polity (or government) refers to those activities centered on allocating resources to achieve goals, for example, reducing
malnutrition or the number of guns available in the population. The family
refers to those activities centered on regulating reproduction and socialization. And education refers to those activities centered on adding to and trans-
mitting knowledge, and also to teaching people dominant values. Strangely,
Professors Messner and Rosenfeld omit religion, which refers to those activities centered on fundamental beliefs and values as they affect socialization,
inequality, and the various forms of tension and contradiction in a society.[16]
Among those values, of course, is the notion that human life is sacred. The
authors of *Crime and the American Dream* argue (correctly) that every society will display distinctive institutional arrangements.

But in the United States, they assert, the economy dominates to an unusual
degree, thus overwhelming activities in the other institutional arenas—not
counting the impact of religion, which they ignore. They observe this domi-
nation in three ways. First, noneconomic positions and goals are devalued.
For example, "it is the home *owner* rather than the home*maker* who is widely
admired and envied."[17] Second, when institutional needs compete, economic
priorities dominate. For example, resistance to parental leave and other policies designed to promote family life is much higher in this country than in
most Western European nations. This is one reason why many "parents worry
about 'finding time' for their families, [but] few workers must 'find time' for
their jobs." Third, norms characteristic of the economy penetrate other institutional spheres. For example, education is viewed as a commodity, no different than any other consumer good; its purpose is less learning for its own
sake than preparing students to earn a living. The overall effect, then, is that
institutional arrangements increase, instead of restrain, criminal tendencies
built into an anomic society. Professors Messner and Rosenfeld summarize
the situation by observing: "This anomic orientation leads not simply to high
levels of crime in general but to especially violent forms of economic crime,
for which the United States is known throughout the industrial world, such
as mugging, carjacking, and home invasion."[18]

The specific crimes referred to here (mugging, etc.) are important, as they
do not comprise the "serious crimes" the authors claimed earlier to be concerned with. At this point in their analysis, however, they assert that as a result
of this institutional imbalance noneconomic institutions are relatively unable

to exert social control over the population. Government, for example, "is constrained in its capacity to mobilize collective resources, including moral resources, to deter criminal choices." This country, they conclude, is overwhelmingly anomic. And this fact "explains, in our view, the unusually high levels of gun-related violence in the United States"; their use merely reflects a willingness to pursue approved goals (economic success) by any means necessary.[19]

Professors Messner and Rosenfeld conclude that high rates of "serious crime" are built into American culture and social structure. They continue by asserting that if their explanation is valid the "logical solution is social reorganization. This will entail, in our view, both institutional reform and cultural regeneration."[20]

At the end of the book, then, the problem becomes how to strengthen social institutions and rethink the cultural values embodied in the American Dream. Before offering some suggestions for "social reorganization," the authors briefly review "conventional strategies for crime control." Political conservatives favor what might be called back-end strategies: deterrence and punishment. For example, they support mandatory minimum sentence requirements and emphasize zero tolerance drug control policies. As you may recall from chapter 1, the data on the effect of incarceration on homicide reduction are mixed. Similarly, draconian drug laws have had little impact on drug availability, use, or sales. On this issue, the authors quote a long-time observer: "When all the King's horses and all the King's men couldn't put Humpty together again, the response was merely to double the number of horses and men, rather than to recognize at some point the futility of the effort."[21] In contrast, political liberals favor what might be called front-end strategies: prevention and opportunity. Professors Messner and Rosenfeld cite the War on Poverty during the 1960s as an example, noting that crime rates increased markedly during this period. It is hard to see how prevention policies can work, they observe, because crime rates do not appear to vary with the level of inequality or unemployment. I do not think this example works very well. It might have been more effective to refer to such other liberal proposals as drug treatment or criminal diversion programs. In any case, the authors assert that the problem with both conservative and liberal approaches is that they fail "to question the fundamental features of American society."[22]

What is needed instead, Professors Messner and Rosenfeld argue, are policies that lead to crime reduction over the long term by strengthening the social structure and weakening the "criminogenic qualities" built into the culture. The result would be less anomie. As a step toward that goal, they make some suggestions for "social reorganization" designed to reduce the rate of "serious crime."

First, the family and schools need to be reinvigorated. For example, "policies that enable parents to spend more time with their children should not only strengthen family controls over children's behavior but also enable the schools to carry out their control functions more effectively."[23] Thus, at work, they recommend family leave, job sharing, and flexible work schedules. At home, they decry the de-emphasis on marriage that seems to be occurring in the United States, arguing that more people should get married because it increases their (and their children's) connections to the larger society. At school, they suggest that education should focus on the "distinctive goal of formal learning," presumably so that students can be better trained, obtain jobs, and thereby see themselves as having a stake in the larger society.

Second, some government policies should be changed. The system of crime control should be reformed by developing a variety of intermediate sanctions that keep people out of prison, thereby reducing costs and relieving overcrowding. In addition, broader patterns of social participation should be required of everyone as they move into adulthood, such as some form of national service corps. Their point is that such experiences can offer "an institutional mooring for young persons during the transition to adulthood."[24]

Third, the corrosive impact of high levels of inequality needs to be reduced because it generates anger and deviance. One way to do this, the authors argue, is by protecting people's incomes and lifestyles. Thus, they present data showing that when societies "tame the market" by guaranteeing minimal levels of well-being to all citizens, the homicide rate declines. They refer here not only to welfare narrowly conceived (as Americans are used to), but also to health insurance and other ways of protecting people's ability to take care of themselves and maintain their lifestyles. As they put it, "to shore up such other institutions as the family, schools, and the polity relative to the economy, a greater share of the national wealth will have to be allocated on the basis of non-economic criteria."[25] This emphasis on the significance of inequality is implicit throughout the book and is fundamental to understanding anomic societies. As I shall note later, it constitutes the primary issue the authors have explored in their subsequent empirical analyses.

Fourth, the regeneration of cultural values must occur. Although the American Dream is beneficial because it empowers everyone to strive for a better life, the authors argue that its exaggerated emphasis on monetary success must be reduced. "Goals other than the accumulation of wealth will have to be elevated to a position of prominence in the cultural hierarchy."[26] They have in mind, here, a situation in which such social roles as parenting, "spousing," teaching, learning, and serving others become ends in themselves.

My conclusion is that Steven Messner and Richard Rosenfeld have succeeded in putting sociology to work. The great strength of *Crime and the American Dream* lies in the fact that one understands more about the cultural and structural sources of crime and other forms of deviance after reading it. Indeed, their book makes a strong argument for the usefulness of anomie as one angle of vision for understanding social life in modern societies. Moreover, it is plainly written. This is no ivory tower screed addressed to like-minded academics. Rather, the authors clearly wished to inform not only criminologists and sociologists but students and ordinary citizens as well. Their book provides a good example of publicly engaged sociology that occurs all too rarely these days. Alas, whether one understands more about the structural sources of homicide is another matter. And whether their suggestions for change would, if implemented, have much effect on the level of lethal violence in this country is still another matter. In fact, with one exception, their proposals seem rather vapid, given their emphasis on the importance of "social reorganization" so as to change "fundamental features of American society."

The exception is significant. Another strength of the book is the focus on the relationship between inequality (item three above) and homicide. This emphasis follows logically from the recognition of the anomic character of American society. Not only does a long cross-national literature deal with this relationship (although Messner and Rosenfeld do not review it), at least one test of "institutional anomie theory," as it has come to be called, has shown the importance of the relationship between inequality and homicide.[27] In addition, in a study published after *Crime and the American Dream*, Steven Messner and Richard Rosenfeld extended their assertion that the impact of the market needs to be tamed by looking at how cross-national variations in income and lifestyle protections affect homicide rates.[28] Note that these variables are specific, directly relevant to the issue, and (at least in principle) can be changed.

It seems to me, then, that their overall interpretation of the nature of American society makes perfect sense. It emphasizes that the United States is inherently anomic, as are all capitalist societies. The ironic implication is that high rates of deviance and crime (including homicide) are normal because they are structurally generated. Having said that, however, I want to comment on some empirical problems and inconsistencies in the argument in *Crime and the American Dream* as they affect the authors' ability to explain the homicide rate in this country.

## SOME CRITICAL COMMENTS

While reading *Crime and the American Dream*, I found myself asking a simple empirical (or observational) question: Given the situation they describe, what specific factors logically related to homicide rates also distinguish the United States compared to other economically developed Western nations? One of them is the degree of inequality, as noted above. There exist additional variables, however, that Professors Messner and Rosenfeld recognize and then fail to consider, even though empirical research shows them to be connected to homicide rates.

One has to do with the impact of guns on the homicide rate. The authors initially observe the importance of the "widespread availability of firearms" as an indicator of the "persistence of a 'gun culture'" in the United States.[29] A few pages later, however, they dismiss the explanatory importance of this issue:

> Although most homicides in the United States are committed with a gun, and most gun-related homicides are committed with a handgun, it is difficult to determine precisely how much of the U.S. homicide rate can be attributed to the widespread availability of firearms. For our purposes, however, such a determination is unnecessary because even if all the gun-related homicides were eliminated . . . the United States would still have a non-gun homicide rate that is higher than the total homicide rates of most other developed nations.

But widespread gun availability is one way in which this country differs from most Western European nations. Nowhere is this more evident than in the Englewood section of Chicago and similar areas in other American cities. Professors Messner and Rosenfeld show that this neighborhood resembles a war zone. In contrast, there exists no part of London nor, indeed, any Western European city, in which people endure four shootings per day and a homicide rate higher than that in medieval times. Yet the authors perform an arithmetical exercise in which they illustrate the point made in the quotation: If one subtracts out the impact of gun-related homicide, the non-gun homicide rate remains higher than the total level of homicide in England. (This means, by the way, that it is possible to estimate how much of the U.S. homicide rate results from "the widespread availability of guns.") Their point is to dismiss the importance of firearms. Yet a long and controversial literature exists on the relationship between firearm availability and homicide rates— which they do not confront. Rather, they simply assert that the anomic character of American social structure explains gun violence. The problem with this argument is not that America is anomic, it is; but the analysis is short-circuited. It seems to me that they need to deal with the extant literature and show how the disjunction between values and legitimate means overrides the importance of gun availability.

There is an alternative interpretation of the relationship between gun availability and the homicide rate. In terms of the baseball metaphor, structurally based limits on the ability to achieve mean that some people will try to cut across the field; but the extent to which they do so with guns reflects deliberate policy choices regulating their level of accessibility. In order to make this case, one could, for example, use the same arithmetical exercise to place the impact of guns in a multivariate framework in which their easy availability explains part of the anomalous American homicide rate. The key word here is "part," not "all." As mentioned before, arguing that gun availability (or any other factor) constitutes a single-cause explanation is an academic siren song; it cannot be right.

The impact of racial discrimination represents another absent explanatory factor. In a discussion of crime control, the authors observe the connection between race and crime in the United States and a few pages later they contrast the high white and African American homicide rates.[30] They know exactly how serious this problem is: "We cannot think of a more alarming set of social indicators in the United States than these measures of risk for lethal violence among black Americans, especially young black males." Nonetheless, they perform another arithmetical exercise and point out that after subtracting the African American homicide rate, that among whites remains higher than in other Western nations. But this result, while accurate, confuses the part for the whole; we are one nation. Their point, as above, is to dismiss the importance of the relationship between race and homicide. But they really know better and cannot quite do it. In this light, their conclusion is oddly telling: "As high as they are, levels of homicide victimization among black Americans do not explain *fully* the differences in homicide rates between the United States and other developed societies." Precisely correct. I italicized *fully* in the quotation to suggest that this factor ought to be considered as part of a more complex and more precise multivariate explanation. Actually, however, the appropriate variable is not race, but racial discrimination. As above, in an anomic society, some people will act out in deviant ways. If more African Americans do so violently, it reflects (in part) the long-term impact of discrimination in an anomic context. The problem of racial and ethnic discrimination occurs in Western Europe as well, of course, but the history of violence directed at African Americans (an especially virulent form of discrimination) suggests that the malign quality of our problem is far greater by several orders of magnitude. We are unique on this variable, too. Once again, an extensive literature exists on the connection between racial discrimination and homicide rates—which Professors Messner and Rosenfeld do not confront. If this relationship is not important or if the anomic character of American society overrides it, then they need to show how that occurs.

The impact of illegal drug markets represents still another rejected variable. As noted earlier, the authors go out of their way to indict the American strategy for dealing with illegal drugs, comparing it to a feckless king trying futilely to put Humpty Dumpty back together. Regardless of one's attitude about drugs or their proper legal status, there is no question that American drug policy creates illegal markets regulated by violence. Illegal drug markets also exist in Western Europe, of course, focusing on essentially the same drugs as in this country, but they are not nearly so violent. Moreover, as the cross-national data on arrest rates presented in chapter 1 suggest, drug policy may be less punitive in Western Europe than in the United States. Again, the issue is not whether America constitutes an anomic society (it does), but how this phenomenon gets expressed in rates of deviant behavior—such as illegal drug use and the markets that cater to it—that are exceedingly violent. And that reflects policy decisions that ought to be considered more systematically. Given their citations, the authors are clearly aware of the extant literature on drugs, drug markets, and homicide rates. This literature should have been confronted, not avoided.

In addition to recognizing but rejecting the importance of at least three potential explanatory variables, the argument in *Crime and the American Dream* displays two other problems that deserve mention. Both suggest limits on the authors' ability to explain the rate of homicide.

First, as mentioned, Professors Messner and Rosenfeld conspicuously fail to include religion in their institutional analysis. To repeat: They argue that, compared to Western European nations, the economy so overwhelms other social institutions in this country that "criminogenic tendencies" are reinforced rather than inhibited. Yet Americans are much more religious than Europeans, as shown by attendance at services (a common indicator of religiosity). For example, table 4.1 shows the percentage of people attending religious services at least once a month during the 1990s in the United States and selected Western European nations. These are the same nations used in figure 3.1.

Attendance is important because there is little doubt that religiosity affects behavior, not just during services but every day.[31] Hence, it seems reasonable to hypothesize that the especially high level of religiosity characteristic of Americans might provide the sort of countervailing institutional pressure that the authors of *Crime and the American Dream* describe as necessary. It

**Table 4.1.   Percentage of Population Attending Religious Services, United States and Western Europe, 1990s**

| Country | Percentage |
|---|---|
| United States | 55 |
| Canada | 40 |
| Switzerland | 25 |
| Netherlands | 31 |
| Great Britain | 25 |
| Former West Germany | 25 |
| France | 17 |
| Sweden | 11 |
| Former East Germany | 9 |

*Source:* Inglehart and Baker (2000:46).

might inhibit crime, although not necessarily homicide. Moreover, as shown below, it turns out that religiosity emerges as a useful explanatory variable in empirical tests of Professors Messner and Rosenfeld's ideas. Further, in a recent essay, they point out that in nations where religion is a (or the) dominant institution, the nature of crime will probably vary.[32] In such social contexts, they suggest, vigilanteeism, hate crimes, and human rights violations might become dominant forms of crime. They contrast this situation with that in anomic societies, like the United States, where much crime has an instrumental motive; it is a means to an economic goal. But this country is highly religious, so this issue should have been considered.

Second, and more important, crime and homicide ought to be considered as separate problems. This is so despite the authors' emphasis on explaining "serious crime" and their presentation of data showing historical and cross-national variations in homicide. Anomie theory tries to account for deviance resulting from attempts at realizing a set of interrelated values that the authors call the American Dream. Hence, as noted above, it focuses on economically motivated crimes. But only a minority of homicides, about one-fourth, involve pecuniary issues, even broadly considered. The banal motives of the vast majority of killers suggest that the high rate of lethal violence in the United States has more specific structural sources than the anomic character of American society.

Professors Messner and Rosenfeld implicitly recognize this fact because, as in the quotation cited previously, they end up offering an account for much less serious crimes: "mugging, carjacking, and home invasion" (burglary). But the United States is not unique with regard to these forms of crime. As I emphasized in chapter 1, cross-national data show that our problem is not crime, but violence. This difficulty may be one reason why Mitchell Chamlin and John Cochran chose to empirically test "institutional anomie theory" by looking at property crimes, such as burglary.[33] But rather than conducting a cross-national study, they focused on variations among American states as the unit of analysis, developed some indirect measures of the institutional-anomie variables, and found that the effect of economic factors on property crime depends on the impact of noneconomic factors. Thus, their findings suggest that the relationship between a high poverty rate (an economic condition) and property crime within the United States reflects the level of membership in religious organizations and the level of electoral participation (noneconomic factors). But, as they emphasize, this is a rather circuitous way of dealing with the theory, and their results are equivocal. So were those of Alex Piquero and Nicole Leeper Piquero.[34] They also used American states as the unit of analysis, developed a variety of indicators of the institutional-anomie variables, and found that the results depended on how the variables were measured. Yet, as Professors Chamlin and Cochran suggest, the most practical way of testing "institutional anomie theory" may be via some indirect method. Otherwise, they conclude, the only "option is simply to reject institutional anomie, along with other approaches which contain unmeasurable, abstract constructs . . . as inherently non-falsifiable."

But this conclusion is not necessary. Moreover, it does not get at the problem, at least the one I am interested in: cross-national variations in homicide rates. Although, as shown in figure 3.3, some states display more homicide than others, the big story is that America is a violent place. Why? The more I thought about the argument in *Crime and the American Dream*, the more I wondered whether anomie theory, by itself, provides a suitable framework for answering this question.


## ANOMIE, MODERNITY, AND HOMICIDE

In trying to understand social life, much depends on the angle of vision from which questions are asked. How, for example, is a sixteen-ounce glass filled with eight ounces of water to be interpreted? Is the glass half full or half empty? In sociology, especially when talking about social problems, the emphasis tends to be on the fact that the "social glass" is half empty. This is the point of view taken by Professors Messner and Rosenfeld. The United States is an anomic society. By focusing on the structural sources of deviance, anomie theory emphasizes (and rightly so) the built-in limitations people face in light of culturally accepted values and the inevitable fact that a certain proportion of people (a rate of behavior) will either retreat from the society, innovate as they strive to succeed, or express their rebellion through anger. Although the accident of birth means that people at the bottom of the class structure feel this pressure greatly, it also affects those at all class levels. This is why the authors of *Crime and the American Dream* argue that such different phenomena as drug dealing and price fixing can be "explained" as flowing from this disjunction between values and opportunity, buttressed by what they see as the peculiar imbalance of social institutions in the United States. In so doing, they push the anomie argument to its limits—or perhaps over its limits.

Their argument provides a compelling vision of modernity, one that, by the way, also underlies Karl Marx's critique of capitalism. As in a Marxian analysis, Professors Messner and Rosenfeld emphasize the need for "social reorganization" by transforming "fundamental features of American society." But, as shown earlier, they avoid proposing really fundamental changes. Their suggestions might more accurately be called adjustments. Yet one of the possible responses to an anomic situation described by Professor Merton, and ignored in *Crime and the American Dream*, is "rebellion." Well, why not rebel? And why not do so violently? Why not overthrow a system that systematically restricts opportunities? The answer is that the economic development characteristic of modern capitalist societies actually provides more opportunities for people and a better quality of life, compared to those in the past. This is why oppressed groups—labor in the nineteenth century, immigrants, members of minority groups, and women in the twentieth century—have always sought to break into the capitalist system rather than overthrow it. It is also why Marx's predictions about the future of capitalism proved to be so wrong.[35] And it is why the fact of anomie cannot account—by itself—for the American anomaly: a high rate of lethal violence.

A focus on the impact of economic development, then, represents a rather different and equally accurate angle of vision for understanding modernity. Unlike anomie, interpreting modernity from this point of view means seeing the "social glass" as half full. Although economic development and its consequences can be studied over, say, the last 750 years, the transformative event was *industrialization*, which changed social life forever in the nineteenth century. The term refers to the change of the economy as new forms of energy were substituted for muscle power, leading to huge advances in productivity and fundamental changes in the occupational structure.

This definition, however, while accurate, is also narrow. Industrialization is linked to a number of other major historical changes that merged together at roughly the same time to form modern societies. First, it is linked to the application of science to problems of economic production, health, and many other difficulties. The significance of this connection has increased in importance over the years. Second, it is linked to the rise of capitalism as an economic system when it reached a critical stage in the nineteenth century. Third, it is linked to the development of the culture of capitalism first described by Max Weber and summarized by Professors Messner and Rosenfeld as the American Dream. Fourth, it is linked to the value placed on personal freedom and democracy that arose in the West in the eighteenth century. Fifth, it is linked to the increasing emphasis on the sanctity of human life that has arisen over time. These developments display what Max Weber called an "elective affinity" for one another; they came into being gradually over the long span of Western history and coalesced in the nineteenth century to produce an engine for economic development and prosperity never before seen.[36] And prosperity has a seductive quality that few who experience it can resist. This is why people do not rebel in capitalist societies.

In this light, I want to pause and return to the baseball metaphor. Economic development means that almost everyone has access to the base paths today, which is to say they have opportunities for success that were not available just a short time ago. Viewed differently than before, this access symbolizes the historical transition from societies in which people's positions and opportunities were mainly determined by birth (the jargon term is *ascription*) to one in which ability and achievement have a much greater impact. Yes, limitations exist; birth still matters. Nonetheless, it is also correct to say that people's starting points in the game have much less influence on where they end up than in the past.

One way to see these changes is to look at mobility rates. In his classic study of the history of stratification, *Power and Privilege*, Gerhard Lenski has shown that mobility rates were very low in all societies before industrialization.[37] With economic development, however, the occupational structure changed and became much more fluid as the number of white-collar jobs rose. Although this process began much earlier, I shall use American data from 1870 and 2000, respectively, to illustrate how much more opportunity has become available with economic development.[38] In 1870, the majority of the population, 53 percent, still worked on farms—probably an all-time low figure to that point in time. About 29 percent worked in blue-collar jobs doing manual labor. Finally, a small middle class had formed, with about 19 percent working in white-collar jobs doing (mostly) non-manual labor— undoubtedly an all-time high to that point. Over the past 130 years or so, however, the occupational structure changed and the size of the middle class increased. Few people work on farms today, about 3 percent at most; 39 percent are engaged in blue-collar and 58 percent in white-collar occupations. This structural transformation carries important implications: It means that upward mobility has become possible over the past few centuries; masses of people have been, in a way, pulled upward by occupational opportunity. This change means that everyone can now share, to varying degrees, in the available technological developments and amenities, from housing and automobiles to cell phones. More people can run the base paths and enjoy a better quality of life than ever before in history.

But not everyone does, however. In fact, the first finding in the literature on mobility is that the mode (what happens most of the time) is occupational stability across generations.[39] The pithy way this pattern is summarized is "from blue collar to blue collar" and "from white collar to white collar" from parents to children. Put differently, a lot of people who, let us say, start in the batter's box or at first or second base, also end there. The second finding, however, is that intergenerational mobility is pervasive, as implied by the data above. People do advance along the base paths, including some of those who begin in the batter's box. But people rarely move from poverty to great wealth (rags to riches), since the third finding is that when mobility occurs it is usually over a short distance. Taken together, these findings mean, once again, that where people start has less influence on where they end up today, compared to the past. Opportunity exists. So most people, as a result, enjoy much better lives. This fundamental change means that modern, class-based societies are liberating because people's ability and hard work can pay off. Western nations are not, of course, purely achievement-oriented societies, and no nation could be. The peculiar task of modernity is to work out an appropriate balance between ascription and achievement. Although the nature of this balance varies considerably from nation to nation, all Western societies emphasize the latter. This was not true in the past.

Thus, the paradox of modern societies is that, on the one hand, they are anomic, which means that structurally based limitations on opportunities generate deviance. On the other hand, however, economic development means that increased opportunity and improved lifestyles (along with other changes) reduce the level of lethal violence. It is the latter that is important for my purpose right now. Recall, for example, the long-term, 750-year transition away from the pathology of violence characteristic of medieval societies. In chapter 3 I summarized the situation with a simple empirical generalization: *The greater the economic development, the lower the level of homicide.* Underlying this finding is Norbert Elias's hypothesis: *The more the use of force is monopolized by the state, the more people have access to the courts to resolve disputes, and the more widespread is formal education and other mechanisms for teaching civility, then the lower the level of interpersonal violence and homicide in a society.* In light of the data presented in chapter 3, it is hard to see how the anomic character of modern societies can be used, by itself, to account for high levels of lethal violence in the United States.

The authors of *Crime and the American Dream* place their analysis squarely in the tradition of anomie theory established by Robert K. Merton. This orientation has provided a rich vein of insight in sociology and criminology, one that has improved our understanding of the nature and characteristics of all Western societies, not just the United States. Perhaps, however, they have dealt with Professor Merton's materials too narrowly—if the purpose is to understand homicide rates.

## BUILDING ON THE
## MESSNER/ROSENFELD STRATEGY

In *Crime and the American Dream*, Steven Messner and Richard Rosenfeld begin their analysis in a straightforward way, by assembling the cross-societal and historical data on robbery and homicide, the "serious crimes" they wish to explain. Although their argument that this social fact can only be explained structurally is not as extensive as mine, as presented in chapter 2 of this book, it is clear and persuasive. Moreover, they are correct that the anomic nature of American society can be used to account for crime and other forms of deviance, especially when connected to the level of inequality. But using anomie as an overall explanatory framework presents several problems when the issue to be explained is cross-national differences in homicide rates. Most important, it leads them to ignore or dismiss the huge literatures that exist dealing with specific variables related to homicide rates. This strategy cannot be right. I am arguing, moreover, that homicide in the United States constitutes a rather special form of crime, partly because it is intrinsically violent and partly because it is so anomalous compared to other economically developed societies.

Given these considerations, it seems to me that we need to move beyond the specific problem Robert K. Merton deals with in "Social Structure and Anomie." The point of that essay is that the various options people face (retreatism, innovation, etc.) are built into the structure of society; they reflect the structural position in which people find themselves. It turns out, as Arthur Stinchcombe observed in an essay too often ignored, that this insight constitutes the underlying theoretical unity in all of Professor Merton's work. Its theoretical thrust is that *people always choose among socially structured alternatives.*[40]

This assertion restates the fundamental sociological insight that I mentioned in chapter 1: Understanding the context in which people make choices is as important as understanding the specific choices they make. In chapter 2 I relied on Emile Durkheim's writings to show that the first characteristic of social structures is that they exist externally to individuals, setting their range of choices. But, depending on the purpose, I could have used Karl Marx's, Robert K. Merton's, or, indeed, the work of any of the classical sociological theorists to make essentially the same point. This possibility suggests that a certain (often unrecognized) similarity exists in structural analyses that appear quite different on the surface.[41]

The implications are important. When Professor Stinchcombe uses the word "choose" he does not refer to rational decision making or obtaining value in an exchange or merely reacting to stimuli. He is making a structural, not a social psychological argument. But any time the word "choose" or "choice" is used the possibility for misunderstanding arises. This is because the existence of socially structured alternatives does not seem salient to most of us as we live our everyday lives. Even though we operate within a social structure, each of us only sees other individuals within it. We come together and separate—forming couples, lobbying political decision-makers, selling drugs—by choice. In this context, it is easy to forget that we have no choice about the family, class, geographical area, nation, or culture into which we are born. Yet these facts are like the house we live in; they provide a context that affects our range of choices. Thus, what Professor Stinchcombe means is that in any society people are presented with a subset of options from the range of all possibilities, these options are meaningful to them, and other imaginable choices are more (often much more) difficult to make. To pick one example, the nation within which one lives provides very specific opportunities and restrictions. Thus, although it is perfectly plausible to argue that any person living in the United Kingdom can, if sufficiently angered, commit murder, this choice is more difficult than in the United States, since it is harder to obtain a gun and more difficult to murder someone with other weapons. The point, again, is that individuals choose among a range of options in a specific social and historical context. As we live our daily lives we do not decide for ourselves what our choices are; rather, they are given by the fact of living at a particular place and time.

But, as described in chapter 2, just as a house can be remodeled, a social structure can be changed. This is its second characteristic. Modernity has meant, among other things, that human beings exercise increasing control over their environment, physical and social. For example, if the level of inequality has been allowed to rise and is now higher in the United States than it is in, say, the United Kingdom, that is because we have chosen to allow this result. This level of inequality becomes, in turn, a new social fact with which ordinary individuals must cope. And if the impact of inequality affects the homicide rate (and it does), then we have also chosen to live with the human carnage that results.

In this chapter, I have tried to show that although Professor Messner and Rosenfeld's analysis of American culture and society is useful in many ways, it does not explain the peculiarly high rate of homicide in this country. In order to build on their work, I would like to take the investigation in a somewhat different direction by constructing a logical experiment that reveals how the United States differs from other nations in fundamental ways that lead to a high rate of lethal violence.

## NOTES

1. Messner and Rosenfeld (2001:viii).
2. Messner and Rosenfeld (2001:18).
3. Merton (1968a).
4. Messner and Rosenfeld (2001:20–25).
5. Messner and Rosenfeld (2001:18–25). Their description of Englewood in the 1980s and 1990s relies on Copeland et al. (1991), on whom I also draw for a more extensive portrayal than they present. The term "hyper-segregation" comes from Massey and Denton (1993) and is explained in chapter 5.
6. All the data in this paragraph are courtesy of the Chicago Police Department and Copeland et al. (1991).
7. Messner and Rosenfeld (2001:33). They take the quotation from Soll (1993).
8. Courtesy of the Chicago Police Department.
9. Messner and Rosenfeld (2001:4–10). The quotation is on p. 5.
10. Messner and Rosenfeld (2001:61–64). In describing these values, the authors draw on Turner and Musick (1985:14).
11. Merton (1968a:200); Messner and Rosenfeld (2001:52–54).
12. Merton (1968a:194).
13. Messner and Rosenfeld (2001:3).
14. Merton (1968a:194, footnote). Italics in original.
15. Messner and Rosenfeld (2001:65).

16. Turner (1997:107).

17. Messner and Rosenfeld (2001:70). Italics in original. The quotation below comes from p. 72.

18. Messner and Rosenfeld (2001:76–77).

19. Messner and Rosenfeld (2001:78). The quotation just above comes from p. 79.

20. Messner and Rosenfeld (2001:92).

21. Messner and Rosenfeld (2001:96). They are quoting Blumstein (1993).

22. Messner and Rosenfeld (2001:99).

23. Messner and Rosenfeld (2001:102).

24. Messner and Rosenfeld (2001:105). The quoted phrase below also comes from p. 105.

25. Messner and Rosenfeld (2001:106).

26. Messner and Rosenfeld (2001:108).

27. Savolainen (2000).

28. Messner and Rosenfeld (1997a).

29. Messner and Rosenfeld (2001:3). The quotation below is from p. 21.

30. Messner and Rosenfeld (2001:4 and 25). The quotations below are from p. 25.

31. Beeghley, Cochran and Bock (1990); Cochran and Beeghley (1996).

32. Messner and Rosenfeld (2001a).

33. Chamlin and Cochran (1995). The quotation at the end of the paragraph is from p. 426.

34. Piquero and Piquero (1998).

35. Marx and Engels (1848). On the problems with Marx's analysis, see Turner, Beeghley and Powers (2002).

36. On these issues, see Berger (1986); Weber (1905); Kuznets (1985); and Lenski (1966).

37. Lenski (1966).

38. United States Bureau of the Census (1975:139); Bureau of Labor Statistics (2001:176).

39. Guest et al. (1989); Blau and Duncan (1967); Featherman and Houser (1978). For a summary of this literature, see Beeghley (2000:42–69).

40. Stinchcombe (1975).

41. Merton (1973).

# 5

## Social Structure and Homicide

Simon's Rock College is a small liberal arts school located in the village of Great Barrington, Massachusetts, in the Berkshire Mountains. The Norman Rockwell Museum is nearby. The campus takes up only a few wooded acres and nearly all the 350 or so students live in college-run dormitories located on site. During the evening in question, many were out and about on campus. Most were preparing for final exams or, as the hour grew later, simply relaxing. In this bucolic setting, eighteen-year-old Galen Gibson was shot and killed just outside the library. He was hit twice. One bullet entered and exited his arm near the elbow. It was not fatal. The other shattered his sternum and passed into his chest cavity; after penetrating a lung and severing blood vessels, it then tore through his trachea and exited his body through the seventh rib. He staggered back into the library and bled to death in just a few minutes as other students watched helplessly.

The shooter was also a student, eighteen-year-old Wayne Lo. Earlier that same day, he presented a valid Montana driver's license at a local gun shop and bought a used version of a Chinese SKS semi-automatic rifle for $130. This was a completely legal sale, as Mr. Lo was of age and had no police record. Although Massachusetts law would have required a thirty-day waiting period after the purchase, an out-of-state resident can bypass this and other restrictions on gun sales.[1]

Alas, young Mr. Gibson was not the first person to be hit with gunfire that winter evening, nor the first to die. Beginning about 10:15 P.M., Mr. Lo shot a campus guard, Theresa Beavers, who was at the front gate. She was also shot twice, but survived and is now a paraplegic. He then killed one of the professors, Ñacuñán Sáez, who was returning to campus in his car. The car rolled into a snow bank. Within moments, other students saw Professor Sáez's body in the wrecked auto and, assuming an accident had occurred, rushed to the nearby college library to get assistance. On the way in, they

103

passed Wayne Lo standing outside the building amid some adjacent trees. Mr. Lo killed Mr. Gibson as he left the library to help. Mr. Lo then moved along, shooting three more students, all of whom survived their wounds. Once alerted, the police responded quickly and Wayne Lo surrendered without a fight, unharmed himself. The entire episode lasted only about thirty minutes.

Although each of the victims knew Mr. Lo, since everyone knew everyone else on this small campus, they had no particular relationship to him. All were simply targets of opportunity. Weeks earlier, Mr. Lo had been told by voices to prepare himself, a fact that even his best friends were not aware of. As part of his preparation, he had looked around and found the SKS semi-automatic to be available at a gun shop near the campus. On the day of the murders, the voices told him that it was time to kill, so he went out and bought the SKS. Although the psychologists who evaluated him prior to his murder trial disagreed in certain respects about his mental illness, they agreed on one thing: Like many mentally disturbed persons, Wayne Lo appeared normal and could function in daily life. As often happens, he was afflicted with a "narrow madness," affecting only part of his psyche. In fact, the rational part of his mind could facilitate the delusion created by the voices. This is why he was able to take a final exam with other students earlier that day and attend a dormitory meeting in the early part of the evening. Superficially, he was behaving normally. But he was in thrall to a "higher" (i.e., delusional) purpose. So he returned to his dormitory room, modified the SKS rifle, and began the shooting rampage. There could have been many more victims.

In addition to locating the SKS, Wayne Lo had also prepared himself ahead of time by purchasing, via mail order, ammunition and parts with which to modify the gun. He needed no identification to make this purchase, only a valid credit card. The 7.62 x 39 mm cartridges were standard military ammunition, designed to wound rather than kill (thereby tying up those who would rescue a soldier). He also obtained several thirty-round magazines (which hold the ammunition) along with the necessary parts to replace the single ten-round magazine that came with the weapon. Thus, as he left his dormitory room with the rifle and extra magazines that fateful evening, Mr. Lo apparently carried more than 200 rounds of ammunition. As it turned out, however, the SKS is not a good-quality firearm and the parts he acquired were not of good quality either. As a result, although it is a high-powered rifle, it presented many problems in use. Each time he inserted a new magazine, the gun fired a few shots and then jammed. He actually fired less than two dozen rounds. The number of victims would have been much higher but for this fortuitous fact. When the students passed Mr. Lo on the way to the library he was probably trying to reconfigure the jammed weapon in order to fire again. By the time Galen Gibson left the building just a few moments later, Mr. Lo had made the gun operational once more. Imagine, for a moment, the carnage that would have resulted if he had possessed a fully functional weapon and been able to smoothly load each new magazine and keep shooting, as he had been directed to do by the voices.

Legally, however, Wayne Lo was sane. He knew right from wrong. Thus, at his subsequent criminal trial, a jury found him guilty of murder and he will spend the rest of his life in prison.

This description of the shooting rampage at Simon's Rock College is taken from a remarkable book, *Goneboy: A Walkabout*, by Gregory Gibson, Galen's father.[2] He describes the "walkabout" as a sort of "finding-out about Galen exercise" in which he tried to discover the truth about how and why his son had been killed. He discovered a lot. In retrospect, it was clear that Wayne Lo had presented warning signs of his mental illness prior to his enrollment at Simon's Rock, but they were subtle and had been disregarded. Even on the day it happened, many decisions were made that inadvertently facilitated Wayne Lo's killing spree that night. For example, early in the evening, one of his friends became fearful and tried, futilely as it turned out, to alert the college that Mr. Lo might possess a gun and intend to use it. The friend called campus security and got an answering machine instead of a person. Similarly, Mr. Lo's package of ammunition and parts arrived at the campus mailroom that morning clearly labeled with the sender's name, "Classic Arms." The package was shown to the Dean of Students, Dr. Bernard Rogers, who nonetheless allowed it to be delivered to Mr. Lo. This is so, even though it is illegal to possess a gun on a college campus in the state of Massachusetts. But these were only two possible points of intervention. As the elder Mr. Gibson came to understand, his son's death, along with that of Professor Sáez and the wounding of four other people, represented the cumulative result of many choices various participants made, any one of which, done differently, might have averted the catastrophe. The people who made these decisions carry a great burden.

Perhaps most important, Mr. Gibson's walkabout was his way of working through his grief over a period of several years. Mere words (mine anyway) can only hint at the depths of his anger and pain; it is an extraordinary, beautifully written, very personal testimony. In the process of finding out what happened, he talked to nearly everyone involved and did a great deal of research. For example, he tracked down not only the owner of the gun store where Mr. Lo obtained the SKS but also the original owner. In so doing, he describes the historical development of firearm technology, the social impact of rising imports of guns (especially from China), and the peculiar fascination guns have on the American imagination.

In addition, Mr. Gibson goes beyond his own travails to explain how the other unwitting and unwilling survivors of this tragedy dealt with their trauma. I mentioned in chapter 1 that every murder victim has seven to ten close relatives and friends. *Goneboy* illustrates how each murder reverberates through family, acquaintances, and neighborhood. In addition to his father, Galen Gibson was survived by his mother and a sister and brother, both younger. This does not count his extended family. The elder Mr. Gibson talked to many of Galen's friends, all of whom were traumatized. Even after several years, for example, his girlfriend "seemed to be drifting through life, unable to catch hold of anything."[3] For most of those involved, the events of that evening will not go away. They have tried to reconstruct their lives, but with varying degrees of success. Mr. Gibson also talked to Wayne Lo's friends. Mr. Lo belonged to a loosely knit group of alienated sorts that exists at many high schools and colleges. They saw phoniness everywhere and took pleasure in outrageous behavior. They made bad jokes about getting rid of all the phonies. Unbeknown to them, however, Mr. Lo took all these antisocial diatribes seriously because he was deluded. For them, the events of that evening will not go away either. Finally, Mr. Gibson talked to Wayne Lo's parents, good people who must come to terms with the fact that their son is a killer. For them, Wayne is a goneboy, too. And remember, there were other victims, including those who were wounded, each of whom had family and friends, each of whom also had to reconstruct their lives. None of these people will ever be the same again. Every homicide in America affects whole communities of people.

And yet what happened that evening in Great Barrington, Massachusetts, is not unusual. Recall that in 1999, about 15,500 Americans became murder victims. And this is a low figure compared to the past. So homicide occurs often in the United States; it is a routine event that reverberates through the population. Consider again the examples presented so far in this book: the murder of Delvin Darnell Carey at a nightclub; the murders of Jennifer Bragg Capobianco, Louis Javelle, and five others at work; the murder of Barry Grunow at a middle school; and now the murders of Galen Gibson and Ñacuñán Sáez at Simon's Rock College. These deaths put a human face on the quantitative data presented in chapter 3 (figure 3.2) and illustrate the range of the homicide problem in this country. Their banal diversity reflects what the poet Robert Penn Warren once called "the murderous innocence of the American people."[4] But remember that Massachusetts, from which two of these examples are taken, displays one of the lowest homicide rates in the nation (figure 3.3). Compare it to the pervasive violence and death that characterize the Englewood section of Chicago and similar sections of any large American city. All these homicides suggest what everyone knows: Anyone living in this country can be murdered at any time or any place. Even though most people reside in neighborhoods, go to work, and attend school in relatively nonviolent places, no one is safe from harm in this country—even if they live in a rustic village in the Berkshire Mountains. This possibility is reflected by the cross-national data (figure 3.1), which show that no other Western nation endures such a high level of carnage. The task in this chapter is to identify the structural sources of homicide, for they do not occur accidentally.

My strategy, you may recall, is to build on Steven Messner and Richard Rosenfeld's work, both theoretically and empirically. Theoretically, based on Robert K. Merton's insights, the goal is to show how the social structure systematically generates rates of behavior by determining the range of choices people face. Empirically, the trick is to isolate the key structural variables affecting the homicide rate and organize them in terms of a logical experiment, after the manner of Max Weber. So in what follows I confront and evaluate the relevant quantitative literature and suggest how each variable is related to the rate of homicide. This task inevitably involves some subjectivity; one makes judgments. Thus, as emphasized in chapter 2, any explanation of the American homicide rate must be interpretive. There is simply no other way to proceed. Even so, it must be reasonably precise. In developing the explanation presented in this chapter, I find it convenient to consider the problem as similar to a multiple regression analysis in a quantitative study. But here it is a metaphor, one that professionals will recognize more often than students. As a metaphor, then, the dependent variable in this study (the $y$ in a regression equation) is the American rate of homicide. The independent variables (the $x$s in a regression equation) comprise a set of structural factors to be described in a few moments. Whether you recognize the metaphor or not, the advantage of thinking about the problem in this way is that each variable must be clearly specified and related to both the homicide rate and one another. The major difference, of course, is that the result is a logically driven model of the American rate of homicide, one in which the variables are manipulated conceptually rather than quantitatively.

With these ideas in mind, the question posed in this book is simple: Compared to other nations (see figure 3.1) and despite significant fluctuations over time (see figure 3.2), how can the high base rate of homicide in the United States be explained? My working hypothesis is: *The high base rate of homicide in the United States reflects the impact of (1) greater availability of guns, (2) the expansion of illegal drug markets, (3) greater racial discrimination, (4) greater exposure to violence, and (5) greater economic inequality.* In considering this hypothesis, remember that no single factor is explanatory. Rather, their combined impact suggests what Steven Messner and Richard Rosenfeld meant when they argued that homicide is built into the social structure of the United States.

## THE GREATER AVAILABILITY OF GUNS

Unlike the situation in other Western nations, the effect of firearm availability on the homicide rate constitutes a great and enduring political controversy in the United States, and a long literature exists on the issue. As a result, this section is the longest in the chapter. The initial structural relationship expressed in the hypothesis is, *the greater the availability of guns in a popula-tion, the greater the homicide rate.* In order to deal with this issue, however, a number of preliminary topics must be discussed: the lethality of guns com-pared to other weapons, the history of guns and homicide, and how many guns circulate in this nation. I also want to outline the opposing argument. Finally, I will summarize the evidence showing that gun availability affects the homicide rate.

## Guns versus Other Weapons

At the present time, guns are the most dangerous personal weapon poten-tially available to people. All the extant data suggest that fatality rates are higher in violent encounters, whether assaults, robberies, or other events, when a gun is used, compared to a knife, club, or bare hands.[5]

Consider knives, which can be exceedingly dangerous weapons. A simple cut of the carotid artery in the neck can cause a person to bleed to death in just a few minutes. But this result is actually not simple to achieve because killing someone with a knife (or club or fist) involves close, hard work. One must physically attack potential victims, who nearly always wish to survive and thus tend to defend themselves. Using a knife, then, requires a high level of psychological commitment, some physical strength, and a willingness to put oneself in danger when potential victims fight back.

A little thought experiment can illustrate the difficulty an aggressor armed with a knife might face. Assume for a moment that either Nathaniel Brazill or Wayne Lo had not had access to a gun. If the fourteen-year-old Mr. Brazill (described in chapter 3) had held only a knife, he would have had to engage his teacher, Barry Grunow, in hand-to-hand combat outside his classroom. Given their differences in age and physique, one or both might have been injured, but it is doubtful that Mr. Grunow would be dead today in this sce-nario or that young Mr. Brazill would have been imprisoned for twenty-eight years. Similarly, if armed with a knife, Mr. Lo would have had to overcome Theresa Beavers at the guard shack, then pull Professor Sáez from his car and kill him, and then turn to his next victim, which probably would not have been Galen Gibson. All this would have been physically difficult and it is unlikely he would have succeeded for very long before being subdued. Not only were many students all around, it is simply harder to get at vital organs with a knife, and even harder with a club or fist.

As an aside, in both these cases one could posit an alternative scenario that some observers think would make America a safer place to live. And that is that one of the victims or bystanders possessed a firearm. Assume for a moment that Wayne Lo's SKS worked properly. Assume further that Professor Sáez saw the shooting of Ms. Beavers as he approached the entrance to the college and that he possessed a loaded nine-millimeter semi-automatic pistol under the seat in his car. Not only are millions of these high-powered handguns in circulation, but 16 percent of handgun owners keep their weapons either in their cars or on their person.[6] Conceivably, he could have surprised Mr. Lo and possibly shot him. Or, more likely, he would have missed and the two might have exchanged gunfire until one of them became incapacitated or gave up. In addition, assume that one of the students carried a gun in her backpack for self-protection. She could have joined the fray as well. As I will describe later on, some observers argue that defensive gun use of this sort provides one way of solving the problem of criminal violence, assuming, of course, that nearby unarmed bystanders would emerge unharmed after the gunfight.

I consider the argument that guns make this a safer society later in the chapter. For now, my point is that guns are more lethal than other weapons because people die less often when knives, clubs, or fists are used. The most conservative estimates suggest that the chances of death from gunshots are between two and five times greater than from knife wounds.[7] But other estimates are higher. For example, one study of emergency room cases compared the impact of gunshots and knifings that resulted from assaults of some sort (attempted suicides and unintentional woundings are excluded). Gunshots resulted in death 17 percent of the time, compared to only 2 percent for knife wounds. In this case, then, the odds of dying from a gunshot wound in a violent encounter are about eight times greater than if a knife is used—at least among victims who survive long enough to be brought into hospital emergency rooms. Wayne Lo, armed with a high-powered rifle, achieved a somewhat higher kill ratio; one-third of his victims died. Moreover, it is possible that the death rate from gunshots has increased in recent years, since the destructive force of guns, especially handguns, has increased during this period.

As I will emphasize later on, the United States is anomalous compared to other nations in that most murders are committed with guns, and most gun-related murders involve handguns.[8] All firearms have become more lethal over the last few decades as the emphasis in manufacturing and use has changed from single-shot accuracy to increased firepower. This new orientation reflects the fact that even though modern guns can be fired accurately over considerable distance, most people fail to kill their target (as suggested by the data above). This is true even for professionals, such as police officers.

In order to increase the odds of at least hitting someone, then, manufacturers have reduced production of revolvers in recent years and increased production of more lethal semi-automatic pistols, which has led to greater involvement of the latter in homicides.[9] *Revolvers* carry five or six rounds of ammunition that are stored in a revolving cylinder. Single-action revolvers must be cocked each time in preparation to shoot. Double-action revolvers are cocked by pulling the trigger, which also rotates the cylinder. In both cases, users can easily fire six shots in just a few seconds; they must then, of course, reload—which takes several moments (even with speed loaders). *Semi-automatic pistols* carry anywhere from seven to twenty rounds of ammunition in a detachable magazine that fits into the grip held by the user. (Although magazines holding more than ten rounds are illegal, millions are available on the secondary market.) After each round is fired, a new bullet is automatically inserted into the chamber, so the user simply keeps pulling the trigger. The advantage of a semi-automatic weapon is that when the magazine empties out, users simply expel it and insert a new one. Smoothly done, the process can take less than a second. Firepower is thus increased, as is the possibility of hitting a vital body part and, hence, disabling or killing a victim. Because I will refer to it later on, one last definition should be included: An *automatic weapon*, such as an assault rifle, is like a machine gun in that it reloads and fires continuously as long as the trigger is pulled and ammunition is available.

These differences mean that semi-automatic pistols are more lethal than revolvers. First, semi-automatics can fire more shots in the same amount of time. As a result, more people can be hit and each is more likely to sustain multiple wounds. This is why data show that the proportion of gunshot victims with more than one wound increased radically in cities around the nation during the 1990s.[10] Galen Gibson and Theresa Beavers were both shot more than once (although with a semi-automatic rifle). Second, semi-automatic pistols often use high-caliber bullets that carry greater killing power, and their lethality is magnified even more because of their design (e.g., hollow point). These characteristics are partly why at-scene mortality rates from gunshot wounds changed during the 1990s. For victims shot with a revolver, death at the scene declined from 42 to 18 percent. By contrast, among victims shot with semi-automatic pistols, the mortality rate at the scene rose from 5 to 34 percent.[11]

In addition to their destructive power, today's firearms are also easier to use than knives or other weapons. They allow more maneuverability, need less strength, and are relatively easy to operate.[12] These characteristics mean that a gun requires less psychological commitment in use, whether one intends to kill another or not. And guns are becoming increasingly simple to load and fire. Moreover, in recent years, domestic gun manufacturers have flooded the market with small, inexpensive semi-automatic pistols designed for concealed-carry use.[13] In addition, a variety of "point and shoot" accessories are now available, such as recoil compensators (to reduce the "kick") and laser aiming devices, that allow inexperienced users to be more comfortable firing guns and more accurate when they do.

The lethality of firearms compared to other weapons is perhaps why ordinary people are not usually allowed to own guns, especially handguns, in most other Western nations (see below). Nonetheless, in every society, a certain number of people have disagreements, become very angry, hear voices, and for other reasons want to hurt others. In such cases, guns provide a quick and efficient means of problem solving. We are armed and ready.

### A Brief History of Guns and Homicide in America

Americans always have been armed. The most reasonable estimate is that about half of all wealth holders owned guns on the eve of the Revolution in 1774.[14] This estimate is probably high for the population as a whole, since it is based on probate data and many people, especially on the frontier, did not possess sufficient wealth to have estates. Even so, guns were widespread in the population. The usual argument is that the early Americans' possession of firearms met their twin needs of hunting game and providing security, whether from attacks by Native Americans, slave revolts, or the threat of outlaws.

But this argument exaggerates the importance of guns during this era. Although many Americans were armed, they were usually not ready—not ready, at least, to use firearms in homicides. Although the evidence is sketchy, it appears that nearly all murderers used weapons other than guns during the early years of the republic.[15] This low level of gun-related homicide probably continued through the first half of the nineteenth century. In 1841, for example, John C. Colt had an ongoing dispute with a printer named Samuel Adams, to whom he owed money. During an argument, Mr. Colt killed Mr. Adams. The name of the perpetrator ought to sound familiar. He was the brother of Samuel Colt, who invented the revolver in 1832. But rather than using one of his brother Samuel's new-fangled handguns, he hammered his victim to death. John Colt's choice of weapon was typical of the time. In his history of homicide in New York City, Eric Monkkonen found that only 14 percent involved the use of guns in the sixty years before the Civil War.[16]

The choice of clubs, axes, knives, and other weapons over guns probably reflects how difficult the latter were to use. Before the Civil War, all guns and the ammunition they needed were handmade by artisans in small shops.[17] Hence, each gun was unique and often ornately beautiful. Guns were not technologically advanced, however, since all displayed three fundamental problems: They were (1) inaccurate, (2) hard to maintain, and (3) hard to use. These characteristics made them ineffective for hunting, only marginally useful in battle, and usually impractical for homicide.

The flintlock musket, which was the most advanced firearm available during the first half of the nineteenth century, was inaccurate beyond about twenty-five yards even under the best of conditions.[18] This is because the ball traveled down the muzzle bouncing from side to side, with its final trajectory determined by the last bounce. Think of it as like a knuckleball that might break in any direction after emerging from the muzzle. For this reason, the flintlock had no sights and soldiers did not aim. Battle tactics employed mass volleys of fire in order to have any impact at all. For example, during the irregular battles around Lexington and Concord on April 19, 1775, which signaled the start of the American Revolution, about 3,763 Americans (not all of whom were armed) hit only 273 British soldiers, killing only a few.[19] Fortunately, the weather was clear that day, since the flintlock would not have fired in the rain. Moreover, the noise and smoke also made flintlocks ineffective for hunting. After one (usually missed) shot, all the game dispersed. Most people farmed and found it much easier to either run traps or slaughter domestic animals (pigs and chickens) to obtain meat. In fact, the use of domestic animals was one of the colonists' great advantages over Native American societies, as it provided a more stable food supply.

The flintlock was also very hard to maintain.[20] Made of iron, it rusted easily unless constantly oiled. In addition, powder accumulated in the barrel after each shot, forming a sludge that increased corrosion and slowed down the flight of the ball. It was supposed to be cleaned after every four shots, a time-consuming chore—especially in battle. Hence, it was easy for a gun to become inoperable, especially without advanced preparation. This difficulty may be one reason why most people were like John Colt and chose to use more immediately available and effective weapons.

Finally, the flintlock was hard to use:

> The process of loading the piece entailed placing the hammer at the half cock, opening the pan, removing a cartridge from the cartridge case which the soldier carried at his side, carrying the cartridge (in the right hand) to the mouth, and tearing the paper with the teeth. A priming charge was then poured from the broken cartridge into the open pan and the steel was pulled back, shutting the pan; the butt of the musket was dropped to the ground; the powder was poured from the cartridge into the muzzle and the ball was inserted; the ramrod was drawn and turned end for end and inserted upon the ball and the wadded cartridge paper; these were rammed home with two forceful blows. The ramrod was then withdrawn from the bore, turned with its small end to the first pipe, and forced down to its place under the barrel. The piece was then ready for cocking and firing. Obviously, in loading the long-barreled musket, the soldier had to stand erect.[21]

Even following this complex procedure exactly still resulted in frequent misfires. It is said, however, that a professional soldier could fire about four rounds in two minutes. But most people were farmers, and even professionals could not maintain this speed for very long. In any case, when the Bill of Rights was written in 1789, the maximum firepower available to an individual amounted to an inaccurate shot every thirty seconds or so. The flintlock musket with its elaborate loading process remained the basic mode for firing a gun from before the American Revolution right through the Civil War.[22] These characteristics made the flintlock an unrealistic tool for homicide. A club was quicker and easier to use, and likely to be much more effective.

Handguns were not practical for homicide, either.[23] Because they were often items of great beauty, the rich collected them. They served as markers of conspicuous consumption, like owning a military vehicle (such as a humvee) today. But they were basically flintlocks with short barrels and, hence, suffered all the defects noted above. In particular, the short barrel made them extremely inaccurate, even at very close quarters. This is probably why most participants survived duels. Samuel Colt's early revolvers did not change this situation very much, which may be another reason why his brother chose a different weapon. They were extremely heavy and rather complex to use, requiring the precise loading of powder, bullets, and firing caps into each chamber. Premanufactured cartridges would not become available until the Civil War and after.

Taken together, these difficulties mean that while the level of lethal violence was higher in this country than in Western Europe during the first half of the nineteenth century, guns had little to do with it. The weapons used in most murders were fists, clubs, knives, axes, and other blunt instruments. Even today, as will be mentioned later on, the United States displays a non-gun homicide rate higher than that in any Western European nation.

The role of the gun in American society and as a murder weapon began changing during the decade before the Civil War. Technological improvements made the revolver more practical to use and other small handguns were invented as well (e.g., those of Henry Derringer). The price of all types of guns fell and they became consumer items for the first time, advertised in mass circulation magazines. It was during this period that Americans became infatuated with firearms as more than tools. And the proportion of homicides involving guns, though still rather low, began rising. This was definitely true in New York City, as Eric Monkkonen shows, and probably true around the nation.[24]

In the years after the Civil War, the use of firearms in homicide accelerated. Gun technology had advanced significantly before the war and continued advancing during it. Breech-loading long guns made of steel with rifled barrels and modern cartridges came into increasing use, a process that became even more widespread in the decades after the war. These improvements increased accuracy and firepower and also made the weapons easier to maintain. Although revolvers were not much help in battle, then and now, because they are designed for personal use during violent encounters, they were commonly distributed to soldiers on both sides during the Civil War. Most important for the homicide rate, ex-soldiers (North and South) kept their weapons at war's end. Ordinary people now possessed effective firearms and began using them. In New York City, for example, the proportion of homicides committed with guns rose to 27 percent during the years after the Civil War.[25] Thus, Americans became both armed and ready—for homicide. As shown in chapter 3, homicide rates were especially high in the South and parts of the West. But even in the North, they were higher than in Western European nations at that time.

And the arming continued, as did technological advances. By the 1880s, gun making had changed from a craft pursued by artisans to a mass-produced industrial product. A few large firms now manufactured hundreds of thousands of handguns and rifles each year for both domestic and foreign sale. In this context, prices fell. One could purchase a gun for $2 or $3, cheap even by nineteenth-century standards. And the quality and reliability of the product improved greatly. As with other industries, American gun technology and manufacturing prowess dominated the world during this period.[26] From this time on, guns became the weapon most often used in homicide. In Chicago, for example, Jeffrey Adler reports that about 61 percent of homicides were gun-related in the years 1875–1899. In the cattle towns of the West and in the South, levels of gun use in homicide were probably comparable.[27] For the nation as a whole, Frederick Hoffman estimates that the proportion of gun-related homicides was 57 percent in 1910, rising to 73 percent in 1921. H. C. Brearley observes that 71 percent of all homicides in this country were gun-related during the 1920s, compared to only 10 percent in England at that time.[28] So, as with other advances during this period, Americans swiftly adopted the new technology.

This pattern—greater lethality as indicated by increasing accuracy and firepower—has characterized weapon technology up to the present. It represents, of course, the successful application of scientific principles to the problem of killing people and is thus part and parcel of what modern societies are like. As you may recall from chapter 3, the United States celebrated its emergence as a modern society at the World's Columbian Exposition in Chicago in 1893 by displaying its advanced technology. Electricity powered Mr. Ferris's wheel and Thomas Edison displayed the phonograph and kinescope—products that continue to affect social life today (albeit in altered form). Gun technology took off as well. Although the invention of another American genius, Hiram Maxim, was not demonstrated at the Exposition, over the long term it had just as great an impact on social life. Mr. Maxim invented the machine gun, the first truly automatic weapon. Easy to operate, it fired 500 rounds per minute for as long as the user depressed the trigger and ammunition was fed on a belt into the firing chamber. This quantum leap in firepower was used to devastating effect in the first modern war, World War I. It has been estimated that 90 percent of the 31 million people who died in that war were mowed down by rapid-firing machine guns.[29]

Rifle technology advanced as well.[30] The major engineering dilemmas at the end of the nineteenth century involved how to improve accuracy over long distance and how to increase the speed with which ammunition could be fed into the firing chamber of the gun. By World War I, bolt-action military rifles had become standard. Accurate up to a thousand yards (ten football fields), the rifles' magazines held bullets that could be fired as fast as a person could operate the bolt. By World War II, semi-automatic and automatic rifles had become predominant. In the more than half-century since then, assault rifles have evolved as a new type of weapon. They employ large-capacity magazines and can fire in either semi-automatic or automatic mode. Compared to earlier long guns, assault rifles combine long-distance, single-shot accuracy with much greater firepower and mobility. The technological problem they solve involves keeping the gun compact and lightweight without reducing barrel length. In both rifles and handguns, longer barrel length increases accuracy while short length decreases it. The Russian inventor Mikhail Kalashnikov developed the most well known assault rifle. Millions of his AK-47 and its successors can be found around the world. It is about thirty inches long, weighs only ten pounds, employs thirty-round magazines, and has a killing range of 1,500 yards (fifteen football fields). It can fire 600 rounds per minute. The American equivalent is the M-16. (By the way, Wayne Lo's SKS was not an assault rifle, as it can only fire in semi-automatic mode.) All these military weapons entered the civilian market in the United States (not in other nations) throughout the twentieth century, often with government encouragement.[31] The federal government, for example, sold weapons to the public, often at reduced prices.

Handgun technology also advanced. As described earlier, over the last two decades or so manufacturers have increased production of semi-automatic pistols compared to revolvers. During this process, the characteristics of pistols have changed significantly as well, leading to greater lethality.[32] Magazine capacity rose. Before 1993, only 14 percent of all handguns held ten or more rounds, the average being 7.6. After that time, 38 percent held ten rounds or more, the average rising to 9.5. This 25 percent increase in capacity probably understates the increase in lethal effects because pistols have become so much more widely available, many with magazines holding up to thirty rounds. In addition, the caliber of these weapons increased, as manufacturers changed from marketing smaller-bore pistols to much larger 9 mm pistols. This change proved to be enormously popular and this type of firearm sells very well; millions circulate on the streets. As one observer concludes, "the 'nine' is [now] the No. 1 [weapon of] choice among gang members, drug dealers, and career criminals on the street." And, of course, what is good for the bad guys is better for police officers and ordinary people, who keep them on their persons and in their homes and cars so they can defend themselves. Finally, several companies have emerged that specialize in the manufacture of small, cheaply made, and easily concealable short-barrel, low-

caliber pistols. The streets have been flooded with these weapons, the so-
called Saturday Night Specials.[33]

This brief history of the relationship between guns and homicide suggests
a clear pattern: Technological advances have led to more guns in more hands,
guns are more lethal, and guns have become the most frequent weapon used
in homicides—at least in the United States. In terms of the house metaphor
used in chapter 2, the door to firearm use is wide open in this country. Guns
are involved in about two-thirds of all homicides in the United States. The
various methods for committing homicide in this country are shown below
for 1999:[34]

| | |
|---|---|
| Firearms | 65% |
| Knives or cutting instruments | 13% |
| Hands, feet, or fists | 7% |
| Other methods or unknown | 15% |
| | 100% |

By contrast, and this is a key point, the use of firearms to commit homicide
is rare in Western Europe. In England and Wales in 1999, for example, the
distribution of weapons used in homicides looks like this:[35]

| | |
|---|---|
| Firearms | 9% |
| Knives or cutting instruments | 30% |
| Hands, feet, or fists | 22% |
| Blunt instrument | 10% |
| Other methods | 21% |
| Unknown | 8% |
| | 100% |

Thus, not only do few homicides occur in England, less than one per
100,000 persons (recall figure 3.2), but those that take place rarely involve
firearms—only 9 percent. In fact, a curious symmetry exists. The data just
above showing the type of weapon used in homicide in England just before
the twenty-first century resemble those in the United States during the first
half of the nineteenth century, prior to the time when guns became effective
weapons. England, then, has chosen to keep the door to gun use closed; its
citizens rarely possess firearms. This same policy exists in most other Western
European nations. By contrast, in this country guns are widely available.

## How Many Guns in America?

Nearly 200 million guns circulate in the United States, about one-third of
them handguns.[36] As all this civilian firepower implies, guns are legal con-

sumer products in this country, bought and sold all the time. An estimated 14 million sales occur each year. Diaz estimates that about 60 percent of sales involve licensed dealers, with the remainder taking place as private transactions in the secondary market. This estimate may be low, however, as all private gifts and sales (via flea markets, gun shows, and through the mail) go unregulated. The story of one gun suggests how easily all guns can be acquired and used.[37]

On a weekend day, sixteen-year-old Nicholas Elliot persuaded his cousin Curtis Williams, a truck driver in his thirties, to take him to Guns Unlimited, a store located in Carrollton, Virginia. Young Mr. Elliot had been infatuated with guns for a long time and did not intend the visit to be a casual one; he knew what he wanted: a Cobray M-11/9 semi-automatic pistol, made by the S.W. Daniel Company. The Cobray came onto the market in 1983, part of a new generation of high-powered semi-automatic pistols. It is nonetheless a cheap weapon, retailing today for about $160. Its design differs fundamentally from other pistols. Dull black in color and very heavy, the grip extends down from the center (not the rear), and a stubby two-inch barrel protrudes from the front. This short barrel means that it is inaccurate, even at close range. But the Cobray carries built-in firepower. Its magazine holds thirty-two rounds of 9 mm bullets, which can be fired at a rate of three per second—about as fast as a human being can pull the trigger. (Inexpensive kits with easy directions are available that convert it to full automatic fire. The kits are legal to sell, even though the resulting submachine gun is not. By definition, a machine gun fires rifle caliber bullets, while a submachine gun fires pistol caliber bullets.) Given its design, the Cobray is useless for hunting or target shooting. As one observer points out, "about the only thing you can do with it is hold it someplace in front of you, pull the trigger as fast as you can, put out as many bullets as you can, and hope like hell they'll hit something."[38] Among gun enthusiasts, this is a called the "spray and pray" strategy. Sometimes it works and sometimes it does not.

After looking around in the gun store, young Mr. Elliot gave his cousin, Curtis Williams, the money to purchase the Cobray. The clerk at Guns Unlimited was standing only a few feet away when this exchange occurred. Mr. Williams thus served as the straw purchaser who made the actual buy. This was necessary because anyone purchasing a firearm from a licensed dealer must fill out a government form that asks whether the buyer is a convicted felon, has a psychiatric record, is an illegal alien, and other questions. Answering yes to any of the questions means the deal cannot be completed, and every potential customer knows this or is so informed by the dealer. In Nicholas Elliot's case, he needed a straw purchaser because he was too young to buy a gun. Even so, he left the store carrying the Cobray.

Several days later, Nicholas Elliot took the Cobray with him to the Atlantic Shores Christian School, which he attended. That morning, he killed a forty-one-year-old teacher, Karen Farley, striking her twice. Her husband survives her, along with their high-school-aged daughter. Another teacher, also hit twice, lived through the ordeal. Still another teacher escaped by running a zigzag pattern through the school yard as Mr. Elliot fired round after round at her, spraying shots across the yard in a back and forth motion. Finally, a teacher tackled Mr. Elliot and thus saved many lives, but not before a bullet whizzed past his head.

Nicholas Elliot's motive for these killings remains unclear. The teacher who tackled him screamed for an explanation and the young man simply said: "They hate me. They make fun of me. They hit me." At least one and possibly several other children had bullied him. Young Mr. Elliot apparently killed Karen Farley because she tried to take the gun from him.[39]

For these banal reasons, then, Ms. Farley is dead and Mr. Elliot will probably spend the rest of his life in prison, at enormous cost to the state of Virginia. Mr. Williams, the straw purchaser, served thirteen months in prison for his role in these shootings. And the families and friends of the victims, along with the survivors, will try to put their lives back together. Although the federal government did not find any violations of law by Guns Unlimited, the family of Karen Farley filed a negligence suit against the dealer and won a judgment of $105,000. Presumably, this amount captures her lost productivity over the next twenty years (?), but what about the family's loss of her love and affection? What about her potential contributions to the society? The family also filed a product liability suit against the gun's manufacturer, S.W. Daniels, but the gun was not defective. As the judge observed, "the weapon worked."[40]

Most do. And, as suggested by the examples in this and previous chapters, data show that most of those who commit homicide with firearms acquire them legally. Many others, like Nicholas Elliot, use straw purchasers to obtain weapons illegally. In fact, most of the guns used in crimes are not stolen; rather, they are bought from dealers.[41] A dual pattern exists. One is for people to obtain guns via purchase (whether legally or not) and use them to commit a crime locally, within a few hundred miles of the sale. The other is for straw purchasers to buy large numbers of guns in Southern states with weak gun control laws and move them up the East Coast to cities and states with stricter laws, where they are resold and then used in crimes. The quantity of guns in circulation and the ease with which they can be purchased means that it is simple for anyone, regardless of age, psychological characteristics, or history of violence (including prison), to obtain a gun.

It should be emphasized, however, that few of the 200 million guns circulating in this country are ever used in a crime, let alone a homicide. Just how many people own all these guns is raised often in sample surveys. From the 1960s through the early 1990s, most studies showed that about 44 to 50 percent of households had guns in them. But gun ownership has declined in recent years; only about 35 to 40 percent of households now have guns in them, usually more than one. Thus, despite the tremendous number of guns available, a minority of households possess them today. [42]

Just as few of the huge number of guns in circulation are used in a crime, very few of those who own guns commit crimes. People keep them in their homes or cars or carry them on their persons, and nearly all are perfectly law abiding. Guns embody many positive associations for owners. They provide recreation and enjoyment. Target shooting is fun and invigorating, giving people a sense of personal power. Guns also constitute potent symbols of individualism, personal autonomy, and freedom from government regulation of their lives. These fundamental rights resonate deeply in many Americans. Further, guns are consumer products of elegance and beauty; this is especially so for high-end products. Finally, guns have been so widespread in the population since the beginning of this nation, and especially since the second half of the nineteenth century, that many owners were raised around guns. In fact, one of the best predictors of current firearm ownership is the presence of guns in the childhood home. For a significant proportion of owners, then, guns are objects of veneration, carefully stored and preserved, used for pleasure. Of course, there is also another reason for owning a gun: About half, 47 percent, of all those possessing guns say their motive is self-protection, whether from personal assault or crime of some other sort. Among those who own only a handgun, almost three-quarters keep them primarily for self-protection. [43]

And this motivation is not irrational. It does not matter that few guns are actually used in homicide or other acts of violence or that few gun owners commit crimes. Because so many guns circulate so easily, almost anybody who wants one can get one. This is one reason why violence in America has a different quality than in other nations, and it is one reason why Americans are afraid. Because they are frightened, it can be argued that if the bad and dangerous people can get guns so easily, then the good people ought to have them, too. Yet, paradoxically, it remains unclear whether households or cars with guns in them are in fact safer. Nor is it clear whether the society as a whole is safer. The good people can easily become bad after they obtain a gun.

Many people, however, do not own guns and are not used to being around them. These people, an increasing proportion of the population, do not attach recreational or pleasurable meaning to guns. They remain, nonetheless, potent symbols—of danger. From these people's perspective, guns, especially handguns, serve one purpose: They provide a means for one person to kill another. So, as Gregory Gibson discovered in his walkabout, for the uninitiated it is "initially weird and scary being surrounded by them." [44] He observes that the language used reflects a fundamental difference in orientation. Gun enthusiasts refer to these products as firearms, while those unfamiliar call them weapons.

This intellectual divide forms the subtext of the political debate about the place of guns in American society. It also underlies scholarly research and controversy about the relationship between gun availability and homicide. In assessing the literature, then, one must ask a simple question: Where does the preponderance of the evidence lie? I use the legal term deliberately because scholars on both sides of the debate over the role of guns in American society present data in support of their arguments. In such a politicized context, all observers can do is recognize the existence of opposing views, and data, and make a sort of juridical judgment.

## The Coincidence Hypothesis

Some scholars argue that guns make the United States a safer society, not a more dangerous or homicidal one. They believe that the correlation between nearly 200 million guns in circulation and a high homicide rate is only a coincidence. There is actually, they assert, no relationship between gun availability and homicide. Two individuals who come to this conclusion and pursue it with special vigor are Don Kates and Gary Kleck, and I shall take them as representative of this point of view.[45] They make four interrelated arguments.

First, they argue that the correlation is a coincidence because any person who intends to kill another will, if denied a gun, simply substitute another weapon. This is also called the "displacement effect." The well-known aphorism, "guns don't kill people, people kill people," summarizes this position. It asserts that those choosing to use a gun must have lethal intentions or they would have selected a different weapon, one less likely to kill. Murderers, it is claimed, are not ordinary people; they are, rather, "aberrants exhibiting life histories of violence and crime, psychopathology, substance abuse, and other dangerous behaviors."[46] This fact is taken as indicating the lethal intention of all murderers.

In reply to this argument, Franklin Zimring and Gordon Hawkins show that lethal intent is unclear in many violent encounters that end in murder, which means the likelihood of weapon substitution seems relatively implausible.[47] Moreover, they argue, even when people intend to kill, as in some of the examples used in this book, their ability to carry out this objective reflects the easy availability of guns. People become enraged and an assault or fight occurs, such as over a debt or after drinking or during a domestic dispute. In such circumstances, the weapon immediately at hand or easily purchased determines the lethal outcome. This interpretation makes sense because at least half (and probably more) of all homicide victims know the assailant, who is an acquaintance, friend, or family member.[48] This fact suggests that households with guns in them are inherently more dangerous than those without.

Even among individuals who do not know each other before the murder, the precipitating event is often a disagreement of some sort followed by one of the parties producing a weapon. As with those who know one another, what appears to happen much of the time is that really angry or delusional people select or purchase the most effective and easily available weapon.[49] And given the huge number of guns in circulation and their ease of purchase, that weapon is often a gun. It thus seems to me that the substitution argument is not persuasive. Some killers do exhibit "life histories of violence." Even so, the structural issue is whether so many of them would have killed if guns were not so readily available in this country. After all, violence-prone people exist in all other nations as well, including those displaying low levels of homicide.

The second argument justifying the coincidence hypothesis is that even when guns are used during a crime, it is said that they are no more likely to result in a victim's death than if other weapons are used. The issue is important because about one-fourth of homicides are committed during a felony, such as a robbery. Professor Kleck presents data showing that while the actual use of a gun increases the odds of a victim's death, its threatened use during a robbery increases an offender's ability to control the situation and reduces the need to fire. Thus, he concludes, the net effect of the presence of a gun on homicide is negligible.[50]

This conclusion, however, is probably incorrect. In general, studies of robbery-homicide indicate that the fatal result was often not premeditated; the goal was the money not the murder. More specifically, Professor Kleck's logic and the methods underlying his analyses seem misbegotten. When his data are reanalyzed, they show that the presence of a gun in a violent incident, such as a robbery, makes homicide much more likely.[51]

The third argument favoring the coincidence hypothesis is that guns are often used in self-defense and, as a result, criminals are thwarted and deterred. The image is that of armed citizens defending themselves and others because they have weapons on their persons, in their cars, or in nightstands next to their beds. From this point of view, if either Ñacuñán Sáez or Karen Farley had carried a semi-automatic pistol, the outcome at Simon's Rock College and Atlantic Shores Christian School might have been different. They could have returned fire, perhaps killing their attackers rather than being killed. The United States, so this argument goes, is actually a safer society because so many people arm themselves. In Professor Kleck's words, "much of the social order in America may depend on the fact that millions of people are armed and dangerous to each other."[52] He concludes that because gun ownership inhibits crime as much (or more) than it generates crime, observers ought to be skeptical of efforts at limiting the availability of guns to the public. Although he does not draw out the implication, others do: America would be a safer place if even more citizens went about armed during the course of the day.[53]

Although the issue of defensive gun use has become very controversial, it appears that Professor Kleck is incorrect. As above, when his data are reanalyzed and juxtaposed with other data, the best available evidence indicates that the use of guns in self-defense is extremely rare.[54] Actually, the reverse is true: Offensive gun use, in which a person displays a gun and uses it to intimidate (and sometimes kill), is much more common.[55] An example would be Nathaniel Brazill's sad behavior at school on the day he shot Barry Grunow.

The fourth argument supporting the coincidence hypothesis is that the evidence simply does not establish the correlation between gun availability and the homicide rate. For example, it is argued that fluctuations in the American homicide rate are not associated with variations in the availability of guns. Thus, the number of guns in circulation has steadily increased over the last few decades while the homicide rate has fluctuated differently, first going up and then down (see figure 3.2). It is also argued that evidence for the relationship is weak because some studies compare only two cities or countries, the measures of gun availability are unsound, and methodological procedures used in some studies are flawed. Hence, Professor Kates and other observers conclude, there is a long-term nonrelationship between firearm availability and homicide in the United States.[56]

The fluctuation argument misses the point. The question, at least in this book, is why the base rate of homicide is so high in this country compared to others, regardless of short-term fluctuations. As a brief sidebar, however, it is worth thinking about the variables that might have affected changes in the American homicide rate over time. I would look at variations in gun availability (by manufacture, import, and sales), level of economic prosperity, the size of the cohort of people aged eighteen to twenty-five, the number of prisoners released each year, aggressive police practices, the effectiveness of emergency medical procedures, and other factors.[57] All this is speculative, of course, and the analysis would have to be worked out in more detail.

Professor Kates's assertion that there is no relationship between gun availability and the homicide rate is, of course, on point. In the next section, I intend to summarize the evidence supporting my assertion that such a relationship does exist. In preparation for that analysis, both the general reader and students might benefit from a brief explanation of what is meant by correlation and causation.[58] A perfect positive correlation occurs when a change in one phenomenon is completely associated with a change in another. For example, when you drive a car down the highway, the rear wheels are perfectly correlated: They both move in the same direction, at the same speed, at the same time. By contrast, a perfect negative correlation occurs when a change in one phenomenon is completely associated with another's change in the opposite direction. For example, the movement of two children on a teeter-totter is negatively correlated: When one moves up the other moves down, at the same speed, at the same time. Nearly all correlations in the social sciences are less (usually far less) than perfect. This is mainly because we do not do laboratory experiments with all the variables controlled. For example, income is positively associated with the value of one's house, which means that one can make the following statement in covariance form: The higher the family income, the greater the value of its housing.[59] But this relationship is far from perfect. Two families with similar incomes may live in houses with quite different values. When no correlation exists, which is what Professors Kates and Kleck argue about guns and homicide, there is no way to tell how a change in one phenomenon is associated with a change in another. For example, the number of leaves falling from a tree in your yard has no relationship to the temperature of your morning coffee. Any relationship that occurs is coincidental.

In thinking about the problem of gun availability and the homicide rate, it is important to remember that correlation is not causation. Some relationships can be correlated (change in one occurs, to some degree, in association with change in another) but are not caused. For example, if I recall correctly, it has been observed that when an AFC football team wins the Super Bowl, the stock market goes up, and when an NFC team wins it goes down. But there is no logic to this assertion. To infer causation requires more than association. It requires that the relationship be temporal; that is, a change in item $x$ (the cause) occurs before the change in item $y$ (the effect). For example, a family must have sufficient income before it can purchase a house. In addition, the relationship should not be spurious; that is, $x$ and $y$ remain associated even when the influence of other factors is eliminated. Finally, a rationale for the relationship must be established; that is, observers must present a logical explanation for why the relationship exists.

Taking these arguments and the criticisms together, my conclusion is that the coincidence hypothesis is implausible. The United States is not a safer place because guns are so readily available. But making the negative case differs from making the positive one. Is the preponderance of the evidence also against it? Can it be shown that a relationship exists between gun availability and homicide such that it must constitute an important part of any explanation of the American anomaly?

## Gun Availability and the Rate of Homicide

Compared to other nations, guns are widely available in the United States and circulate easily. They are involved in about two-thirds of American homicides. And guns are the most lethal weapons available to ordinary citizens. These facts establish a circumstantial reason for believing that the relationship is important. What does other evidence reveal? Consider the following.

*Cross-National Correlations.* Comparative analyses across nations consistently show a positive correlation between the level of gun ownership and the homicide rate. This finding occurs in many works, each of which uses different methods and, hence, reveals different flaws.[60] These methodological differences are important, because the finding occurs regardless of how the variables are measured. For example, in a study of fourteen Western nations, Martin Killias found a correlation of .746 between the percentage of households with guns and the homicide rate. This is a high correlation for a social scientific study. Phrased in covariance form, it leads to the following statement: The higher the proportion of households with guns in them, the higher the homicide rate. Moreover, there appears to be no displacement effect. Thus, nations with low rates of gun ownership do not have more homicides committed with other weapons, which means guns do not substitute for some other means of killing.[61] These studies are cross-sectional, however, and thus they cannot account for a possible spurious correlation between gun availability and homicide. But a third variable would need to produce a high correlation among many nations between gun ownership and homicide rates but only marginally affect murders by other means. As Professor Killias notes, "one can hardly imagine what it might look like." Nonetheless, the conservative conclusion based on these data is that although guns matter, they are not the only things that matter when accounting for the level of lethal violence in a society.

Note, however, that while studies reveal a positive correlation between gun availability and the homicide rate, the relationship is not perfect. Exceptions exist. For example, you may recall from figure 3.1 that Switzerland displays a low homicide rate compared to other Western nations. This is so even though 28 percent of Swiss households have guns in them.[62] I will deal with this issue later. For now, once again, it seems that the availability of guns matters. When their easy accessibility is placed in a multivariate context, even a conceptual one as here, they become an important part of an overall explanation. And other data fit with this conclusion—a fact that reduces the possibility of some third variable being at work.

***Correlations among Cities and States.***   Within the United States, variation in the availability of guns in cities is associated with variations in the homicide rate. A study of fifty large U.S. cities, for example, found a positive correlation between gun ownership and homicide rates. This same study also found that a 10 percent decline in the level of gun ownership in a city is associated with about a 5 percent decrease in the gun robbery rate and a 4 percent decrease in the robbery-murder rate. A subsequent analysis used panel data from the same fifty cities and came to the same conclusion. Other data make the same point: Fewer guns mean fewer gun homicides.[63] More detailed data are available for Detroit, Michigan. In this case, rather than looking at the impact of firearms on robbery and robbery-murder, researchers asked whether their availability affected the overall homicide rate. Since World War II, Detroit has displayed a rather high level of homicide compared to other American cities. One study examined time series data for 1963–1971 and found that nearly all the increase in homicide during this period was associated with increased availability of handguns.[64] Subsequently, David McDowall assembled data for 1951–1986 and had better measures of all variables. He found that "each 1 percent increase in the gun density index is associated with an increase of more than 1 percent in homicides." In an interesting statistical exercise, Professor McDowall asked whether Detroit's homicide rate in 1986, which was fifty-six per 100,000 residents, would differ if the index of gun availability was set at its lowest level from among the years studied and all the other explanatory variables were left at their 1986 levels. With this change, the predicted homicide rate fell to twenty-one per 100,000, a saving of 379 lives. It is, of course, possible that the various measures of gun availability used in these studies are biased or that the relationship between guns and lethal violence is caused by some factor unique to Detroit. But these possibilities seem unlikely.[65] Like other observers, Professor McDowall concludes that if fewer guns were available in Detroit (and by implication other cities), fewer homicides would occur.

A well-known natural experiment illustrates this finding.[66] Although the cities of Seattle, Washington, and Vancouver, British Columbia, are similar in many respects, at the time of the study they differed in the availability of guns and in homicide rates. The weakness of natural experiments is that their validity is hard to assess because the amount of built-in bias is unknown and generalizability to other similar contexts (in this case, cities) is unclear. But this methodology allows researchers to take advantage of situations created by history and politics that resemble those in the laboratory. Thus, Seattle and Vancouver share a common geography, climate, and history. They exhibit similar demographic and socioeconomic characteristics. They display similar levels of assault (but Seattle has somewhat higher burglary and robbery rates). Police and prosecutors in both cities enforce their gun laws in comparable ways (although the laws differ), and when homicide occurs arrest and conviction rates are almost identical. Vancouver has a higher Asian origin population, while Seattle has a higher African American population. In sum, these cities are more comparable to each other than to other cities in their respective nations. For example, Seattle's homicide rate is much less than that of Los Angeles or Detroit, and Vancouver's is much greater than that of Toronto. They endure similar levels of non-gun-related homicide. They differ, however, in the availability of guns and the gun-related homicide rate. About 41 percent of Seattle's residents possess guns, compared to 12 percent in Vancouver. The gun-related homicide rate is five times higher in Seattle. It is possible, of course, that these two cities also differ in some unknown way that produces this result. But what might it be? In addition, it is possible that the implication of this study—that reducing the availability of firearms would reduce the homicide rate—is not generalizable to other American cities, many of which have far higher homicide rates. But the finding does not occur in isolation; it also fits with data on other cities.

A similar finding occurs when the unit of analysis is shifted to states. For example, in a study examining firearm deaths among children, the authors compared the five states with the highest level of gun ownership to the five states with the lowest level. In the former states, children aged five to fourteen were sixteen times more likely to die from an unintentional shooting, seven times more likely to commit suicide with a gun, and three times more likely to be a homicide victim as in the latter. It did not matter how gun availability was measured, and the result remained even after other variables were controlled for (such as a state's level of poverty or urbanization).[67] This finding not only matches the city level data, it also corresponds with the cross-national correlations.

*Restrictions on Gun Availability.*   Just as increasing gun availability increases the homicide rate, studies also show that decreasing gun availability decreases the homicide rate. Thus, imposing penalties for using guns or instituting restrictive policies, either by statute or police action, is followed by declining levels of homicide.

Mandatory sentence requirements try to increase the penalties for gun use and, hence, reduce crime and violence—at least mildly. State legislators like such laws because they do not seem to affect (or offend) ordinary gun owners. One of the best analyses of such efforts is by David McDowall and his colleagues, who looked at six city-specific case studies and found that mandatory sentencing laws reduce gun-related homicide. The effect, however, is not large and varies significantly from city to city. This finding resembles that occurring in other studies.[68]

Statutes restricting gun possession are rare, but one has been analyzed. In late 1976 (the date is important), it became illegal for civilians to purchase, sell, transfer, or possess handguns in the District of Columbia unless they had been registered before enactment of the new law. Colin Loftin and his colleagues took advantage of this natural experiment to analyze the statute's impact and found an immediate and long-term decline in both homicides and suicides of about 25 percent.[69] This effect occurred even though adjacent areas of Virginia and Maryland are part of the same metropolitan area and guns could flow freely into the District. Moreover, these adjacent areas did not show a decline in homicide. In addition, there was no displacement effect; within the District, no changes occurred in non-gun homicides or suicides. This effect, which averaged forty-seven fewer deaths per year, lasted for ten years (the time period is important, as will become clear later).

Finally, it is widely agreed that police action focused on reducing the presence of guns on the street leads to a reduction in homicide. Indeed, such efforts appear to be one (not the only) reason for the decline in homicide over the last decade.[70] One natural experiment shows this effect clearly.[71] In Kansas City, the police selected two reporting areas to test the hypothesis that gun seizures and gun crime are negatively related. Although the two areas were not identical—the target area was smaller and more densely populated, for example—they both displayed high gun crimes and gun-related homicides, and nearly identical numbers of drive-by shootings, before the experiment. For twenty-nine weeks, police made concentrated efforts (via traffic stops and pedestrian checks) to clear guns from the street in the target area. Gun seizures rose 69 percent. Both gun crime and gun-related homicides dropped significantly in the target area. There was no change in the comparison area. Nor did the target area display any change in other kinds of violent and nonviolent crimes. Finally, there was no measurable displacement of gun crimes to patrol areas surrounding the target area, even though guns can obviously be transported the few blocks from one area to another.

These data on the consequences of restricting gun availability need to be interpreted cautiously. But when juxtaposed with the cross-national correlation and city comparisons, the findings display a pattern. And this pattern suggests that the level of gun availability affects homicide rates.

***Some Potential Criticisms.*** Whether this pattern is empirically accurate is important. Several observers have raised questions about it, and I want to pause and review their criticisms.

One line of criticism is that the opposite pattern may occur when guns become more available; that is, placing even more guns in circulation would produce less homicide. For example, at least thirty-one states have passed "right-to-carry" laws that require the issuing of handgun-carry permits to persons meeting a set of criteria, usually age, criminal history, mental status, and sometimes a gun safety course. From this point of view—that more guns make us safer—when citizens carry firearms on their persons, the criminals are deterred by the publicity attending passage of such bills and the rise in legal carrying that follows. For example, John Lott and David Mustard present data showing that such laws reduce crime: homicides by 67 percent, rapes by 65 percent, and assaults by 73 percent.[72] But this claim is probably incorrect, as suggested by the implausibly high estimates of the laws' effects. Furthermore, David McDowall and his colleagues looked at homicide rates in five large urban areas in four states before and after passage of "right-to-carry" laws and found an increase in gun homicides in four of the five. They conclude that such laws do not reduce homicides (they do not make us safer) and may increase homicides.[73] Jens Ludwig replicated this finding in a creative way by comparing differences between gun homicides committed by juveniles and adults. Because juveniles cannot obtain concealed-carry permits, the impact of right-to-carry laws should be evident in differences in homicide victimization rates between adults and juveniles. He found little evidence that such laws reduce homicide. In fact, his data suggest that they increase homicides. Finally, in yet another study, Professor McDowall and his colleagues examined publicity about civilian gun ownership in several cities and found no deterrent effect. Professor Lott, of course, disagrees with these findings.[74]

Another line of criticism involves identifying flaws in the studies referred to in the previous section. Indeed, all display imperfections and can be criticized. Chester Britt and his colleagues focus on the study of Washington, D.C.'s, gun control law referred to earlier.[75] Their remarks, however, reflect a generalized opposition to all the analyses presented above. Those asserting that more guns make us a safer society emphasize the weakness of natural experiments such as this one. Thus, the Britt group asserts that the use of adjacent metropolitan areas as controls was unjustified, that the specification of when the "experiment" began (1976) was arguable, and that the end point of the experiment (ten years later, in 1986) was arbitrary. Hence, they label as "implausible" the Loftin group's conclusion that the gun law is the most likely reason for a decline in homicides in the District.[76] They do not, however, suggest any other factor (a third variable) that might have produced this change. Moreover, even in strictly methodological terms, their critique can be challenged. In a rejoinder, Professor McDowall and his colleagues observe that the controls in a natural experiment are the observations that take place before the intervention (the high homicide rates prior to passage of the law).[77] Moreover, they used the effective date of the law rather than, say, the date of its passage as the beginning of the "experiment" and defend it as a reasonable choice. Finally, they point out that after ten years the situation in the District changed, as illegal drug markets associated with crack cocaine appeared in the District beginning in 1986.[78] In effect, another intervention occurred and homicide rates rose. Although natural experiments cannot be as precise as those occurring in the laboratory, they provide an important means for understanding the impact of historical events on behavior.

## Conclusion

My conclusion is that the preponderance of the evidence reviewed here shows that the availability of guns constitutes one factor explaining why American homicide rates are so high compared to other Western nations. Again, I use this juridical language because the impact of guns has become highly politicized in the United States, although not in other nations. The references to opposing arguments in the text above and in the endnotes suggest that the same scholars consistently appear on each side of the debate, presenting evidence to support their differing points of view. Observers, then, cannot simply "let the data speak," since data exist supporting each side. Rather, observers must evaluate the plausibility of the arguments and data, and come to a judgment.

Structurally, if I am correct, the huge number of guns available in this country changes people's options, making it easier for homicide to occur. Yet people's options differ in other nations as well. As you may recall, the cross-national correlation between gun availability and homicide rates is not perfect. In Switzerland, for example, guns are readily accessible, yet the homicide rate is low. Advocates of the coincidence hypothesis often point to the Swiss situation, asserting that it shows that guns are not the problem.[79] The more likely explanation, however, is that guns are not the only problem, that guns combine with other factors to produce a high rate of homicide in the United States. What the Swiss experience reveals is that a multivariate synthetic approach is necessary. People on both sides of the debate recognize this possibility, often in a throwaway line. For example, in the last paragraph of his book, *Point Blank,* Gary Kleck observes that solving the problem of violence will require looking at economic inequality, injustice, and the life chances of the poor. Similarly, Professors Zimring and Hawkins point out that the impact of guns on violence cannot be understood without knowing more about how gun availability interacts with other factors.[80] Both are correct; neither does the analysis. For example, neither cites any of the literature dealing with the other variables included in the working hypothesis. It is thus necessary to assess how these other factors make the United States unique and show how the availability of guns combines with them.

Here is an interesting exercise as a way of beginning to think about this issue. As observed earlier, guns, mostly handguns, are used in 65 percent of homicides. Other weapons, usually a knife or fists, are used in most of the remainder. The homicide rate in 1999 was a very low (for the United States) 6.1 per 100,000. Thus, 65 percent of 6.1 equals 4.0 gun-related deaths per 100,000 people. By subtraction, other weapons accounted for 2.1 homicides. This exercise suggests that the homicide rate would be far lower if guns were less easily available—under the hypothesis that many of those who were both frustrated and socialized to violence would find it more difficult to kill. Note, however, that the remaining 2.1 homicides are still higher than the average of 1.57 in the nations shown in figure 3.1. The literature on guns contains an implicit assumption that characterizes work on both sides of the issue: that the impact of these weapons constitutes a single-cause explanation. But this assumption cannot be correct. Guns can only explain part of the variance.

## THE EXPANSION OF ILLEGAL DRUG MARKETS

The second structural relationship specified in the hypothesis is: *The more illegal drug markets expand, the more they are regulated by violence and the greater the homicide rate.* Drug policy in this country is designed to reduce the supply of illegal substances by eradicating them in foreign nations, interdicting them as they are smuggled into the United States, and arresting sellers and buyers. According to this criterion, this policy has failed; illegal drugs are readily available to any American who wants them.[81] And many do. My argument, however, is not whether American drug policy is wise or not. Nor is my argument about whether drugs like heroin, cocaine, marijuana, or other substances should be legal or not. Rather, I focus on the paradoxical effect of American drug policy: Because it is against the law to possess or sell these and other drugs, illegal markets exist to satisfy the high demand. Often located in poor neighborhoods, these markets generate crime and violence because they are illegal. And they destroy the fabric of daily life.[82]

Illegal drugs and homicide are connected in three ways.[83] First, the intoxication that occurs when people ingest a substance can lead to lethal violence as users either become aggressive and act out or behave in ways that increase their chance of being victimized. (As an aside, at least one legal drug, alcohol, also leads some users to become violent. Thus, the focus on illegal substances in this section means that I am omitting the impact of rates of alcohol use and the distribution of liquor stores as they might affect the level of homicide.) Second, the desire for illegal drugs can cause people to engage in economic crimes to support their habit. Such crimes (like robbery) can also lead to murder. And third, conducting an illegal business can stimulate homicide. This drug-market-related (or structural) violence includes such issues as disputes between rival dealers, wars between gangs over sales territory, assaults and murders committed within drug dealing operations in order to enforce rules, robberies of drug dealers, elimination of informers, punishment for selling adulterated or bogus drugs, and assaults to collect drug-related debts.[84]

Historically, most of the violence associated with illegal drugs—especially homicide—has been drug-market related. The violent conflicts during the Prohibition era over the distribution of alcohol are well known. But similar battles have occurred over the distribution of marijuana and heroin. Most recently, when crack cocaine appeared in inner cities during the late 1980s and early 1990s, the markets expanded and became exceedingly violent.[85]

A long literature exists on the relationship between illegal drug markets and homicide, and the finding is consistent: They generate violence and contribute to the high American homicide rate. Although I use crack cocaine as an exemplar in what follows, the analysis applies to drug markets generally. Paul Goldstein and his colleagues show, for example, that more than half of the murders in New York City were drug related in the late 1980s, and nearly all of those were connected to selling drugs, mainly crack cocaine. The impact of expanding drug markets is especially clear in Washington, D.C. Crack cocaine began appearing in the District sometime in 1986. One year later, in 1987, only 5 percent of all killings in Washington, D.C., were drug related. In 1988, however, as drug entrepreneurs sought to establish themselves, the proportion of homicides that were drug related rose abruptly to 35 percent and remained relatively high (above 20 percent) for the next four years. Thus, much of the increase in homicides in Washington, D.C., during the late 1980s and early 1990s reflected a rise in drug-market-related murders.[86] The situation in the District is generalizable. It appears that much of the increase in drug-market-related homicide occurred in large cities across the nation during this period, where crack first appeared. For example, in a study of twenty-seven cities, it is estimated that the emergence of crack cocaine led to a 9 percent increase in homicide.[87] Studies of homicides involving youth gangs estimate that 3 to 11 percent are drug related. This connection is hard to assess, of course, because the existence of drug markets brings members of different gangs into contact, and that can stimulate disagreements and violence that are not specifically drug related (more on the neighborhood as a context for homicide later). For the nation as a whole, Professors Zimring and Hawkins conclude that the evidence suggests that "no fewer than 10 percent of American homicides and perhaps as many as 25 percent have important linkages to some illicit drug." This seems like a reasonable overall estimate.[88]

But the link between illegal drug markets and homicide is peculiarly American. All Western nations display problems with drug use and keep the same panoply of substances illegal, which means that all live with the resulting drug markets. But these markets do not seem to be as violent as in the United States.[89] The association between drugs (especially crack cocaine) and homicide in this country exists in a historical context that must be accounted for. One reason for this difference may be that public policy in this country is more punitive; possession and use are treated as criminal acts rather than public health problems. Another reason may be that Americans abuse drugs at a much greater rate than do people in other Western nations. So demand is greater in this country, and competition among independent dealers and drug-selling organizations is keener.[90]

Illegal drug markets providing products in high demand constituted the context in which crack cocaine appeared as a low-priced alternative to powdered cocaine in the late 1980s. Both the timing and price are important, as is the availability of guns as a means of conflict resolution.

The timing is important because a massive restructuring of the American economy occurred over the fifteen years prior to crack's appearance as good-paying manufacturing jobs moved out of central cities to suburbs (and to foreign nations). The impact left large numbers of people, especially many African Americans and Hispanics, with little opportunity to earn a decent living.[91] Teenagers and young adults were especially affected with high rates of unemployment. These changes meant that crack appeared in poor, racially segregated neighborhoods that were also characterized by deteriorating social controls. The latter occurred because impoverished areas of most cities are often disorganized in other ways as well: They display inadequate schools, social services, police protection, and infrastructure. These problems, of course, do not reflect the desires of the residents; they reflect, rather, the distribution of wealth and power in American society.[92] Such neighborhoods are anomic, of course. Recall that the term *anomie* refers to a disjunction between conventional values, such as economic success, and the legitimate means to achieve them. The poor, like everyone else, learn work-oriented values, yet they find that good jobs are hard to obtain, since few businesses locate in impoverished areas. Thus, although most people work in the formal economy (their jobs are on the books), a surplus population exists with nothing to do and little hope for the future. These people must adapt in light of the fact that achieving success in the conventional way, through hard work at a legal job, is unlikely.

The low price of crack is also important. This product originated as a technological innovation. Before 1986 or so, cocaine was sold in powdered form at costs ranging from several hundred to several thousand dollars. Only middle- and upper-class people could afford it. Some unknown entrepreneur (there is no other word for it) figured out that if powdered cocaine is dissolved in water, baking soda is added to it, and the mixture is heated, the resulting pebble-like substance can be smoked; when smoked, it makes a cracking sound. This simple process has several advantages. It expanded the number of potential buyers because crack cocaine can be sold one "hit" at a time, at a cost of $5–10 each. The product thus became available to more people, especially the poor. In addition, although powdered cocaine and crack cocaine are identical pharmacologically, by smoking the product rather than inhaling it through the nose, the alkaloid concentrates in the brain sooner, thus producing a quicker intoxication. Finally, these new consumers purchased the product more often, which increased the total number of transactions. In a capitalist society, of course, sellers will always appear to supply demand and, in this case, crack cocaine can be sold at a very low unit cost with high profit. These characteristics mean that the number of buyers and sellers of crack (and other drugs) expanded in the late 1980s.[93]

It is easy to see why. In an anomic context, some people adapt by retreating from the search for occupational success; that is, they abandon work-centered in favor of leisure-centered activities. As a focus of leisure time, drugs provide meaning and purpose to their lives. Despite stereotypes of drug users and abusers living in poor neighborhoods, their days are full. Their goals simply deviate from the majority. Thus, heroin abusers have been described as always "taking care of business"; they "are actively engaged in meaningful activities and relationships seven days a week" as they seek to obtain their high.[94] Many crack users display similar characteristics. Thus, while most middle-class people try to balance work- and leisure-centered activities, such a balance becomes difficult for the poor in an anomic setting, and some people retreat into drug use and abuse.

As described in chapter 4, another way of adapting to an anomic situation is by seeking occupational success in innovative ways. An informal economy exists in poor communities, where people work off the books doing construction, cutting and styling hair, repairing automobiles, repairing appliances, driving cabs and jitneys, peddling goods, selling food from a cart—anything to make a few dollars.[95] This strategy turns an anomic setting to one's favor by combining work-oriented values with unconventional means. It is not an easy task, requiring the skills of an "adventure capitalist," to use Max Weber's phrase. Most people, however, do not earn much of a living in the informal economy because of legal restrictions. Without a license to cut, repair, drive, or peddle, entrepreneurs must remain circumspect and can only charge low prices.

Selling drugs offers greater economic opportunity, even though it is dangerous. Although part of the informal economy, illegal drug markets are a big industry. Americans spend an estimated $70 billion each year on illegal drugs. As this high figure suggests, illegal drug use occurs among all races and classes as people try to reduce the stress in their daily lives or simply cope with boredom. For middle-class people, especially adolescents and young adults, drug sales depend on word-of-mouth knowledge of who is dealing. In this context, dealers usually keep small supplies available and sell to their friends and acquaintances.[96] At the retail level, however, the sale of illegal drugs has become an important part of the informal economy in poor, racially segregated neighborhoods.

The rewards are significant compared to other jobs. In one study, for example, independent dealers (not gang affiliated) who worked about four hours each day earned an average of $24,000 per year.[97] Although this income seems modest, it is spectacular in neighborhoods bereft of opportunity. It is more than double what one would earn working full time all year long at the minimum wage. It is also dangerous, since independent dealers have less protection from robbery compared to gang members.

In some areas, however, gangs dominate the illegal drug market. Steven Levitt and Sudhir Venkatesh analyzed the structure and finances of an especially well-organized and sophisticated inner-city gang over a four-year period, and found that it resembles that of a franchised company.[98] Gang leaders (four to six individuals) pay two fees to high-level suppliers, one for the right to distribute crack cocaine and the other for the product itself. In this system, the gang leaders profit a great deal, making between $50,000 and $130,000 annually. They become the Bill Gateses (or perhaps the Al Capones) of poor neighborhoods. They organize their employees into teams composed of a team leader, a carrier who delivers the product, two laborers who package it, and a lookout. Over the four years during which the study occurred, gang leaders employed between six and twelve teams. The increase in profits and number of employees occurred when the gang added to its original twelve-block area of influence by seizing control of an adjacent neighborhood of roughly the same size. Professors Levitt and Venkatesh estimate that the laborers and lookouts earned less than the minimum wage, with those above them earning more (wages increased when the new territory was added). Their relatively low incomes over the course of a year mean that street level people in the trade usually combined drug selling with other forms of employment, whether on or off the books.

But, and here is the rub, gangs like this one do not have access to legally enforceable contracts. So when disputes over territory occur or suspicions develop that one of the team leaders is skimming profits, no legal remedies exist. Appeals to the police or courts to resolve disputes are useless. The police are the enemy. To deal with conflict, both internal and external, the gang needed mechanisms of enforcement: guns and fighters. It spent $300–$400 per month on weapons. Early in the study period, it employed mercenary fighters at a cost of $2,000 per month to perform guard duties when sales occurred, protect the gang's turf, enforce rules, and carry out drive-by shootings. Later in the study, weapons expenses increased as the gang stopped hiring mercenaries and used its own members for fighting. Professors Levitt and Venkatesh define gang wars as "a prolonged period of violence involving repeated exchanges of weapons fire between rival gangs."[99] Even though violence is bad for business because it reduces sales, seven gang wars occurred during the time of the study, lasting a total of one year. All this violence means that drug dealing is a dangerous activity, even during more settled periods when no wars are occurring. After all, the teams carry valuable commodities, either drugs or cash, and are subject to the threat of robbery. It has been estimated that up to half of all drug-related murders result from robbery attempts.[100]

Members try to protect themselves—with guns. Over time, many are wounded and killed. Individuals who were active members of the gang for the entire study period had a one in four chance of being killed, mostly by gunshots. Accordingly, the gang leaders maintained funds for funeral expenses and compensatory payments to families of the deceased.

It is important to understand, however, that this gang was exceptionally sophisticated organizationally and financially. Most are less so. But they still require mechanisms of enforcement. For this reason, during the 1980s and 1990s an arms race occurred in urban areas where drugs were sold, as modern-day Al Capones struggled to organize the market for crack cocaine.[101] They recruited adolescents and young adults as street-level dealers, and encouraged them to arm themselves—usually with 9 mm semi-automatic weapons. Possessing a gun can become a status symbol, a statement about one's manhood—even among, perhaps especially among, the young. And because they are immature, they inevitably find reason to use their weapons. Recall from chapter 4, for example, Steven Messner and Richard Rosenfeld's depiction of the Englewood section of Chicago. In this area, as in similar neighborhoods in every American city, the police arrest large numbers of people for possession of drugs and many street-level dealers (the cannon-fodder of the drug trade). Even so, given typical force levels, the police only control the spot on which they stand at the time they stand on it.[102] It should not be surprising, then, that in neighborhoods like Englewood, gunfire and homicide are ordinary events, occurring daily. What happens in such contexts, of course, is that others, young and old, who are not necessarily involved in the drug trade but who must attend the same schools or travel on the same streets, feel the need to arm themselves as well, out of fear for their safety. And the violence escalates. And sometimes it spills over into other neighborhoods, schools, workplaces, and the like. Compared to other nations, no one is safe from being killed in America, no matter where they may be.

Guns are easily available in this country. Drug markets are associated with high homicide rates. The literatures dealing with these two issues exist more or less separately even though, empirically, they are not separate. Thus, when the impact of these two variables is "added" together in a logical way, a step is taken toward explaining the uniquely high American homicide rate. But note that several other factors have been mentioned, at least implicitly, as related to both homicide and American drug policy: racial discrimination, exposure to violence, and economic inequality. The way these variables combine to affect the homicide rate needs to be taken into account as well.

## GREATER RACIAL AND ETHNIC DISCRIMINATION

The third structural relationship specified in the hypothesis is, *the greater the racial and ethnic discrimination, the greater the homicide rate.* The term *discrimination* refers to the unequal treatment of individuals or groups due to their personal (or ascribed) characteristics, such as their race or ethnicity.

In the cross-national literature on homicide, the problem of discrimination is usually dealt with indirectly by looking at the degree of population heterogeneity (defined as differences in language, religion, ethnicity, race, or some combination) and assuming that minority groups suffer unequal treatment based on these qualities. The logic for making this assumption stems from Peter Blau's work, in which he suggests that when ascribed characteristics become salient then the majority prevents minority groups from obtaining valued goals (such as jobs, housing, medical treatment, and other goods and services), social ties between majority and minority groups grow weaker, and intergroup conflict results.[103] In such a context, a higher rate of lethal violence, both between majority and minority groups and within minority groups, becomes one predicted outcome. And, indeed, cross-national studies consistently find that a positive relationship exists between population heterogeneity and homicide.[104] In covariance form, then, the finding is that *the greater the population heterogeneity, the higher the homicide rate.*

Rosemary Gartner, for example, shows that ethnic heterogeneity is positively related to homicide in eighteen economically developed nations—including the United States, which is one of the most heterogeneous societies in the world.[105] Even though reliance on Professor Blau's logic makes good sense, it would be better to avoid the assumption and examine the impact of discrimination on homicide directly. So far as I know, only one study does this. Steven Messner examined the impact of various forms of economic discrimination against minority groups in fifty-two nations, including the United States, and found a positive correlation with the homicide rate.[106] These findings suggest that the third relationship specified in the hypothesis is correct.

The impact of population heterogeneity within the United States is not new. For example, Eric Monkkonen shows that the homicide rate in New York City rose radically during the second half of the nineteenth century, just as Irish and German immigrants appeared in the city in large numbers. By comparison, as mentioned in chapter 3, homicide rates in Liverpool, England, remained very low—less than one per 100,000. During this same period, wealth inequality in New York and other cities was spiking. As will be suggested later, the level of economic inequality also affects the homicide rate.[107]

Now, however, I want to examine the nature of the relationship between racial discrimination and homicide in the United States in more detail. More than two hundred years of slavery and one hundred years of legal segregation make the situation of African Americans utterly unique. As shown in previous chapters, African Americans display a much higher rate of homicide than do whites, and the historical data presented in chapter 3 showed that this pattern has existed for many years. Given the cross-national findings and the underlying logic stemming from Professor Blau's work, this result should not be surprising. Nor should it be surprising that a long literature exists linking racial discrimination to economic inequality, high levels of poverty, the emergence of norms that encourage aggressiveness, and other factors. These variables, in turn, are positively correlated with high African American homicide rates.[108] Although I am simplifying, the underlying rationale in all this work is that racial discrimination leads to restricted life chances and neighborhood disorganization.[109] Hence, people must adapt, and they do so in the usual variety of ways. A few commit homicide, usually with guns, and often in the context of illegal drug markets.

As Douglas Massey observes, one of the keys to understanding violence among impoverished African Americans lies in the impact of residential discrimination and the segregation that results. Throughout the twentieth century, African Americans endured more housing segregation than any other racial or ethnic group. Today, for example, the average white person living in a metropolitan area resides in a neighborhood that is 80 percent white and 7 percent African American. By contrast, the typical African American person living in a metropolitan area resides in a neighborhood that is 51 percent African American and 33 percent white. But these data understate the level of African American residential segregation because they refer to all metropolitan areas. According to Douglas Massey and Nancy Denton, thirty metropolitan areas in which about 40 percent of all African Americans live are "hypersegregated" such that virtually everyone in their neighborhood is also African American. This high degree of social isolation occurs in every large city, including New York, Chicago, Washington, D.C., Philadelphia, Atlanta, Los Angeles, and St. Louis. It affects every facet of daily life for many African Americans in the twenty-first century.[110]

A detailed analysis of the reasons whites have imposed residential isolation on African Americans would take us too far afield. I would, however, like to mention three interrelated factors: (1) a high level of prejudice against African Americans as potential neighbors, (2) discriminatory policies pursued by whites in the banking and real estate industries, and (3) discriminatory public policies implemented by whites at all levels of government. Although the last has declined since the 1960s, the other two continue today.[111]

Regardless of the reasons, the results are catastrophic: *The greater the residential segregation, the greater the African American homicide rate.* For example, Ruth Peterson and Lauren Krivo analyzed 125 central cities and found that the level of residential segregation displayed a much greater impact on homicide rates than other variables (such as poverty and occupation). They also found that the greatest effect occurred with homicides among acquaintances and strangers, rather than within families. They conclude that housing segregation leads to violent interaction outside the home, in the public sphere. The finding is very stable.[112]

Housing segregation means that a significant proportion of the African American population resides in neighborhoods characterized by multiple and accumulated disadvantages. As a result, there emerges what Douglas Massey calls "a racially distinctive ecological niche of violence."[113] Thus, housing segregation signifies limited educational and economic opportunities. Schools are poorer. Large numbers of teenagers and young adults find school to be meaningless. A high proportion drop out. Such persons have limited skills, and the jobs they can obtain are often located so far away as to involve unrealistic commutes. Even finding out about jobs is very difficult. Many residents of inner-city neighborhoods rarely travel outside of their immediate neighborhood and have few friends who live outside of it. So they have few contacts with white society and little information about jobs that white society provides. In central cities, then, a high proportion of men are out of the labor force, unemployed, or underemployed. With crowded apartments that are too cold in winter and too hot in summer, street life is active. This situation inevitably means that high levels of impoverished people are concentrated in small ecological niches. And wherever it occurs, poverty is correlated with a high rate of crime because, in an anomic environment, the number of people turning to illegal or deviant activities goes up. It is not accidental that illegal drug markets develop in residentially segregated inner-city areas, since they offer economic opportunity. Partly as a result, rates of homicide in racially isolated inner cities can be very high, as illustrated by the Englewood section of Chicago.

But more is going on here than the violence associated with illegal drug markets. The sociological issue is this: Given barriers to residential mobility, how are people to adapt to living in an impoverished and harsh environment characterized by widespread crime and violence, where the very real threat of assault and death is felt on a daily basis? Such neighborhoods resemble war zones. It seems to me that Elijah Anderson provides the answer in the title of his book, *Code of the Streets*; that is, people develop a set of informal but widely known norms governing interpersonal behavior in public places.[114] He studied an impoverished African American neighborhood in Philadelphia over many years, one that displays both hyper-segregation and a very high homicide rate. He shows that those living in this area adhere to rules (or codes) that prescribe how people are to comport themselves while on the street and how they should respond if challenged. This is an environment in which the phrase "police protection" is oxymoronic because residents see the police as abusing the people they are supposed to protect. Thus, inhabitants of racially segregated inner-city neighborhoods believe they must protect themselves. Hence, the code of the street constitutes an attempt at regulating the use of violence in a context where the law is viewed (and is often in fact) irrelevant to daily life. Such contexts are inherently more lethal because everyone is made hostage to the most violent among them.

The norms embodied in the code of the street dictate that people, especially males, should carry themselves in an assertive manner that communicates the willingness and ability to be violent. So they use gait, facial expression, and talk to promote "respect" and deter aggression. For example, people do not make eye contact; it can be taken as a challenge. Seeking "respect" (or honor) in these ways is more than mere vanity; it constitutes a form of social capital that is designed to help people keep themselves physically safe in public places. One way to protect oneself is to carry a gun because its display can intimidate others and thus provide a means of self-protection. Nationwide, about 5 percent of all high school students admitted to carrying a gun at least once during a thirty-day period in 1999, a figure that is probably much higher in impoverished inner-city neighborhoods where violence is pervasive.[115] As a result of so many people going armed on the street all the time, however, the violence takes on a life of its own. Inevitably, some people use their guns.

This social context, then, is one in which the norms of civility with which middle-class people are familiar, based on mutual trust and the rule of law (buttressed by police protection) do not apply. It is, rather, a peculiar social niche in which honor can only be established and preserved by the strategic use of violence. As Professor Anderson explains, from early childhood individuals growing up in this environment are socialized to fight to protect themselves. In this social context, aggressive and violent behaviors are not aberrant; rather, they constitute a rational response to a hostile environment. As he also explains, impoverished African American neighborhoods like the one he studied are divided between those whom he calls "decent families" and "street families." Even in the poorest areas, decent families constitute the majority of the population. They value hard work and self-reliance (what I called the American Dream in chapter 4), employ strict child-rearing practices, ally themselves with churches and schools, and try to teach their children norms of civility. Street families, by contrast, lack jobs and education, seek "respect" as an indicator of self-esteem, and feel bitter about the pervasive discrimination (it is not rocket science to look around one's segregated neighborhood and see racism at work). At the extreme, the most alienated and embittered people show contempt for others, especially anyone representing "the system." They become predators. But this difference between "decent" and "street" oriented families turns out to be irrelevant in public places in inner-city neighborhoods, where everyone must live by the code of the street; everyone must fight.

Geoffrey Canada opens his memoir of growing up in the Bronx section of New York City by telling how he first learned about the need to fight.[116] He was four years old; his two brothers were five and six. The older boys came home from the playground without the five-year-old's jacket. A bigger boy had taken it. His mother told the oldest to go back out and get the jacket; if he did not come back with it, she would give him a beating worse than might occur in any fight he might have. The crying boy left, confronted the child with the jacket, and got it back. Afterward, his mother told the boys that they had to stick together and protect themselves, that "she would not tolerate our becoming victims." Fight or become a victim: This is the basic lesson of the streets that every African American child growing up in segregated neighborhoods must learn. Mr. Canada grew up in the 1960s, a time when the rules were brutal but clear, taught by older children to younger ones. Since the mid-1980s, however, he describes the streets as becoming much more lethal because so many kids (and adults) now have guns:

The rules of conduct on when to shoot, or when someone else might shoot you, are unclear. In some places there has to be a physical conflict, in some a nasty verbal conflict or just a wrong look can get you shot, and in some places you could be shot just for being there. So . . . you have tens of thousands of kids with guns, trying to protect themselves, but there are no clear rules to follow.

As a result, he writes, children (and adults) learn that it is better to act quickly and decisively when on the street, to kill and live—even if it means going to jail. They also learn to become cold; to survive, they must dominate their emotions and hide their basic humanity. This is what happens in a rigidly segregated environment produced by housing discrimination; the code of the street has become an engine of violence and homicide—sometimes at rates much higher than in medieval Europe or sixteenth-century London.

Gangs represent an organized response to the code of the street. Martín Sánchez Jankowski studied thirty-seven gangs over more than ten years.[117] He found that people join gangs as a way to earn a living, as a source of comradeship and leisure time (like a fraternity or sorority), and—most important—as a means for personal protection. As a gang member, one is not facing the predators in the neighborhood alone. Of course, in order to survive, these organizations must generate revenue. Professor Jankowski shows that gangs provide a variety of goods and services to their communities. For example, they sell car parts, protection, demolition (arson), and prostitution. But "the biggest money maker and the one product every gang tries to market is illegal drugs." Depending on their size, how long they have existed, and neighborhood characteristics, some gangs function as drug wholesalers obtaining their revenue via franchise fees, whereas others sell directly to consumers. Guns are another profitable product. Although some are stolen, most are purchased from gunrunners and resold. Of course, these markets are not regulated by law or contract. Survival requires that gangs use force against rivals who attempt to enter their areas of influence, and honor requires retaliation if a member is threatened or harmed. Gangs, then, become a collective engine of violence in racially segregated, impoverished neighborhoods.

Because of housing segregation, everyone gets trapped in a self-perpetuating system, "a racially distinctive ecological niche of violence."[118] This peculiarly American niche of violence constitutes, however, only a specific example of a more generalized sociological phenomenon. As Donald Black argues, widespread violence reflects attempts at self-help in a context where the law is unavailable, and (as suggested by the cross-national findings) members of minority groups in every society often find themselves in this situation.[119] He asserts that codes of honor (which take various forms) thus constitute a logical response to a malign social structure. This is not a unique development. You may recall from chapter 3, for example, the vignette of *Romeo and Juliet*. It describes an environment in which a code of honor regulated violence, and feuding and brawling provided the only means for resolving conflicts. This is precisely the situation today in impoverished, hyper-segregated African American neighborhoods, where people view the police as repressive (an occupying force), give the courts little legitimacy, and have access to guns (instead of swords). So, like sixteenth-century Londoners, they settle disputes on their own. The result is lethal for many. Such neighborhoods provide a practical model of what happens when many people go about armed, ready to defend themselves.

Minorities display higher homicide rates in all Western nations. Yet, just as the overall American rate is anomalous, so is the very high African American rate. Their situation is anomalous, as well, compared to minority groups in other nations. But in thinking about this fact, notice again how all the variables considered in this chapter are interrelated. When the impact of racial discrimination is, in a conceptual way, added to the impact of gun availability and illegal drug markets, I am arguing, the reason for the uniquely high American homicide rate becomes clearer. Notice again that the protagonists on each side in the gun literature do not deal with the impact of racial discrimination and the possibility that discrimination might combine with gun availability to produce lethal effects. Similarly, scholars writing in the literature on drug markets and homicide usually do not confront the possible importance of racial discrimination as a factor. The clue is that scholars in each discrete area do not cite one another, which suggests they are not aware of each other's work. Thus, each of these literatures exists independently of the other, even though the phenomena to which they refer are empirically interrelated. It is not clear, at least to me, how we are to understand the American anomaly of high homicide rates unless these interrelationships are examined and interpreted.

## GREATER EXPOSURE TO VIOLENCE

The fourth structural relationship specified in the hypothesis is that *the more the population is exposed to violence, the greater the homicide rate*. This variable, exposure to violence, is conceptualized as comprising four contexts in which people endure or witness it: the media, family, neighborhoods, and government. The degree of exposure to violence in a population, I am arguing, seen as the cumulative impact of these specific agents of violence, leads a small proportion of people to act violently, sometimes with lethal consequences. Exposure to violence is, of course, interrelated with all the other variables considered here.

### The Mass Media

Consider first the mass media as agents of violence, contributing to the population's exposure to violence. Children and adolescents today grow up in a media-dominated society. Television is the most popular medium to which they are exposed. Children watch, on average, about four hours of television each day and in so doing witness about 12,000 violent acts in a year. And this figure does not count movies, music videos, and video games, which are generally more violent. For example, in 1998 the top-grossing movies averaged forty-six scenes of violence, most of them life threatening. Music videos averaged one violent act per minute. In general, then, a large segment of the American population enjoys violent media presentations.[120]

This enjoyment follows from certain peculiar qualities characteristic of media violence compared to the real world. Whether on the tube, in the theater, or at the arcade, violence often seems glamorous: Many perpetrators go unpunished and few show any remorse. Media violence is also sanitized: Most victims do not seem to suffer and no long-term trauma to victims' families and friends occurs. Finally, media violence often appears trivial: Even though the result is often death, many scenes of violence are portrayed as humorous.[121] Think about the Dirty Harry movies, which still get a lot of play on television. In each one, Harry imposes his own righteous solution in situations where the law is hapless. "Make my day," he tells the bad guy, a phrase that has entered the national consciousness. Harry is not a unique character in the media. Partly because of these peculiarities, people learn to accept violence as normal, as inconsequential, which makes the effect of witnessing so much of it very significant.

The literature on the impact of exposure to violence on television, at the movies, and in other venues comprises hundreds of studies and displays clear results: Witnessing violence in the media increases people's aggression.[122] And the more people watch, the greater the impact. Aggression, here, does not refer to the kinds of assertive behavior people admire in, say, business executives; it refers to behavior intended to harm others, often violently.

The social psychological processes that result in aggression are very straightforward. The media's effect is greatest on children. As Brad Bushman and Rowell Huesmann observe, "childhood is the cradle of social behavior" eventually displayed in adulthood. What happens is that children who watch a great deal of television and other forms of the media learn to use violence as a problem-solving strategy (they learn a "script," in the jargon). The media, in short, socialize people to respond violently when they become frustrated. Moreover, viewers, especially heavy viewers, also learn to see the world as a hostile place, one in which it is often necessary to carry a weapon for self-protection—like Harry does. And like Harry, they learn to justify aggressive behavior as a morally right response. Most viewers want him (and characters like him) to pull the trigger. And the more they see the deaths that result, the more used to it viewers become. Compared to light viewers, heavy viewers display an emotional desensitization such that violent episodes result in less psychological arousal. As I will comment later, this response can be a useful survival mechanism in contexts where real violence is pervasive.[123]

Longitudinal studies, in which the same people are followed over time, show clearly how chronic exposure to television violence also carries long-term consequences for behavior. For example, in one study researchers interviewed and tested about 400 elementary age children in the 1970s and again fifteen years later when they were in their early twenties. Those who were heavy viewers of television as children were more aggressive as adults. Similarly, in another study, researchers followed more than 700 individuals over seventeen years and found that those who watched more television as adolescents and young adults were more likely to act aggressively in later life.[124]

Although this literature is long and the findings reported above clear and stable, some observers disagree. The most well known critic is probably Jonathan Freedman, who argues that the causal nexus between media violence and aggression still remains unclear. Most scholars, however, think he sets the bar for certainty so high that it is unattainable. Dolf Zillman and James Weaver, for example, note that Professor Freedman and others who reject the data would only be satisfied with "longitudinal experimental studies in which, within gender and a multitude of personality variables, random assignment is honored and exposure to violent fare is rigorously controlled—that is, with research that in a free society simply cannot be conducted."[125] If this degree of certitude becomes the standard, then it is hard to see how social science can ever inform public policy—on this or any other topic. Economists justify macroeconomic policies based on far less information. In fact, consider relationships that most people take as so clear as to be obvious. For example, it seems like common sense to assert that condom use will prevent infection with the HIV virus and that calcium intake will increase bone mass. Yet in study after study, the correlation between television viewing and aggression is higher than in studies of these and other relationships. No one expects a commercial on television to affect everyone. In fact, if it stimulates one in a thousand persons to purchase a product, that commercial would be considered a wild success. Similarly, only a small proportion of viewers display aggression after watching media violence. But that is enough. My conclusion is that media violence does affect people's level of aggression.[126]

On this basis, it can be argued that the impact of media violence on aggression constitutes part of a process by which the population is exposed to violence and, in combination with the other variables considered here, leads a few people to commit violence against other human beings. This is partly because they become desensitized to violence. Yet, despite what you may think, such desensitization is a very unnatural state because most people have an ingrained inhibition against killing other people. This is so even in combat, even when the enemy is firing. Thus, the military historian S.L.A. Marshall showed that during World War II only 20 percent of individual riflemen actually fired their weapons at enemy soldiers in combat. Thirty years later, however, during the Vietnam War, this figure had increased to about 90 percent. Why? New training methods were developed that break down soldiers' inhibitions about killing. Before World War II, the military trained soldiers by having them shoot at bull's-eye targets. But in light of Professor Marshall's findings (and those of others) the military began using operant conditioning techniques to teach trainees to kill on command. For example, trainees are placed in simulated battlefield situations and taught to shoot at lifelike human pop-up targets. In the civilian world, the mass media provide a step in this process. Guns are the featured tools for solving problems, of course, especially semi-automatic weapons. Apart from kissing (and perhaps sexual intercourse), nothing seems easier on the screen or at the arcade than pulling a trigger.

But the arcade may be a special situation. According to military psychologist David Grossman, video games take the process of desensitization much farther, as players become used to the idea of killing one another in an active way. In the arcade, children (and adults) do not merely witness others using firearms, they hold a gun and shoot at pop-up targets, the "enemy" on the screen. Professor Grossman suggests that the development of interactive "point-and-shoot" video games mimics military conditioning without military discipline. He suggests that, under certain social conditions, chronic exposure to these games can be observed on the streets.[127] This result may become more likely when people witness or endure violence in other contexts (see below) and the overall impact combines with easy access to real guns, drug markets, and racial discrimination, among other factors.

Ultimately, it must be recognized that hardly anyone who watches a lot of violence on television and in the movies becomes a murderer. Few of those who play a lot of point-and-shoot video games murder anyone, either. But, then, hardly anyone becomes a murderer, even in the United States. For the moment, I am simply arguing that the effect of lots of people watching lots of media violence contributes to the population's exposure to violence. As such, in a large population, some (small) proportion of people will be affected, especially those who witness and experience violence themselves, in their families and neighborhoods. Risk factors cumulate.

## The Family

Consider next the family as an agent of violence, a second contributor to the population's exposure to violence. Some children who are victimized become violent themselves. And some children who witness family violence learn to use violence themselves.

About 826,000 children were victims of maltreatment in 1999, a figure that is down significantly from earlier in the decade.[128] This translates into a victimization rate of about twelve per 1,000 children. About 60 percent of them were neglected, 21 percent physically abused, and 11 percent sexually abused, with the remainder suffering other forms of maltreatment. These data are conservative estimates, of course, since they refer to cases that come to the attention of state agencies. The casual beating of children to enforce behavior or to teach them to defend themselves will not usually appear. Note, however, that victimization varies by race and ethnicity, as shown in table 5.1 in terms of rates per 1,000 children.

The impact of child maltreatment on children is clear: A "cycle of violence" exists such that when children are neglected and victimized, they learn to use violence themselves. In one of the most comprehensive studies, Cathy Widon followed a matched set of children, about half of whom were abused or neglected and half not, over twenty-five years. She found that those who had been maltreated as children were more likely to be arrested as juveniles and as adults, and they were more likely to be arrested for violent crimes. Those who had been abused or neglected were younger at first arrest and arrested more frequently. Other researchers report similar findings.[129]

Among adults, violence between intimates occurs often. About 25 percent of women and 8 percent of men say they have been raped or assaulted by a spouse, partner, or date at some point in their lives.[130] As above, these data are conservative. Although both women and men can be violent, men initiate the violence in most families. And women suffer much more than men when violence occurs. Recall from chapter 1, for example, that homicide is one of the leading causes of death for women between the ages of fifteen and forty-four. Husbands and boyfriends commit many of these murders. And they often use guns.

The traumatic impact of witnessing family violence, as when children see and hear their mother being beaten, can lead them to become violent themselves. The witnessing constitutes an overwhelming experience, destroying children's sense of safety and trust. One response consists of what psychologists call post-traumatic stress disorder (PTSD). The term refers to people's response to the shock of watching violence: intense anxiety, an inability to concentrate, being easily startled, flashbacks, and nightmares, among other

**Table 5.1.   Child Abuse Victimization by Race and Ethnicity, per 1,000 Children**

| Race/Ethnicity | Number per 1,000 |
|---|---|
| African American | 25 |
| Native American | 20 |
| Hispanic American | 13 |
| White (non-Hispanic) | 11 |
| Asian American | 4 |

*Source:* United States Dept. of Health and Human Services (2001a).

symptoms. Another response, also reflective of PTSD, is an increased likelihood of drug abuse. Still another response is to become aggressive and violent; this is more characteristic of men than women. It occurs because the sense of helplessness leads to a need to assert power.[131]

Taken together, all the data suggest that the lesson children learn from violence in the family (and neglect, as it turns out) is to use aggression themselves. In this regard, consider the high level at which African American children are victimized, as reported in table 5.1. Part of this race-related difference in rates may reflect an awful paradox. When African American parents living in impoverished, segregated neighborhoods that can only be described as war zones deliberately teach their children to fight in ways that white authorities might define as abusive, they are trying to equip their children with an essential survival mechanism. The result can lead to a higher homicide rate.

It is a long way, of course, from being beaten or witnessing one's mother being beaten to committing homicide. Much depends on the frequency and severity of such events. But most children who endure some form of family violence do not commit murder. Many children, in fact, break the cycle of violence. I am arguing, however, that the level of family violence in a population constitutes a second risk factor constituting the "variable" "exposure to violence." I am also arguing that it combines with witnessing mass media violence: When those who watch a lot of violent media are combined with those who experience family violence (either as victim or witness), the result is a certain (undoubtedly small) number of people who are prone to violence. A few of them commit homicide.

## The Neighborhood

Now consider neighborhoods as agents of violence, a third contributor to the population's exposure to violence. In some neighborhoods, violence is pervasive. Whether a "subculture of violence" exists is unclear. It does seem clear, however, that areas exist in many cities where people use violence as a means to an end. Consider the following, some of which has been described before. A significant number of homicides in large cities are either committed as part of gang activities or by gang members. Gang-related homicides usually occur on the street and have several participants. Both perpetrators and victims are usually young males who nearly always use guns. Among adolescents, gang members are more likely to possess guns than non-gang members. In this context, however, non-gang members arm themselves as well—leading to more violence. This process is why homicide rates among juveniles have risen in recent years, even as overall rates have fallen. Thus, violence becomes common in some neighborhoods, especially where gangs exist and drugs are sold.[132] As mentioned in chapter 1, homicide is the second leading cause of death among adolescents and young adults.

In social contexts like this, elementary school children witness murders, shootings, and stabbings; they see dead bodies in the street. In one sample of low-income, mainly African American children, 47 percent had witnessed a homicide. In similar samples, about one-quarter of children report seeing someone killed, nearly always on the street. In some public housing complexes, every child knows a victim of homicide. These children live in neighborhoods where gunfire is an everyday occurrence. But the violence goes beyond homicide, of course. In samples of African American urban children, the majority of them report witnessing stabbings and shootings. Even more than vicarious media experiences, directly observing violence and its aftermath on the streets where one lives is traumatizing. It leads to psychological distress (PTSD and other symptoms) along with drug use. Yet when people's sense of trust in the world around them is destroyed, the wounds are rarely obvious. They resemble "Snowden's secret" in Joseph Heller's novel, *Catch-22*.[133] While on a mission during World War II, Snowden, a bomber navigator, seems to suffer from a minor wound. But when Captain Yossarian opens Snowden's flak jacket, he finds a hideous and, indeed, fatal injury. Similarly, the psychological wounds experienced by children, who are cheated of their childhood by neighborhood violence, are deep and long lasting. Such wounds fuel fear and rage. Children become desensitized to violence. It seems acceptable and is perpetuated over time—sometimes with fatal consequences.[134]

Considering the impact of neighborhood as generator of lethal violence apart from other factors dealt with in this chapter (e.g., racial discrimination and drug markets) is tricky. It opens up the possibility of what would be called multi-collinearity in a quantitative piece—several variables measuring essentially the same thing. Part of the reason I analyze neighborhood effects separately is because the literature on the socializing impact of witnessing violence in the neighborhood constitutes a separate line of inquiry, and that fact needs to be highlighted. Authors in this literature do not cite the literature on guns, drug markets, or racial discrimination (and vice versa). Moreover, a case can be made, I believe, for thinking about the various contexts in which a population is exposed to violence as having an independent, cumulative impact: Some people see lots of violence in the media, at home, and on the streets where they live, thereby increasing the risk factor for homicide. And some of them (it does not take many) become more prone to use violence as a problem-solving tool.

## The Government

Finally, consider the government as an agent of violence, a fourth contributor to the population's exposure to violence. In this country, unlike others, one can argue that government violence occurs sufficiently often that it provides a model for what happens in the media, in some homes, and in some neighborhoods. I use two indicators of government violence: the death penalty and military campaigns.

The United States is the only Western nation still imposing capital punishment on criminals. As are most other topics considered here, this one is very controversial. The question is whether executions and publicity about them have a deterrent effect (that is, it suppresses the homicide rate) or a brutalization effect (it increases the homicide rate). The media, especially television and newspapers, provide the public with most of its information about crimes of violence and their aftermath: executions. John Cochran and his colleagues reviewed the literature and show that the evidence, while inconsistent, suggests that capital punishment does not have a deterrent effect. Moreover, in a natural experiment they examined murders in Oklahoma before and after a well-publicized 1990 execution. They found that while executions had no deterrent effect on felony homicides, Oklahoma experienced an abrupt and long-term increase in stranger homicides of about one every three weeks. As always with a natural experiment, this relationship might be spurious; some unknown variable could have produced this effect. It is, however, unclear what that variable might be.[135]

As with executions, homicide rates increase after wars. After reviewing the literature, Ted Robert Gurr concludes that this relationship is invariant over time and across societies. For example, in one of the best studies, Dane Archer and Rosemary Gartner compared homicide rates in various nations before and after World Wars I and II, and found significant (albeit brief) increases in nearly all cases. Professor Gurr opts for the Archer-Gartner interpretation: War legitimizes violence, directly for those who fight (and are socialized to violence) and indirectly for those who find in war a license to act on their feelings of anger. He notes, wryly, that while "this interpretation is difficult to prove" it is consistent with the evidence. Thus, it is not accidental that each of the four military campaigns engaged in by American armed forces during the 1980s was followed by an increase in criminal violence. Similarly, as illustrated in figure 3.2, it is not accidental that American homicide rates spiked after World War II and during the Vietnam War, the most televised war in our history (although other factors were undoubtedly at play during the Vietnam era).[136]

Thus, in the case of both the death penalty and military campaigns, research shows a correlation with increases in the homicide rate. I am suggesting, however, that the reason for this relationship is that government is providing a model of appropriate behavior, much as occurs in the media, some families, and some neighborhoods. Government is showing some people that a connection exists between using force and getting what they want. It is showing that violence works and using it is legitimate. Of course, this effect would only occur in a small number of people, perhaps especially those who are exposed to a lot of media violence and have either been subjected to or witnessed violence in the home or neighborhood.

In *Crime and the American Dream*, Steven Messner and Richard Rosenfeld argue that noneconomic institutions are dominated by the economy and, hence, constitute weak bulwarks against "criminogenic tendencies" in this country.[137] Perhaps. But the reverse effect may be the real problem: Exposure to violence in the media, family, neighborhood, and government may contribute to the uniquely high rate of homicide in the United States. When so many people in the population learn from violence in all these contexts, it should not be surprising that some proportion of them become desensitized and resort to violence—some of it lethal. Not all, of course. Not most. Only a few. But enough. Now one way of using violence is to hit someone. But death occurs rarely from hitting. Another is to shoot someone, which increases the odds of death. Easy gun availability thus provides part of the context in which exposure to violence occurs. When the impact of these two variables is, in a conceptual way, "added" together, we take a step toward explaining the high American homicide rate. Other parts of the context comprise the expansion of illegal drug markets and racial discrimination. When all these factors are combined, they suggest how the American anomaly can be explained.

## GREATER ECONOMIC INEQUALITY

The fifth structural relationship specified in the hypothesis is, *the greater the economic inequality, the higher the homicide rate.* In assessing this relationship, I initially use the degree of income inequality as the indicator of economic inequality and then turn to the moderating impact of various lifestyle protections provided by the state.

A common measure of income inequality used in cross-national studies is the Gini Coefficient. It provides a standard index that varies between 0 and 100, with a higher number indicating greater inequality. Thus, a score of 0 would mean that all incomes are completely equal, while 100 would mean that one person receives all the income. Of course, these extreme results do not occur in any nation. In practical use, the standard interpretation of the Gini is that values between 20 and 24 indicate a "small" level of income inequality, 25 and 29 a "moderate" level, and 30 and 34 a "high" level. Any nation with a Gini above 35 displays a "very high" level of inequality.[138]

Shown in table 5.2 are Gini Coefficients for the same eight Western nations included in figure 3.1. All the data are for 1995, except for Switzerland, which is for 1992.

As these data reveal, the United States displays greater income inequality

**Table 5.2.  Gini Coefficients for Eight Western Nations**

| Country | Gini Coefficient |
|---|---|
| United States | 36 |
| United Kingdom | 34 |
| Switzerland | 31 |
| France | 31 |
| Canada | 28 |
| Netherlands | 27 |
| Germany | 27 |
| Sweden | 21 |

*Note:* All data are for 1995, except for Switzerland, which is for 1992.

*Source:* Ritakallio (2001:15). For Switzerland, the Gini is based on calculations by Veli-Matti Ritakallio from the Luxembourg Income Study database. My thanks to Professor Ritakallio.

than does any other Western nation. Although some of the cross-national differences displayed in the table seem small, such as between the United States and the United Kingdom, the nature of the Gini means that they are both statistically and substantively significant. The disparity between the United States and other nations has been stable for many years. On this issue, America is consistently described as being in a world of its own. In fact, changes in tax law over the last quarter-century have increased inequality in this country to a point not seen since just before the Depression. In considering the data in the table, note that income inequality understates the overall level of economic inequality. Using cross-national wealth inequality as the indicator would mean that the difference between the United States and other Western nations would be even greater than shown.[139]

The level of economic inequality is associated with the homicide rate. A large body of cross-national literature establishes a positive relationship between these two variables, and the connection is especially strong in nations that are more democratic.[140] The finding is very stable regardless of how the variables are measured. This is significant because it is not at all clear whether the overall degree of income inequality or the number of people at the extreme, indicated by the level of poverty, provides a better predictor of the homicide rate. But trying to answer this question is probably a fool's errand. They are highly correlated, which means their separate impact will be hard to parcel out in quantitative terms. More important for my purpose, compared to the other nations shown above, the United States displays the highest level of both income inequality and poverty.[141]

Subnational American data are consonant with the cross-national literature. As long ago as 1942, Clifford Shaw and Henry McKay examined poor and non-poor areas of twenty-one cities and showed that impoverished neighborhoods displayed consistently high crime rates among juveniles even though their racial and ethnic composition changed completely over time. In Detroit over a fifty-year period, people who were poor for long periods displayed higher rates of homicide. Similarly, another analysis of Detroit used the infant mortality rate as a proxy for poverty and found that it had a large influence on homicide—again over a fifty-year period. Finally, many studies show that cities with higher levels of inequality display higher levels of homicide.[142]

But in modern societies, the impact of inequality can be moderated via public policies, and the homicide rate is also affected. The issue is the degree of lifestyle protection citizens enjoy. The logic is that a stable (even if low) income means that people's lifestyles will be stable as well. Their range of choices will remain about the same even if their job disappears, so the level of anger and lethal violence should be less. Welfare in the narrow American sense of providing aid to the poor constitutes an obvious mechanism for protecting people's income. And, as it turns out, a body of cross-national literature shows that welfare expenditures are negatively related to homicide rates: The greater the welfare expenditures, the lower the homicide rates. The United States, of course, spends less on welfare than do other Western nations, and its efforts are more focused.[143]

The vicissitudes of economic inequality, however, go beyond income to general issues of lifestyle protection. When the state grants services and resources to citizens as a matter of right, then they enjoy some protection from the forces of the job market. The jargon term describing this state of affairs is *decommodification*, which refers to people's ability to act unconstrained by market considerations stemming from their jobs or lack thereof.[144] For example, in a relatively decommodified society, people can obtain day care and education for their children; medical treatment; pensions in old age; income protection if they become disabled, sick, or unemployed; and other benefits as rights of citizenship, thereby reducing their reliance on the market as a source of lifestyle protection. In a study of forty-five nations, Steven Messner and Richard Rosenfeld hypothesized that the level of decommodification of labor would be negatively related to the homicide rate. After looking at the impact of welfare arrangements, pensions, sick leave, disability insurance, and unemployment compensation, they found that nations with the lowest level of decommodification also displayed the highest rates of homicide. The United States, of course, epitomized this relationship. Their analysis has been replicated at least once.[145]

The stability of the relationship between inequality and homicide led Judith Blau and Peter Blau to the chilling conclusion that "high rates of criminal violence [including homicide] are apparently the price of racial and economic inequalities" in America.[146] The reason for this conclusion, as the Blaus make clear, is that inequality generates alienation, despair, and pent-up aggression that find expression in frequent interpersonal conflicts. One result of these conflicts is that some people commit homicide, enough so that the overall American rate is much higher than in other nations. This result occurs in part, I would suggest, when a high level of inequality combines with easy access to guns, expanding illegal drug markets, greater racial discrimination, and greater exposure to violence. Implicit in this argument is the notion that the impact of racial discrimination and inequality can be separated, at least analytically. Professors Blau and Blau are among the few who have shown their different effects empirically as well. Note that the Blaus' data set allowed them to deal with two of the variables affecting the homicide rate. This is rare. Of course (and this comment should not be taken as a criticism), neither the Blaus nor Professors Messner and Rosenfeld could confront the issues of gun availability, illegal drug markets, or exposure to violence, even though these factors are also related to the American anomaly. Similarly, data limitations mean that scholars working on those issues cannot confront the literature on economic inequality. Yet, once again, all these variables are empirically interrelated.

The level of economic inequality is significant in a larger sense as well, for it provides a precise measure of how anomic a society is. Recall from chapter 4 that anomic societies are based on an internal contradiction: Everyone is supposed to strive for material success, yet built-in limits restrict their ability to achieve. In his analysis in "Social Structure and Anomie," Robert K. Merton stresses that in any capitalist society legitimate opportunities for success are unequally distributed by social class.[147] This fact means that those near the bottom of the class structure have fewer and less effective choices than do those near the top. Such inequality means that millions of people endure the sometimes debilitating consequences of restricted life chances and lifestyles. So they must adapt, as illustrated by the baseball metaphor developed in chapter 4. Most, you will recall, keep striving, keep trying to do the best they can. Some withdraw from the competition, into drug use for example. A few find deviant ways to succeed; in Professor Merton's evocative word, they innovate. These last responses often involve turning to selling drugs or other forms of crime. Both can lead to murder. Moreover, people who have few choices also develop a lot of free-floating anger, and their disputes with one another sometimes become violent—with lethal results.

## UNDERSTANDING HOMICIDE

We have a problem. Homicide is a routine event in the United States. Thousands of Americans are killed each year who happen to find themselves in the wrong place at the wrong time, who happen to confront a very angry or mentally ill person. Even though homicide is concentrated among the poor and occurs disproportionately among African Americans, victims can be of any class or race. No one is safe. People are afraid. The impact is enormous. As suggested in chapter 1 and portrayed by Gregory Gibson in *Goneboy*, the trauma to those who witness and survive these events is incalculable. Chapter 1 also described the profound economic consequences that follow, as indicated by the huge medical costs, legal costs, incarceration costs, and productivity losses. Cross-national and historical data presented in chapter 3 show that this situation is anomalous; no other Western nation endures this level of carnage and its consequences. In this book, I argue that in order to understand the peculiarly high rate of homicide in the United States, observers must ask the right question.

Was Wayne Lo simply a "nut with a gun"? Well, yes. Hence, understanding the events that occurred one evening at Simon's Rock College requires assessing how his mental illness, combined with the mistakes and misjudgments of various college officials, led to two murders and four serious injuries. Was Nicholas Elliot a young kid who became really, really angry? Yes again. Hence, understanding the events that occurred one day at Atlantic Shores Christian School would require figuring out how his experiences at home and school led him to commit homicide. Such understanding is useful. Moreover, much can be gained by asking some underlying generic questions: Why do individuals kill? How do killers differ from those who do not kill? I submit, however, that answering such questions explains nothing whatsoever about the American anomaly. This is because a social psychological understanding of a killer's motivation deals with each homicide in isolation from all the others. As long as observers ask this type of question, the routine nature of lethal violence in this country will remain inexplicable, and the police sergeant's lament following the murder of Delvin Darnell Carey will remain sadly true.

Taken together, do the deaths of Mr. Carey, Barry Grunow, Jennifer Bragg Capobianco, Louis Javelle, Galen Gibson, Ñacuñán Sáez, Karen Farley, and the thousands and thousands of unknown others killed each year reveal a pattern that can be understood? This is a structural question. And it can now be answered, at least provisionally. Thus, the working hypothesis presented at the beginning of this chapter was that *the high base rate of homicide in the United States reflects the impact of (1) greater availability of guns, (2) the expansion of illegal drug markets, (3) greater racial discrimination, (4) greater exposure to violence, and (5) greater economic inequality*. The data are clear. In every case, the extant literature shows that the bivariate relationship between each factor in the hypothesis and homicide is empirically demonstrable. The widespread availability of guns makes the United States unique, the expansion (and violence) of drug markets makes it unique, the level of racial discrimination makes it unique; the degree of exposure to violence makes it unique, and the level of economic inequality makes it unique. In addition, however, when, in a conceptual way, the impact of these variables is added together, it should hardly be surprising that the American rate of homicide is anomalous. As described in chapter 2, this "adding together" reflects a specific strategy: to develop what might be called a logical experiment in the form of a "synthetic multivariate analysis" in which the variables are manipulated logically rather than computationally.

Moreover, this answer has theoretical implications. One of the typical complaints among professionals in the social sciences is that quantitative research lacks a theoretical basis. Although there is merit to this assertion, the literature reviewed in this chapter implies a theoretical orientation: The social structure generates rates of behavior by determining the range of options available to people. From this point of view, it becomes clear that Steven Messner and Richard Rosenfeld are quite correct when they assert that homicide is built into the social structure of American society—although not in the way they suppose. As I argued in chapter 1, one of sociology's most important insights is that knowing the social context in which people make choices is as important as (or more important than) knowing the specific choices they make. Thus, just as understanding the reasons for the high rate of automobile deaths increased when the focus shifted from the "nut behind the wheel" to the context in which driving occurs, understanding the peculiarly high rate of homicide in the United States improves with a shift from analyzing the "nut with a gun" to the context in which so many murders occur.

In addition, this answer and the conceptual strategy used here also bring up the eternally vexing problem of method. Another common complaint among professionals in the social sciences is that, regardless of topic, quantitative research often features powerful tests of trivial ideas.[148] But that is clearly not the problem with the disparate literature on the correlates of homicide. The issues raised in these studies are important, indeed fundamental, for understanding the nature of American society. It should be clear, moreover, that the variables included in the working hypothesis were not randomly selected. In fact, as the citations show, there is little in this chapter that sociologists and criminologists dealing with these relationships have not been saying for years. But the problem with all this research activity is that studies showing how each of these variables is related to the homicide rate (a set of bivariate relationships) are not connected to the other variables included in the working hypothesis. As indicated, the clue to this intellectual incoherence is that scholars studying each relationship do not cite each other.

I believe, however, that understanding the anomalous American homicide rate is too important a problem to be left in such a disjointed state. In some of the more progressive schools, children are encouraged to "color outside the lines." This is a metaphor, of course, designed to encourage the young to think creatively. I would like to suggest that sociologists and criminologists ought to try to "color outside the lines" as well. Such intellectual leaps are difficult, however, because most social scientists are so well trained quantitatively that their natural response is to look for a better, meaning more inclusive, data set. But this solution cannot work—if the goal is to understand the homicide rate. If we wait for a better data set, one that includes all the variables in the working hypothesis, we will wait forever. As mentioned before, one of the paradoxes of sociology and other disciplines is that many of the most important questions are not susceptible to precise measurement even if, as shown in this chapter, their component parts are. I am arguing that the five variables discussed here are interrelated and have a cumulative impact that sets the United States apart. Well, how is this claim to be evaluated? We must consider what Seymour Martin Lipset, with a bow to Max Weber, once called the "method of dialogue."[149] As described in chapter 2, this "method" is precisely how economists assess the impact of global warming on agriculture, how physicists debate the consequences of nuclear winter, and how demographers consider alternative explanations for the modern rise of population. The strategy I am using is unique only to sociologists and criminologists.

In a way, I began the sort of dialogue Professor Lipset proposes in chapter 4 with the critique of Steven Messner and Richard Rosenfeld's *Crime and the American Dream*. Now, after presenting my strategy for building on their analysis and evaluating the hypothesis, we need to move forward. The task of understanding why so much homicide occurs in this country remains incomplete. Thus, I would like to close by raising some ticklish questions about the argument presented here; it is called a "working hypothesis" deliberately.

First, have I misread or misinterpreted the findings in the literature? Scholars arguing that guns make the United States a safer society will undoubtedly have something to say about this issue. My interpretation of the role of the media in promoting aggression and the way the media combine with other "agents of violence" will probably also be questioned. In effect, that section of the chapter constituted a sort of sub-multivariate analysis: The degree of exposure to violence reflects the impact of all four of the variables considered (the media, family, neighborhood, and government). Exposure to violence, in turn, contributes to the homicide rate. At least that is the argument. Other interpretations of the literature considered in this chapter might be questioned as well, and that is all to the good.

Second, have the variables affecting the high homicide rate in the United States changed over time? This is a real possibility. For example, understanding homicide in America today differs from understanding its origins. Where did the high U.S. rate come from? Eric Monkkonen, for example, suggests that American and English rates were roughly similar prior to 1850, diverging in the quarter century that followed.[150] He offers a tentative structural account for this change: The Civil War increased access to guns, punishment was feeble, and immigration was high. Roger Lane proposes that the American rate has always been higher and points to the overriding importance of slavery and its aftermath.[151] Others have observed the interaction between slavery and the violent culture of the Scots-Irish immigrants who settled the Southern states and argued that this factor contributes to the problem.[152] Another possibility is that the variables (or their values) affecting homicide may well have changed over the course of the twentieth century. For example, it is likely that the impact of immigration (both internal and external) was great in the early 1900s, but it became less as the years passed.[153] Similarly, the impact of American drug policy on illegal drug markets may have been greater over the last thirty years or so than it was earlier. The problem of changes over time in the variables affecting the homicide rate ought to occupy us for quite awhile.

Third, what additional variables, if any, both distinguish the United States and affect the homicide rate? One candidate is the high American divorce rate, since the strong emotions connected with this phenomenon may affect homicide. And there is some suggestion in the literature that this is so.[154] Similarly, the potential effect of the Southern culture of violence needs to be considered, although for reasons suggested in chapter 3 I suspect that the impact of this factor may never be resolved.[155] Finally, as indicated previously in passing, the spatial distribution of liquor stores in cities and neighborhoods and the role of alcohol consumption almost certainly ought to be considered.[156] There are probably other variables, too.

Fourth, do some of the factors described here affect certain types of homicide rather than others? Again, this is a real possibility, one raised by Rosemary Gartner with regard to the age and sex distribution of homicide.[157] My discussion focuses on murders resulting from interpersonal conflict or predatory encounters, such as robbery. But not all of these events are alike. Moreover, other types of homicide (e.g., due to unsafe merchandise) may be less applicable to this analysis.

There are undoubtedly additional questions that can be raised about the argument presented here. And sorting them out will take a lot of work. But questions like these must be addressed if we are to understand the high American homicide rate. Let the dialogue continue. The carnage certainly will.

## NOTES

1. Gibson (1999:ix–x).
2. Gibson (1999). See also DePalma (1992).
3. Gibson (1999:192).
4. Quoted in McWhorter (2001:11).
5. Cook (1991). See also Zimring (1972); Vinson (1974); Saltzman et al. (1992); and Sarvesvaran and Jayewardene (1995).
6. Cook and Ludwig (1997:7).

7. Reiss and Roth (1993:260–61). The emergency room study is by Miller and Cohen (1996).

8. Federal Bureau of Investigation (2001).

9. See Wintemute (1996) and Diaz (1999:91–109) on gun production. On the use of semi-automatic pistols, see Stone et al. (1995); Hutson et al. (1995); and Hargarten et al. (1996). On the definitions, see Wintemute (1996) and Diaz (1999:34–35, 98–99).

10. Wintemute (1996); Diaz (1999:103–4).

11. Wintemute (1996). Another part of the explanation for the decline in at-scene mortality is probably improved emergency medical services; see Harris et al. (2002).

12. Wintemute (1996); Zimring and Hawkins (1997); Diaz (1999:91–105).

13. Wintemute (1996); Diaz (1999:50–88).

14. Lindgren and Heather (2002). Belleseiles provides a much lower estimate of gun ownership (2000), but Lindgren and Heather show conclusively that his data are unlikely to be correct. Roth confirms their findings (2002).

15. Roth (2002).

16. On Colt's murder of Adams, see Monkkonen (2001:26–27) or, for a more detailed description, see Tucher (1994:99–107). Monkkonen's estimate of New York City gun-related murders is on p. 35.

17. Kennett and Anderson (1975); Monkkonen (2001).

18. See the experiments done by Given (1994:93–111).

19. French (1925).

20. Given (1994:93–111).

21. Russell (1975:162–63); Given (1994:93–111).

22. Kennett and Anderson (1975).

23. Russell (1975:82–96); Monkkonen (2001:28).

24. Monkkonen (2001:39–40); Kennett and Anderson (1975:108–32).

25. Monkkonen (2001:35).

26. Kennett and Anderson (1975:83–108).

27. Adler's report is a personal communication based on his Chicago data, as cited in chapter 3. On the West, see McGrath (1989) and McKanna (1997). On the South, see Vandal (2000) and Butterfield (1996).

28. Hoffman (1925:70); Brearley (1932:68). Estimates of the homicide rate in Rome at this time resemble Brearley's estimates for England; see Boschi (1998).

29. Ellis (1975); Gibson (1999:184).

30. Kennett and Anderson (1975:187–216); Gibson (1999:163–65).

31. Kennett and Anderson (1975:187–246); Gibson (1999:165–69); Diaz (1999:68–88).

32. Cook and Ludwig (1997:6); Diaz (1999:96–105). The quotation below is from Diaz, p. 105.

33. Wintemute (1994); Cook and Ludwig (1997:6).

34. Federal Bureau of Investigation (2001).

35. Intelligence and Security Committee (2001).

36. Cook and Ludwig (1997:1). On the marketing and sales of guns, see Diaz (1999).

37. The next five paragraphs are from Larson (1993; 1994). I found the $160 sale price referred to in the text by searching the Internet for a Cobray M-11/9.

38. Larson (1993:51).

39. Larson (1994:159).

40. Larson (1994:201).

41. Butterfield (1999; 1999a).

42. The recent data are from Cook and Ludwig (1997:2). Kleck compiled the survey data over the last four decades (1997:98).

43. Cook and Ludwig (1997:3).

44. Gibson (1999:47). I shared Mr. Gibson's reactions. For the record, I have never belonged to or contributed money to any organization interested in gun-related issues.

45. Kates and Polsby (2000); Kleck (1991; 1997).

46. Kates and Polsby (2000:192).

47. Zimring and Hawkins (1997).

48. Federal Bureau of Investigation (2001:17). The nature of the relationship between the victim and assailant is often unknown early in the police investigation, which is when the data that go to the FBI are tabulated. Later on, for example, by the time an arrest occurs, the police often know a great deal more about the victim-assailant relationship (Reidel, 1998; 1999). Decker analyzed data for St. Louis and showed that the murder was committed by a stranger only 18 percent of the time (1993).

49. Baker (1985); Anderson (1998).

50. Kleck (1991:182–83).

51. On the studies of robbery, see Zimring and Hawkins (1997). For the reanalysis of Kleck's data, see Alba and Messner (1995). Kleck disagrees, of course; see his exchange with Alba and Messner (Kleck, 1995; Alba and Messner, 1995a).

52. Kleck (1991:143). See also Kleck (1997a).

53. See, for example, Browne (2000).

54. Cook and Ludwig (1997); Cook et al. (1997); Hemenway (1997). Again, Kleck disagrees; see the citations in notes 49 and 50.

55. Hemenway and Azrael (2000).

56. Kates and Polsby (2000); Kleck (1991; 1997).

57. See Blumstein and Wallman (2000); LaFree (1999a); Fagan et al. (1998); Blumstein (1998); Butterfield (1998, 1999b); Winship and Berrien (1999); Harris et al. (2002).

58. A confession: I have lost track of where the examples used in this paragraph come from.

59. Beeghley (2000:216–19).

60. Etzioni and Remp (1973); Curtis (1974); van Dijk et al. (1990); Lester (1991); Killias (1993a; 1993b); Krug et al. (1997); United Nations (1998).

61. Killias (1993a; 1993b). The correlation above is reported in 1993b:1723 and the quotation below comes from 1993a:300.

62. Killias (1993b:1723).

63. The city studies are Cook (1979) and McDowall (1986). For other data, see Duggan (2000).

64. Fisher (1976); McDowall et al. (1991). The quotation below is from McDowall, p. 1090.

65. On issues related to the measurement of gun availability, see Azrael et al. (2001).

66. Sloan et al. (1988). On natural experiments, see Campbell and Stanley (1963).

67. Miller et al. (2002).

68. McDowall et al. (1992); Deutsch and Alt (1977); Hay and McCleary (1979); Pierce and Bowers (1981); McPheters et al. (1984); O'Carroll et al. (1992).

69. Loftin et al. (1991).

70. See Blumstein and Wallman (2000); LaFree (1999a); Fagan et al. (1998); Blumstein (1998); Butterfield (1998, 1999b); Winship and Berrien (1999).

71. Sherman et al. (1995); Sherman and Rogan (1995).

72. Lott and Mustard (1997; see Table 11); Black and Nagin (1998).

73. McDowall et al. (1995); Ludwig (1998).

74. McDowall et al. (1991). See Lott's replies to Black and Nagin and others (1998:122–58; 1998a). Finally, see Ludwig's dismissal of Lott's comments (1997; 1998a).

75. Britt et al. (1996).

76. Loftin et al. (1991).

77. McDowall et al. (1996).

78. Zimring and Hawkins (1997:248); Grogger and Willis (2000).

79. Kopel (1992).

80. Kleck (1991); Zimring and Hawkins (1997).

81. United States Department of Health and Human Services (2001). For a structural account of the high demand for drugs in this country, see Beeghley (1999:134–39).

82. National Institute of Justice (1995); Simon and Burns (1997); Hagedorn (1998).

83. Goldstein (1985).

84. Goldstein et al. (1989).

85. Fagan and Chin (1990); Goldstein et al. (1989); Blumstein (1995); Blumstein and Cork (1996); Grogger and Willis (2000).

86. On the date of the appearance of crack in the District, see Grogger and Willis (2000). On the percentage of homicides that were drug related, see Zimring and Hawkins (1997:248–51).

87. The study of twenty-seven cities is Grogger and Willis (2000). For studies of gang-related homicide and its connection to drug markets, see Block et al. (1996); Venkatesh (1996); Block and Block (1993); Sanders (1994).

88. Zimring and Hawkins (1997:144).

89. Zimring and Hawkins (1997:146).

90. Goode (1989); Falco (1994).

91. Kasarda (1988; 1989; 1995); Farley (1987); Wilson (1996).

92. Beeghley (2000).

93. United States Sentencing Commission (1995); Blumstein and Cork (1996).

94. Preble and Casey (1969); Faupel (1991).

95. Sassen-Koob (1989); Hagedorn (1998).

96. On the size of the illegal drug market, see Ostrowski (1989). On the demog-

*Chapter 5*

raphy of drug use, see Kandel (1993). On the neighborhood impact of drug sales, see Sullivan (1989); Williams (1990); Simon and Burns (1997). On the middle class, see Hagedorn (1998).

97. Reuter et al. (1990).

98. Levitt and Venkatesh (2000).

99. Levitt and Venketesh (2000:757).

100. Jacobs (2000:2).

101. Blumstein (1995); Blumstein and Cork (1996).

102. Simon and Burns (1997).

103. Blau (1977).

104. Braithwaite and Braithwaite (1980); Hansmann and Quigley (1982); Avison and Loring (1986); Krahn et al. (1986); and Gartner (1990).

105. Gartner (1990).

106. Messner (1989). On homicide rates among Hispanic Americans, see Martinez and Lee (1999).

107. Monkkonen (1989). On economic inequality in American cities in the second half of the nineteenth century, see Soltow (1975).

108. Blau and Blau (1982); Blau and Golden (1986); Rose and McClain (1990; 1998); Hawkins (1999).

109. Bursik (1988).

110. On segregation today, see Lewis Mumford Center (2001). On the history of residential segregation and its impact, see Massey and Denton (1993) and Massey (1995). On hyper-segregation, see Massey and Denton, pp. 76–77.

111. My language in this paragraph parallels Douglas Massey's (1995:1207). On these three points, see Massey and Denton (1993). For more recent studies, see Emerson et al. (2001); Association of Community Organizations for Reform Now (1999).

112. Peterson and Krivo (1993); Shihadeh and Flynn (1996); Shihadeh and Maume (1997); Parker and McCall (1999); Jacobs and Wood (1999).

113. Massey (1995); Massey and Denton (1993); Massey and Fischer (2000). See also the sources cited in note 105.

114. Anderson (1999; 1994). On residents' relationship to the police, see 1999:320; see also Simon (1991).

115. Centers for Disease Control (2000:Table 6).

116. Canada (1995). The quotations below are from pp. 4 and 100.

117. Jankowski (1991:37–63, 120–23). The quotation below is from p. 120.

118. Massey (1995).

119. Black (1983). See also Cooney (1997; 1998).

120. Barry (1993); Groves (1997); Federal Trade Commission (2000). On the level of violence in movies and music videos, see Center for Media and Public Affairs (1999).

121. National Television Violence Study (1996; 1997; 1998). See also Bushman and Huesmann (2001:228).

122. Reviews of this literature are in American Psychological Association (1993); Paik and Comstock (1994); Centers for Disease Control (2000); and Bushman and Huesmann (2001). Some data suggest that the impact of media violence can be

reduced when children watch less television and play fewer video games; see Robinson et al. (2001).

123. Bushman and Huesmann (2001:236–41). The quotation comes from p. 241.

124. Huesmann et al. (1998); Johnson et al. (2002).

125. Freedman (1988; 1994); Zillman and Weaver (1999:147).

126. The examples used here come from Bushman and Huesmann (2001:235). On condom use, they cite Weller (1993); on calcium intake, they cite Welten et al. (1995). They also provide many other examples of "common sense" in which studies show a lower correlation than that between media violence and aggression.

127. Marshall (1978); Grossman and Siddle (1999:149); Grossman (1996).

128. United States Department of Health and Human Services (2001a). All the data in this paragraph come from this source.

129. Widon (1992); Widon and Maxfield (2001). See also Athens (1989); Zingraff et al. (1993); Smith and Thornberry (1995).

130. National Institute of Justice (2000). On men as the initiators of family violence, see Kurtz (1993).

131. See Straus et al. (1980); Athens (1989); Attala et al. (1995); Gelles (1997). On post-traumatic stress disorder, see van der Kolk et al. (1996); Erwin et al. (2000).

132. On homicides by gang members, see Maxson (1999). On gang members possessing and using guns, see Lizotte et al. (1994); Bjerregaard and Lizotte (1995). On homicide rates among juveniles, see Blumstein and Cork (1996); Fagan et al. (1998). On the drug-violence connection, see Blumstein (1995).

133. Heller (1961).

134. On the urban sample, see Fitzpatrick (1997). See the review of the literature in Buka et al. (2001). On the impact of witnessing violence, see Garbarino (1992); American Psychological Association (1993).

135. Sorenson et al. (1998); Cochran et al. (1994).

136. Gurr (1989:47); Archer and Gartner (1984); Bebber (1994).

137. Messner and Rosenfeld (2001).

138. Gottschalk et al. (1997).

139. Such data are more difficult to obtain, but see Wolff (2001:31–36).

140. Messner (1980); Avison and Loring (1986); Gartner (1990); Land et al. (1990); Cutright and Briggs (1995). See the review of the literature in Krahn et al. (1986).

141. Ritakallio (2001:14).

142. Shaw and McKay (1942); Loftin et al. (1989); Messner (1986); Blau and Blau (1982:126). See the review of the literature in Kovandzic et al. (1998).

143. Fiala and LaFree (1988); Gartner (1990); Pampel and Gartner (1995).

144. Esping-Anderson (1990).

145. Messner and Rosenfeld (1997a). For the replication, see Savolainen (2000).

146. Blau and Blau (1982).

147. Merton (1968a).

148. This line paraphrases one used by Glenn Firebaugh shortly after he became editor of the *American Sociological Review*. It appeared in the sociology newsletter, *Footnotes* (May/June, 1996, pp. 9–10).

149. Lipset (1968:51).

150. Monkkonen (1989; 2001).

151. Lane (1997).

152. Fischer (1989); Butterfield (1996).

153. Lane (1997); Adler (2000).

154. See Gartner (1990). For a structural analysis of the American divorce rate, see Beeghley (1996).

155. There is a long literature on this issue. The most well known contributors are Hackney (1969); Gastil (1971); Loftin and Hill (1974); Butterfield (1996); Nisbet and Cohen (1996).

156. Parker (1995).

157. Gartner (1990).

# 6

## Is Change Possible?

Two African American children, Lafayette Rivers and his younger cousin Dede, were on their way to the store where Lafayette planned to buy radio headphones with $8.00 he had received as a birthday gift. Gunfire erupted around them. The children fell to the ground and Lafayette restrained Dede from running for home, a dangerous act when bullets are flying. After a few minutes, when the shooting subsided, the children held hands as they crawled through the dirt toward home. When they finally got inside, Lafayette found that he had lost all but fifty cents of his birthday money. They had, however, survived the day's volley of gunfire.

This scene opens Alex Kotlowitz's book, *There Are No Children Here*, in which he describes a summer in the life of two brothers, Lafayette and Pharaoh Rivers, who live in a housing project in Chicago.[1] As in other cities, violence is common in Chicago's housing projects, where guns, illegal drug markets, racial discrimination, and poverty combine to create a miasmic environment. Other neighborhood residents that summer were not as lucky as Lafayette and his cousin; several were murdered, and children living in the project witnessed the shooting death of one of them. Although Lafayette is only twelve years old, Mr. Kotlowitz describes him as looking "like an old man" because there appears "bottled up inside him a lifetime's worth of horrors." This is the reason for the book's title; they have seen too much to be children. When asked what he wanted to be, Lafayette may have been unconsciously reflecting all that he had experienced up to that moment when he replied: "If I grow up, I'd like to be a bus driver." His mother has already purchased burial insurance for him.

The parents of eleven-year-old Natalie Brooks had not purchased burial insurance for her. They saw no need to. They live in Jonesboro, Arkansas, a town of 46,000 people located about 130 miles northeast of Little Rock. This is one of those classic small towns that residents describe as "a good and

163

decent place." Although hunting is a way of life in this section of rural Arkansas, for both adults and children, those residing in Jonesboro see it as a safe, bucolic setting in which to live and raise their kids. They describe homicide as rare in Jonesboro, since it occurs only about twice per year.[2]

There has been, however, one notorious exception to that pattern, which affected Natalie Brooks and many others. One of those affected was thirty-two-year-old Shannon Wright. On the day in question, Ms. Wright and her husband, Mitchell, woke early and played with their two-and-one-half-year-old son, Zane, for awhile, as they did every morning. Ms. Wright grew up in Jonesboro, married, and taught English at Westside Middle School. The school is virtually all white. When she dropped Zane off at her mother's house on her way to work, Ms. Wright used her son's nickname, saying, "Bye, bye, Cowboy Tex. See you this afternoon." But Shannon Wright would not return to her son or husband that evening, nor will she ever again. She, along with Natalie Brooks and four other middle school children, were shot and killed that day. Ms. Wright would have had, on average, about fifty-one years of life ahead of her; young Ms. Brooks and the other children killed would each have had about seventy years. In addition to the six killings, ten other children and one other teacher were wounded in the same incident. All of these victims had relatives and friends who were also traumatized. Although the frequency of school shootings has decreased over the last decade, this one captured the nation's attention, not only because of the number of victims but also because of the characteristics of the perpetrators.

The shooters were Mitchell Johnson, age thirteen, and Andrew Golden, age eleven, both of whom attended Westside Middle School. That morning, young Mr. Golden broke into his grandfather's glass-enclosed gun case and stole a variety of weapons: several semi-automatic pistols, a couple of revolvers, a .30-caliber carbine, a .44-caliber semi-automatic rifle, and a .30-6 deer hunting rifle fitted with a telescopic sight. All the ammunition he needed for these weapons was stacked on top of the refrigerator. Young Mr. Johnson, in turn, stole his parent's van, which the boys drove to a wooded area near the school. Mitchell pulled a fire alarm and then retreated to a hiding place the boys had established about 100 yards from the school's main exit. After the students and teachers left the building and began milling about, the boys fired a minimum of twenty-six shots in less than fifteen seconds. Given their weaponry, it was easy to hit a lot of people. Andrew, moreover, had had plenty of practice. He began hunting at age six. In addition, he and his father belonged to the Jonesboro Practical Shooters Club, where they competed with other fathers and sons by shooting at moving or pop-up targets. After they stopped firing their guns that morning, the boys ran off, only to be arrested within minutes.

In the aftermath, residents were shocked—numb, really. In various ways, they wondered how such a thing could happen in their little town. Most blamed the boys, which makes perfect sense. People, even young people, need to be held responsible for their acts. Although their motives remain unclear, the two children were, indeed, very angry. Mitchell Johnson, in particular, had stated in advance that he was going to shoot people, especially some girls who had rejected him. The reporters dealing with the story, however, tried to raise some of the larger issues inherent in such events. In response to questions, townspeople seemed at first surprised and then angry at the implication that the boys' easy access to guns may have contributed to this tragedy. As a spokesperson for the state police pointed out: "This is a part of the country where it's unusual if a child doesn't have a gun growing up. People here enjoy their hunting privileges and don't want this [tragedy] ruining those privileges."[3]

Perhaps not. But homicide is routine in America to a degree that is inconceivable in other Western nations. And the fear that results is realistic. This is so even though deaths from homicide are not randomly distributed; they are higher in some areas than others. A few states, for example, such as Massachusetts and North Dakota, display rather low rates; while others, such as Louisiana and Mississippi, display very high rates (recall figure 3.3). Arkansas is above average for the nation as a whole, with 7.9 killings per 100,000 residents.

Homicide rates are also higher among some groups of people than among others. African Americans are especially vulnerable, as the vignette from *There Are No Children Here* suggests. But the vignette merely illustrates a larger truth that can be stated quantitatively. The historical data presented in chapter 3 show that the extreme rate of homicide victimization among African Americans has been a constant phenomenon over the years. The current homicide rate for African Americans of about twenty-one per 100,000 persons summarizes the situation today.[4] Recall, however, that in some urban neighborhoods the level is significantly greater than that, well above rates last seen in other Western nations in medieval times. So simply having dark skin is and always has been dangerous in this country, and this is so no matter what city or state they live in.

By comparison, the homicide rate for whites is "only" about four per 100,000 persons. On the one hand, compared to African Americans, this level means that people with white skin are usually safer in this country, no matter where they live. On the other hand, however, this "low" white rate is four times higher than that in some other Western nations (recall figures 3.1 and 3.2). This difference means that even though the odds of death from homicide vary a great deal in this country, by region and race, for example, cross-national comparisons show that in America everyone is at greater risk of being murdered, whether going to a museum or store, to work or school. The spasm of carnage at Westside Middle School in Jonesboro constitutes an extreme example, of course, an aberration even by American standards—

which is why it became newsworthy. But the aberrant highlights the normal: The average of two homicides that occur in Jonesboro each year translates into a rate of about 4.3 per 100,000 persons. The fact that residents of Jonesboro consider it to be a safe place to live only indicates Americans' peculiar definition of safety—at least compared to citizens of any Western European nation. Considered in cross-national terms, this relatively "safe" rate of homicide in Jonesboro and other American communities represents a high level of annual trauma, in terms not only of lives lost but also of the suffering of surviving family and friends as well as economic costs (in adjudication, medical expenses, and lost productivity).

But public places are not the only settings where homicide occurs. In America, even the home is dangerous, especially for women. Men are typically killed away from home, rarely by someone with whom they are sexually intimate. Women, by contrast, are more likely to be killed at home, usually by a spouse, companion, former boyfriend, or other intimate acquaintance. For example, as mentioned in chapter 1, among women aged fifteen to twenty-four, homicide is the fourth leading cause of death for whites and the second leading cause of death for African Americans and Hispanics. Among women aged twenty-five to forty-four, homicide is the fifth leading cause of death in all three groups.[5] Yet this level of lethal violence in American homes is anomalous. For example, the overall homicide rate among women in this country is 3.2 per 100,000. Although this figure may seem low, it is three times greater than in Canada (.96 per 100,000), four times greater than in France (.72), five times greater than in Germany (.66), and eight times greater than in England and Wales (.40). Women are much more likely to be murdered in the United States than in any Western nation. Moreover, in this country most homicides against women are committed with guns, whereas use of firearms is rare in other nations.[6]

Whether in public or private spheres, we live with lethal violence. It is routine. And its consequences—in lives, trauma, and cost—profoundly alter the nature of social life in the United States. We have a problem. Must we live with it?

## SOCIOLOGY AND SOCIAL CHANGE

The answer is, no, we do not have to live with a high rate of homicide. We choose to live with it. As emphasized at the beginning of this book, the story of the last two centuries is one of increasing control over every dimension of life. Such control is the essence of modernity. But even given increasing control, social change is not easy, mainly because we are handcuffed to history. This is a metaphorical way of restating Emile Durkheim's dictum that "social facts are things." It suggests that the possibilities for changing social organization are limited by the context in which proposals occur. Think of the problem as like remodeling a house. It exists, it is real, and it can be changed. But its current structure places limits on the changes that can be made.

I believe that sociology can help in the process of "social remodeling" by identifying both possibilities and potential pitfalls of change, not only with regard to the homicide rate but also other matters. As an intellectual enterprise, *sociology* can be defined as a systematic attempt at seeing social life as clearly as possible, understanding its various dimensions, and doing so without being swayed by one's personal hopes and fears. This is a textbook definition, of course, one taken from Peter Berger.[7] Even so, it seems to me that it represents a generalizable goal that characterizes the modern mind; in fact, Professor Berger includes it in a book titled *Facing Up to Modernity*. Substitute a different subject matter for "social life" in the definition and it describes what any discipline that claims to be scientific tries to do.

Given our particular subject matter, if sociologists are indeed able to see social life clearly and to understand its dimensions and their interrelationships, research results have implications for people's hopes and fears about the future. This possibility also occurs, of course, as mentioned in chapter 2, when observers in other disciplines (such as economists, physicists, and demographers) try to understand their topics. Paradox follows, especially for sociological research and perhaps research in other disciplines as well, for the results often seem contradictory: They appear politically radical yet also conservative, liberating yet also constraining. This paradox, Peter Berger suggests, is inherent to sociological inquiry.[8]

On the one hand, knowledge liberates people by opening up the possibility for change. It is, after all, fairly obvious that implications for change follow from any explanation of the anomalous American homicide rate. Based on their analysis, you may recall, Steven Messner and Richard Rosenfeld emphasize the importance of "social reorganization" so as to alter "fundamental features of American society" and thereby reduce the homicide rate. This prescription is correct, which is partly why their study marks a real contribution to understanding. In this book, I have tried to build on their analysis by showing how the five variables in the working hypothesis (gun availability, illegal drug markets, racial and ethnic discrimination, exposure to violence, and economic inequality) contribute, individually and in combination, to the high American homicide rate. I am arguing that they constitute fundamental features of American social structure, and that research suggests what needs to be changed in order for citizens to live in a less homicidal society. This fact stimulates people's hope for progress in the future. As mentioned before, unlike the social institutions on which Professors Messner and Rosenfeld focus, the "score" of each of the variables in the working hypothesis is manipulable, at least in principle. They each represent policy choices. And in modern societies, choices made can be unmade. We can lower the homicide rate. Other nations that resemble our own culturally and in terms of their level of economic development have succeeded in this task. We do not need to weep and wail about the supposed meaninglessness of homicide.

On the other hand, sociological analyses also show that improvement does not always follow from change. The issue of unanticipated consequences looms like a dark specter over all social science–generated policy proposals, especially those implying the need for structural changes. And this possibility carries conservative implications along with it, because disorder, disorganization, and greater costs sometimes result from attempts at change. Such prospects make people fear the future, which constrains them. After all, most individuals are enmeshed in structures of norms and roles with which they are both familiar and comfortable. The residents of Jonesboro like living there. The state police spokesperson quoted earlier used an unfortunate phrase when he referred to "hunting privileges"; it sounded unfeeling in light of the tragedy that had just occurred. What he really meant, I suspect, is that the local people like their particular traditions (such as hunting and the centrality of guns in their daily lives) and that these traditions have many positive qualities. Similarly, members of urban gangs often find comfort and solace in their participation and the accompanying lifestyle. Yes, the environment is miasmic; yes, they know they might die at a young age. But this way of life is what they have grown up with and familiarity breeds a sense of acceptance, if not well-being. Few persons dislike everything about their lives, which means they want to preserve what is good, maintain their traditions, and retain a sense of orderliness and continuity from one generation to another. This orientation militates against change, even if its goals are well intended. It suggests that our ability to reduce the level of lethal violence is limited not only by what people will accept but also by the efforts of organized interest groups to prevent change. Some people always benefit from the status quo, and they will try hard to retain it.

The result of these contradictory impulses, as Professor Berger comments, is that sociology often produces a paradoxical, but by no means irrational, stance on the part of its (more sensible) practitioners and others exposed to it: that of people who think daringly but act prudently. Put differently, even though most of the key variables are known, reducing the high American homicide rate will not occur easily. All the issues raised by the working hypothesis are controversial and changing them will involve both benefits and liabilities, some of which may not be obvious. Even so, we as a nation need to begin discussing some alternatives that might lead to a reduction in the homicide rate.

## TWO ILLUSTRATIONS

Chapter 3 traced the history of homicide in America and compared it to that in various Western European nations. The results show that this country is a very lethal place in which to live. Chapter 5 explained why: The "scores" attached to each of the variables in the working hypothesis are high. They make this country unique among modern societies. How, then, can these scores be reduced? The answers, of course, are uncertain. But I intend to start the conversation by focusing on two of the most important variables. This brief discussion provides a way of illustrating the structurally based choices this country faces as it attempts to deal with the problem of homicide.

## Gun Availability

The United States is unique among Western societies in the widespread availability of guns. The evidence shows that the ease with which guns are acquired contributes significantly to the anomalous American homicide rate. It follows that one way to reduce the level of carnage might be to reduce the availability of guns in the American population.

In this country, however, unlike other Western nations, any proposal to reduce gun availability generates controversy. This is partly because, as the historian Richard Hofstadter argued some years ago, America is a gun-oriented culture.[9] The origin of this fetish for guns, he suggests, lies in the frontier experience, especially as it has been idealized in the media. Guns emerged as an important part of everyday social life in the second half of the nineteenth century when they became widely available, easy to use, and accurate. In the days before spectator sports and competitive athletics developed into basic elements of popular culture, hunting and fishing were probably the chief American sports. Shooting contests were common, especially in rural communities. Jonesboro is not all that different, even today. But the United States is not the only nation with a frontier history. Canada and Australia, for example, were both frontier societies. Although Japan did not have a frontier, it does have a long history of feudal violence. Professor Hofstadter observes that while these and other nations "have succeeded in modifying their old gun habits" during the course of economic development, we have not.

We continue being a gun-oriented culture. As Steven Messner and Richard Rosenfeld point out, "high rates of gun-related violence . . . result in part from a cultural ethos that encourages the rapid deployment of technically efficient methods to solve interpersonal problems."[10] One of the cultural values they mention is activism, people's desire to overcome obstacles and master the situations in which they find themselves. Americans, especially, want to do so in the most direct and efficient way possible. Another value is individualism. Not only do Americans want to "make it" on their own, they want to be left alone to do as they please in their private lives, as long they do not harm others. Thus, compared to other Western nations, Americans emphasize the importance of individual rights and individual autonomy. It is the individual, we think, who achieves or fails; it is individuals who protect themselves. Connected to this value is a third one: personal freedom. This orientation refers, of course, to political independence and civil rights. But, in addition, in the United States the notion of personal freedom carries with it a strain of antipaternalism that is especially resonant: Others, we think, especially the government, should not tell individuals what is in their best interest.

Although these ethical standards characterize all Western democracies, they are exaggerated in the United States. Whether correctly or not, Americans believe these values help make this country great, that they lead to technological advances, economic development, and other good things. They also, however, lead many people to want to own guns. Thus, for the citizens of Jonesboro, who hunt and fish as a way of life, the gun provides a practical (albeit unrealistic) symbol of self-reliance and independence. But they are not alone. Both suburbanites with permits to carry and urban gang members are fascinated with guns. In this country, more than others, Professor Hofstadter argues, citizens resonate with the isolated individual—whether detective, sheriff, or even villain—seeking to solve problems. And all too often, compared to other nations, the solution does not come from reason or thought, but from action, from the use of a gun. In some way, all the Walter Mittys in America imagine they can be like Dirty Harry. It is a powerful fantasy. It is also self-destructive. When Kareem Robinson killed Delvin Darnell Carey (chapter 1), he had a problem to solve, and he went about it in a very American way. So too, did all the other perpetrators described in this book. So too, do all the killers of 15,000 American citizens each year. But this huge loss of life troubles many observers because it conflicts with another fundamental value: the belief in the sanctity of human life and the dignity of each individual that characterizes every modern society, including the United States. When values conflict—as when the desire to be left alone conflicts with the need to protect human life—a resolution in the form of public policy becomes tricky. But it is not impossible.

Assuming for the moment that protecting lives requires that some limits be placed on the availability of guns, the key to moving in that direction is to recognize that guns are ordinary consumer products bought and sold, new and used, just like automobiles. Americans are fascinated with cars, just as they are with guns, because in certain ways cars also reflect our peculiar emphasis on individualism and personal freedom. Even so, in this area the government tells citizens what is in their best interest by limiting their freedom to drive down the road—precisely in order to save lives. Thus, as for many other products, Americans accept without question that the design, manufacture, marketing, sale, and possession of automobiles should be regulated in the public interest. For example, Americans accept as necessary the registration of automobiles and the requirement that owners carry insurance. They also accept as necessary that individuals wanting to drive must obtain a license—and wait until they are sixteen years of age to do so. They accept these limitations because operating a vehicle can cause harm to self and others, even though cars are not intended to be harmful. Many other consumer products are similarly regulated. By contrast, guns are not so regulated; it is easier to buy, own, or use a gun than to buy, own, or operate a car. Yet guns are designed, manufactured, and marketed for the express purpose of harming and possibly killing other living things.

The "biography" of one gun not only illustrates this purpose, it also suggests how firearms are transported around the country and end up in neighborhoods characterized by pervasive violence.[11] This particular weapon is a twelve-shot Jennings 9 mm semi-automatic made mostly of plastic. It is six inches long with a two-inch barrel, weighs sixteen ounces, and was manufactured by Bryco Arms in Costa Mesa, California. After manufacture, a gun wholesaler in Ohio purchased this particular Jennings. The wholesaler sold it to a dealer in Georgia for $90. The dealer sold the Jennings for $150 to a straw purchaser working for a gunrunner. The straw purchaser also bought eight other weapons at the same time. These purchases were all illegal, not because of their quantity, but because the true buyer was a convicted felon. The gunrunner transported it to New York City, where he resold it (illegally) to Demeris Tolbert, reputed to be a member of a street gang called the Bloods. Shortly after acquiring it, Mr. Tolbert used the Jennings to shoot and kill sixteen-year-old Jermain Wilson, who was said to belong to another gang, called the Crips. It is not known if this murder resulted from a personal dispute or a gang-related conflict. In any case, young Mr. Wilson would have lived, on average, another fifty-four years if he had not been killed. A few days after that, Mr. Tolbert robbed and killed Mr. Savinder Oberoi, a forty-eight-year-old businessman and father of four children, outside his shop. Mr. Oberoi had, on average, about thirty-two years of potential life snuffed out. His wife and children, of course, are forever deprived of his loving presence. Finally, later that same day, Mr. Tolbert shot and wounded a New York City police officer who was attempting to arrest him. Despite this shooting, Mr. Tolbert was indeed arrested at that point and the gun recovered. Luckily, neither the gunrunner nor Mr. Tolbert bothered to file off the gun's serial number, which allowed its movements to be traced. By the way, this list of the Jennings's travels and uses is not exhaustive; law enforcement officials estimate that it was employed in at least thirteen crimes, including the two murders.

Despite their express purpose, few guns are ever used in a homicide. Most are bought perfectly legally and kept in the home or car. They are tools for hunting or target shooting, or admired for their craftsmanship. As mentioned earlier, most people purchase guns, especially handguns, to provide themselves with a sense of safety from personal or home attack. As an aside, note that some people buy guns because they fear the rise of an authoritarian American government and believe that their weapons can protect them.[12]

Regardless of motive, in nearly all cases, possessing guns is benign in the sense that they are not used to threaten or kill anyone. Gary Kleck, for example, estimates that of the millions of handguns currently circulating in this country, only about 1 percent are used in a crime in any year. He also estimates that only between 2 and 7 percent of the guns sold in any one year will ever be employed in a crime over their usable life. Other estimates are similar.[13] These data show that almost all guns just sit around most of the time. Like millions of others, Andrew Golden's grandfather has owned guns all his life. Until young Andrew broke into his gun case, not one of them had ever been used in a crime.

Even so, because they are bought and sold as ordinary consumer products, a small proportion of guns will be used in crimes and some of them will involve homicide. As noted previously, at least 200 million guns circulate in this country, with at least 14 million sold each year. And these are conservative estimates; the real number of both is probably much higher. This volume means guns are easily accessible to anyone who wants one. If Professor Kleck's estimate is used, then 1 percent of the 200 million guns in circulation means that at least 2 million of them are involved in crimes each year, probably more.

The large number of guns used in crimes each year reveals why the high level of gun-related homicide occurs so often in this country compared to others. The lethal results that followed from the purchase of the Jennings semi-automatic and the Cobray M-11/9 described in chapter 5 merely illustrate what these numbers mean in practice. Clearly, as also shown by the Jennings, the ability of gang members and other violent people to obtain firearms constitutes a major problem that needs to be discussed. Recall also that gang members not only use guns themselves but also buy and sell them as a source of revenue. Guns are also intrinsic to illegal drug markets and part of the code of the streets characterizing some neighborhoods. Unfortunately, these neighborhoods are afflicted with many individuals like Demeris Tolbert, who live and work in them. Such persons often have long criminal records and are used to employing violence to solve their problems. They prey on other people. These are the "high-risk" users of guns, who often acquire them illegally.

But the real problem goes beyond gunrunners, gang members, criminals using guns in robberies, illegal drug sales, and generalized violence in some poor communities. It is not "just" gang members and drug dealers who murder one another. (Are their lives unimportant? This question ought to be asked.) Innocent bystanders who find themselves in the wrong place at the wrong time get killed, too. Lafayette Rivers's mother purchased burial insurance for him because of the pervasiveness of this problem in her neighborhood.

The real problem is that any gun can be used at any time by anyone to kill another human being. A child can break into a gun case, as Andrew Golden did, or simply pick up a weapon left in a drawer, as Nathaniel Brazill did (recall chapter 3). A mentally ill person, such as Wayne Lo (chapter 5), can buy a gun at a store and modify it with parts ordered through the mail. Very angry persons, such as Michael McDermott (chapter 2), only have to drive to the next state and purchase weapons. A couple argues, and one of them picks up the gun designed to protect them from intruders and uses it on the other. All of these guns were owned by people deemed "low-risk" users. They acquired their guns perfectly legally. These ordinary citizens, or their children, became criminals only when they killed someone.

Regardless of the "risk level" of those possessing guns, gun-related murders constitute about two-thirds of the overall American homicide rate, roughly 10,000 human beings each year. All of the victims have names. All of them have families, companions, and friends.

Even though it is perfectly reasonable to try to understand the psychological impulses that lead the "nut with a gun" to kill, the argument in this book is that it would be smarter to change the social structure in order to lower the rate of gun-related homicides. In light of the evidence, it seems reasonable to believe that reducing gun availability would help to achieve this goal. If so, this product ought to be regulated just like any other manufactured good. The question is how. Given the conflicting values described earlier, what reasonable limits should be placed on this product, if any?

And that question leads to the meaning of the Second Amendment of the Constitution, the touchstone of the debate over guns in this country. It states, rather ambiguously, "A well regulated Militia, being necessary to the security of a free State, the right of the people to keep and bear Arms, shall not be infringed." There are huge scholarly and political disagreements over whether the Amendment applies to individual ownership of guns or to the use of guns by members of the militia. And disputes occur about what the term "militia" means, too. Moreover, unlike other sections of the Bill of Rights, the Second Amendment has not been applied to the states; in legal jargon, it has not been "incorporated." This signifies that the Amendment applies only to the federal government, not states or cities, which suggests that they are free to either ban citizens from possessing guns or require them to possess guns. There have been and will be disputes about this possibility as well.[14]

At the risk of sounding blasé about an important set of legal issues, I want to pause only briefly to consider the meaning of the Second Amendment. It seems to me that two tentative conclusions emerge from thinking, more or less dispassionately, about the Amendment and its history.

First, regardless of what the framers of the Constitution "really" intended, the Amendment protects and (I predict) will be interpreted to protect the right of individuals to possess guns. I am, of course, perfectly aware that this conclusion does not follow from a reading of the Amendment's history or previous interpretations by the Supreme Court. Moreover, new court cases will undoubtedly proceed and everyone from constitutional scholars to liberal and conservative ideologues will debate the issue over the next few years. But several social facts underlie the debate and will inevitably influence the conclusion: The most important is the minimum estimate of 200 million guns circulating in private hands in this country. In addition, a complex manufacturing and retail chain exists that underlies the buying and selling of this product. For example, eighty-one different companies manufacture pistols in the United States and ninety-seven manufacture rifles. Some of these, as well as other companies, produce revolvers, shotguns, and miscellaneous firearms. In 1995, more than 4.2 million new guns were manufactured in this country. This total does not include foreign imports.[15] At the other end of the chain, every city and county in America has multiple retail outlets for the sale of guns to the public. Within thirty miles of my home are thirteen gun shops, not counting sporting goods stores where guns are also sold. On top of that, of course, firearms are also bought and sold at gun shows, swap meets, and through the mail. These realities signify that the meaning of the Amendment has been resolved: Americans can, do, and will own guns, and they will buy and sell them, too. But these rights (like that of free speech and owning or operating a motor vehicle) are not unlimited.

Thus, second, every case that has made its way to the Supreme Court has affirmed the government's ability to protect the public health in general and, more specifically, to regulate the availability of guns and the conditions of their possession. The courts will undoubtedly resolve the precise nature and extent of these limits over the next few years. In the meantime, it seems to me, observers should avoid the tendency for the discussion to get hijacked by the invocation of the right to own guns based on the Second Amendment. In practical terms, as Robert Spitzer comments, the "constant and misplaced invocation of [this right] only serves to heighten social conflict, cultivate ideological rigidity, and stifle rational policy debate."[16] The Second Amendment, he concludes, does not pose an obstacle to regulating guns by imposing reasonable limits on their availability.

At least five (and perhaps other) areas of potential intervention ought to be discussed. None is new; each is controversial. All have some support from the public and, indeed, reflect a public health approach to the issue of guns and homicide.[17]

**Design.**    Design changes can make guns safer and reduce the odds of their being used in homicides or suicides or leading to accidental deaths and injuries. Over the years, greater lethality has been far more important to manufacturers than safety. Lethality, someone remarked, is like the nicotine of gun design and manufacture. But this orientation can be changed. About two-thirds of the public, including gun owners, favor some sort of government regulation of firearm design.[18]

The most common design change that is talked about in the literature involves personalizing each gun so that only the authorized user can fire it.[19] About 71 percent of the public and 59 percent of gun owners support this strategy in some form.[20] Personalization can be achieved by equipping the gun with a coded computer chip and requiring that the owner possess one as well, in a ring, pin, or watch. Fingerprint-reading technology will soon be available, which would eliminate the need for a second piece of equipment. In other industries where product-related injuries and deaths occurred (autos, for example), the federal government has required them to develop safer designs. The advantage of built-in safety features is that the consumer does not have to do anything to the gun.

Such design changes might reduce access by making it more difficult for thieves or straw purchasers to obtain guns and resell them in neighborhoods where violence is widespread. They might also make it harder for children to obtain and use guns. Under current law, however, the Consumer Product Safety Commission is prohibited from exercising jurisdiction over the design of firearms. Is this wise?

***Manufacture.*** The manufacture of specific weapons could be regulated so as to reduce the number of certain types of new firearms coming onto the market each year.

Some guns, called Saturday Night Specials, are inherently unsafe because they are made of poor quality materials and prone to malfunction.[21] The mostly plastic Jennings semi-automatic pistol provides an example. So does the Cobray M-11/9 that Nicholas Elliot used to kill Karen Farley (recall chapter 5). Such guns have no discernible sport or hunting purpose and are unreliable. But criminals and gang members like them: For example, young adults with arrest records (e.g., for misdemeanors) who purchase handguns legally are more likely to select a Saturday Night Special. Similarly, young adults with no previous arrest record who purchase Saturday Night Specials are more likely than other gun buyers to commit crimes after their purchase.[22] Under current law, such weapons cannot be imported into this country because they are so defective. But they can be manufactured domestically. More than 90 percent of the public, including gun owners, support the requirement that domestically manufactured guns meet the same quality standards as imported guns.[23] Some evidence indicates that a limit on Saturday Night Specials might reduce the rate of homicide. In 1990, for example, Maryland banned their sale within the state, with the result that homicides committed with this type of weapon dropped significantly.[24] This result fits with the data reviewed in chapter 5.

Other firearms are especially lethal and, again, have little use other than as weapons for killing human beings. The Second Amendment was passed when the flintlock was the most dangerous gun available to citizens. Perhaps the manufacture of semi-automatic rifles and assault weapons intended for military use ought to be more strictly regulated so as to keep some of them from falling into civilian hands. Wayne Lo walked into a gun shop and bought a semi-automatic rifle. He used the mail to increase its lethality. Eleven-year-old Andrew Golden easily obtained two semi-automatic weapons from his grandfather's house. Ordinary criminals obtain them easily, too. Is it wise to allow companies to manufacture either poorly made or extremely lethal weapons? Is it wise to allow the unregulated mail order shipment of parts designed to increase the firepower of weapons?

*Marketing.*  The Federal Trade Commission could regulate gun-related advertisements, especially those promising home protection.[25] Marketing efforts in the national media, not just gun-oriented magazines, promise homeowners that—when armed with a gun—they will be protected from intruders. But these marketing efforts fail to identify the risks inherent in having guns in the home. For example, they display unlocked firearms on night-stands or in drawers with ammunition nearby. The clear implication is that the gun should be kept immediately available and loaded. These advertisements compare ownership of a semi-automatic pistol with homeowners' insurance. This is so even though the evidence shows that defensive gun use against intruders is actually very rare. Moreover, homes with guns in them are much more likely to experience a homicide (as well as a suicide or accidental shooting), usually by a family member or intimate acquaintance, than are homes without guns.[26] The Federal Trade Commission is empowered to regulate and prohibit "unfair or deceptive" advertisements, especially those that mislead consumers or increase their risk. If manufacturers were required to point out, for example, the dangers involved in having guns in the home, fewer people might purchase them. At present, compared to most other products, guns are unique in that their marketing is totally unregulated. Is this wise?

*Sale.*  The sale of weapons could be regulated more than is currently the case. The relationship between dealers and straw purchasers who buy in bulk is especially important. Because only a few dealers persistently sell guns that end up being used in crimes, law enforcement efforts should focus on them.[27] All dealers could be trained to spot straw purchasers. Perhaps more important, would it make sense to limit the freedom to purchase guns to one per month or one every six weeks? This strategy might make bulk purchases intended for eventual illegal resale to high-risk users (like gang members) more difficult.

Some evidence supports this suggestion. Although theft of guns (via burglary, for example) is an important issue, it appears that most guns used in crimes are bought from dealers.[28] What happens is that straw purchasers buy weapons in quantity for gunrunners in states with weak gun control laws, and the latter resell them in states where gun laws are stricter. Most of these guns appear to end up in violence-prone neighborhoods where homicide rates are high. The Bureau of Alcohol, Tobacco, and Firearms, in fact, refers to Interstate 95, which runs north and south along the East Coast, as the "iron pipeline" because it constitutes one of the most important gun-trafficking routes in this country.[29] For example, at one time guns originally sold in Virginia, Georgia, and Florida accounted for 65 percent of all successfully traced firearms used in crimes in New York City. The Jennings semi-automatic that Demeris Tolbert used to kill Jermain Wilson illustrates the pattern. In 1993, however, Virginia enacted a law limiting handgun purchases by one individual to one in each thirty-day period. As a result, the number of crime guns traced to original sale in Virginia dropped significantly. Of course, those wishing to purchase weapons in bulk for resale in violent neighborhoods simply switched to other states. Thus, it is plausible to argue that a nationwide limit on the number of guns that can be purchased at any one time might reduce the trafficking in this product. By the way, the Virginia law included an exception that allowed bulk purchases for legitimate reasons, such as when a collector wants to buy a set of antique guns.[30]

There are other questions surrounding the sale of guns that also ought to be discussed. Should waiting periods be longer or more strictly enforced? Should background checks be required for sales at gun shows, through the mail, and between private individuals? Requiring that private sellers have a dealer do the background check and making the seller liable for the subsequent use of the gun if this procedure was not followed might be a way to regulate sales between individuals. Should the sale of guns be prohibited to people with previous arrest records, such as for domestic violence, possession of drug paraphernalia, driving under the influence of alcohol, and possibly some other crimes? The majority of the public favors all these policies in some form.[31] The point of regulating the sale of guns would be to slow down their movement into the hands of high-risk persons, those prone to commit crimes—especially crimes of violence. Is it wise to allow the current situation to continue?

*Possession.*   The question here is whether there should be limits on the possession of guns or the conditions of their possession.

One answer is no. For example, a typical observer argues that "access to firearms for self-protection is a constitutionally protected right. Analysis of the risks and benefits of this right belongs to individual citizens, not the federal government." Similarly, after sketching the existence of "hotheads" who might pull out a gun during a traffic dispute (road rage), another observer argues that "our founding fathers meant for us to defend ourselves from these people and not be dominated by them."[32] These types of assertions are pretty common; they appeal to the values of activism, individualism, and personal freedom described in chapter 4. In so doing, the arguments resemble those made about other issues. For example, as the government sought to make automobiles safer beginning in the 1960s, the installation and use of seat belts became controversial. Some observers asserted that individuals have or ought to have the right to decide for themselves whether to buy a car equipped with them or to use them.[33] Today, of course, mandated design changes mean that all vehicles come with these devices, and people can be ticketed if they fail to "buckle up." The logic, of course, is to protect human lives. The relative success of such policies constitutes one reason why auto fatalities declined over the last few decades. More generally, arguments like those above attempt to close off debate by appealing to the Dirty Harry lurking inside many Americans. They assert that, unlike other economically developed nations, Americans should not try to reduce the availability of guns regardless of their known lethal consequences.

But to reduce the homicide rate and thereby save lives, we need to open the debate and consider options for placing limits on the possession of guns. This is because the evidence shows clearly that when fewer guns are available in a nation, state, or city, the homicide rate is lower.

Several options exist. One possibility would be to ban the possession of certain kinds of weapons, such as those that are unsafe or especially lethal. One way to do this might involve a buy back. Every person who turned in a Saturday Night Special could be given $100, no questions asked. Every person who turned in an assault rifle could be given $500, no questions asked. As an aside, this strategy might also work in impoverished neighborhoods where violence is high. Although expensive, a buy back might be cheaper than paying for the medical and legal costs associated with gun use. If these weapons could no longer be manufactured and those turned in were melted down, it might be possible to reduce their presence on the street.

Another possibility is to regulate the terms of possession. Sales could be registered and owners required to purchase liability insurance. In this country, as in other nations, automobile owners must do these things. In a related way, those who wish to own guns could be required to store them in safe locations (i.e., in a safe) or equip them with trigger locks, or both. Owners who followed such policies would be protected from liability if gun theft occurred because of a burglary; those who failed to store their guns properly would expose themselves to civil and criminal penalties. Similarly, if children like Mitchell Johnson and Andrew Golden were able to obtain guns, their owners would be liable—again, both civilly and criminally—if they had failed to take the storage precautions required by law. Finally, children could be restricted from possessing or using guns. Under current law, it is illegal for an eleven-year-old child like Andrew Golden to drive a car because he is too immature for that responsibility. It was perfectly legal, however, for Andrew's father to take him shooting and to give him military-like training designed to break down his inhibitions about killing people.[34] Whether the residents of Jonesboro wish to admit it or not, Shannon Wright, Natalie Brooks, and four other middle school children paid the price for their young killers' easy access to guns and the training at least one of them received. So do thousands of other victims each year. And so, of course, do the killers who spend their lives in jail.

We need to ask ourselves whether it is wise public policy to allow citizens unfettered access to lethal consumer products. If it is not, then options for limiting possession and specifying the terms of possession, like those mentioned here, ought to be considered. Although it can be argued that possessing a gun is a constitutionally protected right, it can also be argued that those wishing to exercise that right should take responsibility for doing so. Every owner of an automobile does just that, and no one thinks twice about fulfilling this obligation. It saves lives.

In addition to considering how to prevent firearms from being purchased and resold in neighborhoods where homicide rates are catastrophically high, such as the Englewood section of Chicago, the possibility of proactive measures to remove them from circulation should be discussed. As indicated previously, every large city in the United States has areas that display pervasive violence. But evidence suggests that when the police take concerted action to get guns off the streets of violent neighborhoods, the homicide rate falls. In chapter 5, I reviewed the Kansas City experiment to illustrate the impact that police activities can have on the possession of guns and the homicide rate in high-crime areas.[35] It constitutes an example of what is called in the jargon "problem oriented policing." Other examples exist. Thus, in Boston, Operation Ceasefire was more broadly based and produced better results. The Boston police worked in cooperation with various state and federal agencies, as well as with neighborhood residents, for the sole purpose of stopping gun-related violence. The agencies employed massive police presence and legal methods to remove from the streets guns and people who engaged in violence. Gang members and others were informed clearly and unmistakably that the way to keep the police off their backs was to avoid violence. Although the evidence should be interpreted cautiously, such proactive tactics have worked in other cities as well.[36] The keys to success for such strategies appear to be (1) the long-term application of significant police resources in small geographical areas, (2) honesty in communication with the objects of attention (the gangs), (3) cooperation among agencies (federal, state, and local), and (4) positive relationships with the community as a whole (not only leaders but also ordinary citizens).

But developing and implementing such strategies is easier said than done.

One difficulty is that local authorities may only superficially implement a plan that appears well crafted on paper. This problem appears a lot in police work.[37] Another difficulty is that people of color populate many of the areas characterized by high levels of violence, and African Americans and other minorities have learned over the years, often with good reason, to distrust the police.[38] But if these difficulties can be overcome, and the experience in Boston suggests they can be, then police efforts at removing guns from the streets might make a difference. Even so, while a "police solution" may have an impact, all observers agree that it will be limited unless coupled with changes in the degree of racial discrimination (especially housing segregation), the level of inequality, and other factors affecting the homicide rate.[39]

If the goal is to reduce the homicide rate, then these and other gun-related options need to be considered. If, on the other hand, Americans wish to live with a high rate of homicide, then these options should be rejected. But consider the following:

Would Barry Grunow (chapter 3) be dead today if the gun used to kill him had been personalized so that only its owner could use it?

Would Karen Farley (chapter 5) be dead today if the clerks at Guns Unlimited had been trained to spot and motivated to prevent straw purchases?

Would Galen Gibson and Ñacuñán Sáez (chapter 5) be dead today if the state of Massachusetts had required that anyone purchasing a gun, including out-of-state residents, had to wait thirty days?

Would Jermain Wilson be dead today if bulk purchases by gunrunners or their representatives were prevented?

Would Natalie Brooks and Shannon Wright be dead today if the guns used to kill them had been stored in a locked safe?

The answers to these questions are, of course, unknown. And these examples should be taken as illustrating some of the many ways people are murdered in America. In these and other cases, perhaps the killers were so motivated that they would have used other weapons. But this alternative would have made the murders more difficult. Or maybe the outcome would have been different if the victims had been carrying weapons of their own. Would a better solution have been for them to return fire? Gunfights happen in places like Englewood and the housing project where children like Lafayette Rivers live. Do such neighborhoods provide the model of how to make America a safer place? Some observers believe that it does. Gary Kleck, for example, argues that social order in this country may depend on millions of people going armed and being dangerous to one another.[40] Everyone going out and about armed is an option, one considered in some states. Given the inevitable uncertainty that accompanies proposals for change, the question becomes which type of proposal is more likely to reduce the homicide rate:

some reasonable limits on gun availability or encouraging everyone to arm themselves. Although the outcome cannot be known, if the latter policy is pursued, I fear we will end up hostage to the immature, the crazy, the angry—to every pretend Dirty Harry.

I have focused on some proposals for reducing gun availability because this variable is the most important factor producing a high homicide rate. In a multivariate analysis, it would be said to explain most of the variance. But it does not operate alone. The American anomaly results from other factors interrelated with gun availability, as shown by the working hypothesis.

## Illegal Drug Markets

Assume for the moment that no changes are made in gun availability or that guns become even more accessible; the question then becomes whether changes in other variables, such as the endemic violence associated with drug markets, can lead to a reduction in the homicide rate. Although there are no easy solutions to the drug problem in America, alternatives do exist if we are willing to consider them, if we are willing to think outside the lines of conventional wisdom. I use this variable as a second illustration of the structurally based choices this country faces if it wants to reduce the homicide rate.

In considering the possibilities, it should be recognized at the beginning that reducing the supply of illegal drugs to the extent that markets cannot function probably will not work. The cost of producing drugs is so low and the profits so great that a push-down, pop-up process occurs in which the suppression of drug production in one nation or region leads to its appearance in another. In addition, keeping drugs out of the country is extremely difficult, mainly because open borders are essential to trade.[41] One border-crossing site provides an example: At San Ysidro, California, the gateway to San Diego and beyond, more than 40 million people enter the United States legally each year, nearly all of them honest travelers. And this entryway is only one of thousands. It only takes a few individuals hidden among the masses entering this country every year to smuggle in large amounts of illegal substances, and if some are caught, that is merely a (very small) cost of doing business. Hence, while continuing to work with other nations to reduce production and continuing to interdict drug shipments coming into the United States, we should not have unrealistic expectations about success on these fronts. It is a truism in economics that supply will always rise to meet demand, and experience has shown that drugs are no different than other consumer products.

In this context, it seems to me, our most practical choice is to focus on reducing demand. The United States, it is said, consumes 60 percent of the world's supply of illegal substances.[42] Although it is not clear how this figure is obtained, there is little doubt that Americans consume a lot of drugs—legal and illegal. Our goal should be to reduce the level of drug use and abuse in this country in as humane a way as possible and at the lowest cost. If demand falls, the markets will atrophy and the violence should fall as well.

One option might be to continue the current emphasis on zero tolerance, which focuses on locking up people involved with certain drugs. Arrest data illustrate how this policy has been pursued over the past few decades. In 1980, local, state, and federal authorities arrested almost 600,000 persons for drug law violations. By the year 2000, however, this figure had risen to 1.6 million persons. More than 80 percent of these arrests were for possession, and more than half of them were for marijuana possession. Of those arrested for selling illicit substances, nearly all were low-level dealers, such as the gang members described in chapter 5. The capture of low-level dealers is common. The drug industry is very decentralized, such that the key players who make most of the profit remain hidden—and safe from arrest.[43] They do not care about the violence inherent in the markets; it is in fact one basis for their profits.

It follows from the arrest data that the state and federal prison population has been transformed during this same period. Among state prisoners in 1980, violations of drug laws constituted the most serious offense for only 6 percent. By 1999, this figure had risen to 21 percent; again, this refers to the most serious offense for which they were imprisoned. And again, most of these convictions were for possession. Among federal prisoners, only 16 percent were convicted of drug offenses in 1970. By 2000, this figure had risen to 57 percent. Of these, more than half of the convictions were for possession. As a result of all these arrests and convictions, prisons are over capacity in the federal system and twenty-two states. The other twenty-eight states are at capacity. This result exists despite massive prison construction around the country over the last thirty years.[44] As mentioned in chapter 1, the United States now imprisons five times more people than do all of the countries in the European Union. Even allowing for plea-bargaining, most of them are in prison for nonviolent offenses. The logic underlying this strategy is that the threat and reality of arrest and imprisonment will deter both sellers and users of illegal drugs.

The current emphasis on zero tolerance, however, carries with it unintended consequences that support the existence of illegal drug markets. First, illegal drugs cost pennies to grow, manufacture, and smuggle into this country, but their illicit nature keeps prices—and profits—very high. In effect, keeping cocaine, heroin, and marijuana illegal amounts to imposing a tariff that supports the markets by raising the prices consumers pay to astronomical levels. Second, locking up street-level dealers has little deterrent effect; it merely produces job openings. It is a little like jailing a corporate executive: The possibility of good pay in an anomic context where few legitimate jobs are available means that someone will move into the vacated "office" rather soon. Third, in addition to the development of crack cocaine in the 1980s, in at least one other case the illegal nature of the product along with enhanced enforcement has led to scientific advance that stimulates illegal drug markets. Thus, also in the early 1980s, the government systematically went after domestic marijuana growers, using aerial surveillance and other methods to capture them. The result was a horticultural revolution as production moved indoors and underground, and new high-potency strains have been developed and entered the marketplace. Fourth, and most important for my purposes, such markets remain exceedingly violent without affecting either drug supply or demand. The reason for the violence, of course, is that the distribution and sale of certain substances occurs outside the law. In comparison, as Superior Court Judge James Gray points out in one of the better critiques of current drug policy, if a distributor of Coors beer had a dispute with a distributor of Budweiser over sales territory or products, it is unlikely they would resort to a shootout. They would meet in court rather than the street. There may be a lesson here.[45]

Nonetheless, some argue that the United States should live with these consequences—including the high rate of homicide in many urban neighborhoods—and expand on "lock 'em up" policies to give zero tolerance real teeth. First, penalties for possession could be increased. For example, under current law, possession of 5,000 grams of cocaine leads to a mandatory prison sentence of ten years; 500 grams means five years. Why not require ten years for 500 grams and five years for 50 grams? Second, penalties for dealing could be increased. For example, drug dealers could be sentenced to death. Third, "humiliation sentences" could be imposed, such as hanging signs on people's houses spelling out their drug-related crimes. Fourth, unrelated penalties could be imposed, such as driver's license suspension or denial of student loans. Fifth, search and seizure rules could be eased even more than they have been. Thus, the police could search anyone at any time for any reason. All these and other proposals have been suggested over the last few years, often in bills placed before Congress but not passed.[46]

In one form or another, zero tolerance via arrest and imprisonment has represented the standard wisdom underlying drug policy in America for nearly a century. Although rarely stated explicitly, the radically increased emphasis on incarceration over the last three decades or so constitutes a policy experiment designed to reduce drug use. One wonders, however, whether it will ever succeed. Moreover, even if zero tolerance eventually reduced drug use from current levels, perhaps if proposals like those described just above are enacted, it is hard to see how the markets would become less violent. The question is whether it is wise to continue pursuing the same type of policies over and over again, always hoping for different results. Maybe we should consider trying something else, especially if we wish to reduce the homicide rate.

The difficulty with trying something else, however, is that the notion of zero tolerance is imbued with a certain moralism that leads both government policy makers and other defenders to refuse to discuss alternatives and demonize as "soft on drugs" those proposing to do so. This attitude is counterproductive. As Judge Gray comments, the discussion of various options to reduce the demand for certain drugs does not mean that observers espousing one or another point of view approve of drug use and abuse.[47] It is possible that one lesson that can be taken from the last three decades of drug policy is that the United States never will be a drug-free society. If this conclusion is correct, as Judge Gray (and others) suggest, then perhaps we ought to abandon the moralist stance and adopt a managerial one. Perhaps we can manage the drug problem so as to minimize harm, not only to users but also to the community in the form of lethal violence. The question is, how? Are other strategies available that might help the United States reduce the level of drug use and abuse in a humane way and at a lower cost (in lives as well as money) than zero tolerance policies?

Among the alternatives to zero tolerance, the most radical option to think about would be to legalize marijuana, cocaine, and heroin in a regulated way analogous to alcohol or cigarettes—or guns. Although this strategy may seem imprudent in the current moralistic context, how does the notion of a state store for drugs differ so much from the state-regulated gun shops that exist in every city? Moreover, this option is worth considering if only to highlight the structural choices we face. For example, this option embodies a basic insight from economics: The only way to destroy an illegal market is to offer the same product legally at a lower price. If adults (not children) could purchase, say, cocaine, at a state store similar to a gun shop, the illegal dealers would have far fewer clients. Some potential advantages are that (1) deaths and injuries due to impurities would fall, (2) profits would stay in the country and be taxed, and (3) most important, the lethal violence characteristic of many urban neighborhoods would decline. Other benefits might ensue.[48] Even if use rates went up, which is a major potential disadvantage, it is possible that people would consume less dangerous drugs than alcohol and cigarettes. The point to remember in thinking about this and other options is that making a product legal does not imply approval. Simply because tobacco is legal does not imply approval of smoking. Simply because alcoholic beverages are legal does not imply approval of getting drunk. Most generally, thinking about the legalization of certain drugs does not make their use right—or healthy. Remember the goal: to manage the problem of drug use so as to reduce harm and save lives.

In this regard, if legalization in the form of regulated distribution were coupled with honest educational campaigns and increases in the availability of treatment facilities for those wishing to stop abusing drugs, overall use rates might not rise; they might decline. That has certainly been the American experience with cigarettes and the experience of other Western nations with illegal substances.[49] For example, let us say that a unit of cocaine selling on the street for, say, $10 was sold to adults at a state store for $2.50. Of this amount, $0.75 could go to the grower/producer, $0.75 could go to the retailer, and $1.00 could be a tax used for education about and treatment of drug abuse. The long-term impact of the campaign against cigarette smoking provides a good model of how educational efforts that provide accurate and practical information can change behavior (and it is more difficult to stop using tobacco products than these other substances). Moreover, as I will suggest later, for those who are or become addicted, treatment is much more effective and costs less than incarceration. Of course, the numbers in this example merely illustrate the general principle of destroying the illegal market by underpricing it and using the proceeds to reduce demand for the products. If many of the street dealers could not compete, then fewer of them would be walking around with lots of cash, vulnerable to robbery, and fewer of them would disagree over sales territory and other matters. In such a context, the homicide rate might fall and parents would not feel the need to spend precious resources on burial insurance for their children.

Another option is to keep marijuana, cocaine, and heroin illegal to provide leverage for dealing with disruptive drug-related conflicts, but direct the police to overlook private behavior. The idea, here, as one observer comments, is that "we should reserve our prison space for people we are afraid of, instead of people we are mad at."[50] So drug users would be arrested when they endangered others or acted out by disturbing the peace in some form. Otherwise, users would be directed into treatment. Treatment facilities would have to be widespread and easily available, preferably at little or no charge. At present, a huge prison-industrial complex exists that lobbies for increased prison funding—at great expense to the public. Although the numbers vary from state to state and in the federal prison system, it costs between $20,000 and $30,000 to house each inmate for a year. But many nonviolent drug offenders will grow old in prison, mainly because of three-strike laws, and outlays for them will more than double, to an estimated $69,000 per year.[51]

Consider these huge costs in light of the fact that studies show that treatment is effective. For example, one estimate of the impact of outpatient treatment shows that weekly use of cocaine declined from 42 to 18 percent and weekly use of marijuana declined from 25 to 9 percent. Similarly, one estimate of long-term inpatient treatment shows that weekly use of cocaine fell from 66 to 22 percent and weekly use of heroin fell from 17 to 6 percent.[52] Note that use rates did not fall to zero. Anyone who has tried to quit smoking knows that relapse is common and it often takes several attempts to really quit. As Mark Twain once said, "giving up smoking is easy. I've done it lots of times."[53] So expectations of the impact of drug treatment need to be realistic. It is not like taking out an appendix: here today and gone tomorrow. It is more like treating someone with high blood pressure, diabetes, hypertension, or asthma: a continuing process that takes time. No one thinks it odd that many people find it hard to comply with the medication regimen for such ailments. In fact, noncompliance rates for these four diseases and drug relapse rates after treatment are roughly similar.[54] Moreover, from a policy (but not necessarily individual) angle, "successful" treatment does not always mean abstinence. Just as people with high blood pressure may sometimes eat foods they should not, those who go through treatment sometimes use drugs—but they do so less often and in smaller amounts than before. They also commit fewer crimes, especially crimes of violence. The Dutch experience with treatment and education is instructive. Over the past few years, use of marijuana by teenagers in the Netherlands has fallen to about half that in the United States; use of hard drugs like cocaine and heroin has declined as well. The average age of drug users in the Netherlands has risen, suggesting that fewer young people are becoming addicted.[55] Homicide rates in the Netherlands are very low (see figure 3.1). Is this fact accidental?

Compared to prison, the savings that follow from an emphasis on treatment are potentially spectacular. Shown in table 6.1 are yearly cost estimates per addict for various forms of treatment, compared to the cost of keeping a person in the federal prison system.

These data suggest that treatment (depending on its form) costs the public only 10 to 25 percent as much as imprisonment. And most prisoners are there for possession violations. Moreover, additional savings would accrue because health care expenses for addicts plunge after treatment.[56] Is it wise to pursue zero tolerance policies by continuing to spend billions of dollars of public resources on law enforcement and prisons, year after year, hoping for a different result? Hoping the violence will decline?

Although other options undoubtedly exist for reducing the demand for drugs and the violence associated with the markets, the last one I want to

**Table 6.1. Estimated Annual Costs per Person for Various Medical Treatments and Imprisonment**

| Treatment | Cost |
|---|---|
| Regular Outpatient Treatment | $ 1,800 |
| Intensive Outpatient Treatment | $ 2,500 |
| Methadone Maintenance | $ 3,900 |
| Short-Term Residential Treatment | $ 4,400 |
| Long-Term Residential Treatment | $ 6,800 |
| Prison | $25,900 |

*Sources:* Physician Leadership on National Drug Policy (2000:16). Other estimates are similar; see Gray (2001); Falco (1994).

mention suggests one way in which drug markets are connected to other variables in the working hypothesis: increasing employment opportunities and reducing the level of inequality in the United States. This country, you will recall, displays greater inequality (as revealed by the Gini Coefficient) than any of the nations shown in figure 3.1, and studies reveal that this factor is directly associated with the homicide rate. Inequality is also, of course, related to drug use and the expansion of illegal drug markets. Hence, a strategy aimed at reducing inequality would be designed to have both direct and indirect effects: to reduce the homicide rate directly by reducing the level of frustration and anger in the population and reduce demand for illegal drugs. Those who are most successful at getting off drugs have jobs and other external supports.[57] The more people who have income, hope, stability, something to do, and meaning in their lives, the fewer will retreat or seek alternative means to success.

Alas, alternatives to zero tolerance policies are rarely discussed in any meaningful way. It has been said that you can outlaw political corruption but cannot make it unpopular. Zero tolerance policies, I suspect, are similar. Even so, given what is known and allowing for its possible imperfections, the question that should be asked is what types of proposals are likely to reduce the viability of illegal drug markets—and their violence. And then we need to talk about them without ideological or moralistic blinders.

The two illustrations described in this chapter are designed to suggest the types of structural changes that are necessary to reduce the homicide rate in the United States. Just as the availability of guns, illegal drug markets, and the other variables in the working hypothesis are interrelated, so are potential changes. Assume for the moment that this country moved to reduce the availability of guns and, at the same time, undercut the economic basis of illegal drug markets. One suspects that the level of lethal violence would decline compared to that in Western Europe. It is a thought to consider.

## CONCLUDING COMMENTS

Of course, nothing is sure. Change can have unexpected and unforeseen consequences. But is it prudent to retain the status quo? If the United States continues with the same policies that produce high gun availability and illegal drug markets and makes no changes in the other variables included in the working hypothesis, the odds are that homicide rates will remain high as well. Expecting a different result from current policies is unrealistic. In chapter 1, I outlined some of the consequences of the American anomaly: (1) Lives are lost, which means that talent is wasted and whatever people would be—wives, husbands, parents, and all the other mundane aspects of living and contributing to the community—just does not happen; (2) the public's exposure to violence is high, which continues the cycle of violence in our cities and towns; (3) the medical and legal costs are staggering, and productivity is lost; (4) finally, the trauma to the survivors is profound. Is this the kind of society in which we wish to live?

This is, of course, a value-laden question. Although Max Weber may have misinterpreted the nature of modern societies, he understood clearly the nature of social science and its relationship to values. Is there, he asked, a scientific basis for deciding about public policy toward issues like guns or drugs? His answer was simple: No. Social science, he argued, informs and explains. Only values guide action.[58]

Again: Is this the kind of society in which we wish to live? Failure to consider alternative ways of organizing our society means, quite bluntly, that every American's personal safety and survival will remain hostage to the crazy, the immature, and the violent—whether at home, at school, at work, or visiting the Art Institute in Chicago. The opening scenes of this chapter symbolize the dilemma we face. A society in which children living in poor neighborhoods must crawl through the dirt to avoid being shot by the day's volley of gunfire has something deeply wrong with it. A society in which eleven-year-olds and their teachers place their lives on the line each day they go to school is terribly damaged. Change is possible.

## NOTES

1. Kotlowitz (1991:3). The quotations below are from p. x.

2. On the events in Jonesboro, see Kifner (1998); Bragg (1998; 1998a; 1998b); Verhovek (1998; 1998a); and Chen (1998). The quotation below from Shannon Wright is from Kifner, p. 16.

3. Quoted in Verhovek (1998:14).

4. On the history of homicide victimization of African Americans, see Lane (1997). Monkkonen (1989) argues that significant differences between African American and white homicide rates did not occur until the second half of the nineteenth century. The current African American homicide rate is from Federal Bureau of Investigation (2000).

5. National Center for Health Statistics (2000:26); Bailey et al. (1997); Violence Policy Center (2000).

6. Hemenway et al. (2002). All the cross-national data presented here come from this source.

7. Berger (1977:vii).

8. Berger (1977a).

9. Hofstadter (1970). See also Kennett and Anderson (1975).

10. Messner and Rosenfeld (2001:3). In what immediately follows, I draw on Turner and Musick (1985:14).

11. Blair and Weissman (2000).

12. See Gibson (1999:143–55), who describes the logic of this orientation.

13. Kleck (1991:44–45). See also Cook (1981).

14. See Bogus (2000). For good chapter-length treatments, see Spitzer (1998:17–43) and Carter (1997:23–36).

15. Diaz (1999:24).

16. Spitzer (1998: 41).

17. Vernick and Teret (2000).

18. Teret et al. (1998a).

19. Teret et al. (1998); Cook and Leitzel (2002).

20. Teret et al. (1998a).

21. Wintemute (1994).

22. Wintemute et al. (1998).

23. Teret et al. (1998a).

24. Webster et al. (2002).

25. Vernick et al. (1997).

26. Kellerman et al. (1993).

27. Office of Juvenile Justice and Delinquency Prevention (1999); see also Butterfield (1999a).

28. Butterfield (1999; 1999a).

29. Weil and Knox (1996). All the material in the remainder of this paragraph comes from this source.

30. See the exchange between Blackman (1996) and Weil (1996).

31. Teret et al. (1998a).

32. Orr (1997); Marvel (2000). Dr. Marvel, by the way, practices medicine in Jonesboro, Arkansas.

33. Waller (2000:102).

34. Recall the work of military psychologist Dave Grossman (1996).

35. Sherman et al. (1995).

36. National Institute of Justice (2001). This remarkable document is worth reading. Also on Boston, see Patterson and Winship (1999). For other examples, see Office of Juvenile Justice and Delinquency Prevention (1999).

37. Eck and Maguire (2000:245).

38. Anderson (1999:321).

39. Eck and Maguire (2000). They provide an appropriately cautious review of the literature on the ability of the police to prevent crime.

40. Kleck (1991:143).

41. Nadelman (1988); Ostrowski (1989); Gray (2001:47–61); Brzezinski (2002). The 40 million figure is from Brzezinski, p. 29.

42. Goode (1989).

43. Brzezinski (2002).

44. State and local arrest and conviction data are from Bureau of Justice Statistics (2001d). Federal data are from Bureau of Justice Statistics (2001a:526). Reasons for conviction are from Bureau of Justice Statistics (2001d). Capacity data are from Bureau of Justice Statistics (2001e).

45. First, Brzezinski (2002); second, Reuter (1991) and Shenk (1995); third, Pollan (1995); fourth, Reuter (1991) and Gray (2001:68). Many others have made all these points.

46. Gray (2001:91–123, 151–65).
47. Gray (2001:142–49).
48. Ostrowski (1989).
49. Gray (2001:218–21). The following example of the cost of cocaine is taken from Gray, p. 223.
50. Quoted in Gray (2001:182).
51. Gray (2001:37).
52. Physician Leadership on National Drug Policy (2000:29–34).
53. Quoted in Gray (2001:197).
54. Physician Leadership on National Drug Policy (2000:41).
55. Gray (2001:218–21).
56. Physician Leadership on National Drug Policy (2000:21).
57. Falco (1994).
58. Weber (1904).

# References

Adler, Jeffrey S. 1997. "'My Mother-in-Law Is to Blame, But I'll Walk on Her Neck Yet': Homicide in Late Nineteenth Century Chicago." *Journal of Social History* 31:253–76.

———. 1999. "'The Negro Would Be More Than an Angel to Withstand Such Treatment': African American Homicide in Chicago, 1875–1910." In *Lethal Imagination: Violence and Brutality in American History,* edited by Michael A. Bellesiles, 295–314. New York: New York University Press.

———. 2000. "'Halting the Slaughter of the Innocents': The Civilizing Process and the Surge in Violence in Turn-of-the-Century Chicago." *Social Science History* 25:29–52.

Adler, Patricia A. 1985. *Wheeling and Dealing: An Ethnography of an Upper-Level Dealing and Smuggling Community.* New York: Columbia University Press.

Akers, Ronald L. 2000. *Criminological Theories: Introduction, Evaluation, and Application.* 3d ed. Los Angeles: Roxbury Press.

Alba, Richard D., and Steven F. Messner. 1995. "*Point Blank* Against Itself: Evidence and Inference about Guns, Crime, and Gun Control." *Journal of Quantitative Criminology* 11:391–410.

———. 1995a. "*Point Blank* and the Evidence: A Rejoinder to Gary Kleck." *Journal of Quantitative Criminology* 11:425–28.

Allen, James, Hilton Als, John Lewis, and Leon F. Litwack. 2000. *Without Sanctuary: Lynching Photography in America.* Santa Fe, NM: Twin Palms Press.

American Psychological Association. 1993. *Violence & Youth: Psychology's Response.* New York: American Psychological Association.

Anderson, Craig A. 1998. "Does the Gun Pull the Trigger?: Automatic Priming Effects of Weapons Pictures and Weapon Names." *Psychological Science* 9:308–15.

Anderson, Elijah. 1994. "The Code of the Streets." *The Atlantic Monthly* 273(May):80–110.

———. 1999. *The Code of the Street: Decency, Violence, and the Moral Life of the Inner City.* New York: Norton.

Archer, Dane, and Rosemary Gartner. 1984. *Violence and Crime in Cross-National Perspective.* New Haven, CT: Yale University Press.

191

Associated Press. 2000. "Grief, Disbelief Follow Teacher Shooting." *Gainesville Sun,* May 16:1.

Association of Community Organizations for Reform Now. 1999. *Giving No Credit Where Credit Is Due: An Analysis of Home Purchase Mortgage Lending in Thirty-Five Cities, 1995–1997.* Washington, DC: Association of Community Organizations for Reform Now.

Athens, Lonnie. 1989. *The Creation of Dangerous Violent Criminals.* New York: Routledge.

———. 1997. *Violent Criminal Acts and Actors Revisited.* Chicago: University of Illinois Press.

Atkinson, Anthony B., Lee Rainwater, and Timothy M. Smeeding. 1995. *Income Distribution in OECD Countries.* Paris: Organization for Economic Cooperation and Development.

Attala, Janice M., Kerry Bauza, Heather Pratt, and Denise Vieira. 1995. "Integrative Review of Effects on Children of Witness Domestic Violence." *Issues in Comprehensive Pediatric Nursing* 18:163–72.

Avison, William R., and Pamela L. Loring. 1986. "Population Diversity and Cross-National Homicide: The Effects of Inequality and Heterogeneity." *Criminology* 24:733–49.

Azrael, Deborah, Philip J. Cook, and Mathew Miller. 2001. "State and Local Prevalence of Firearms Ownership: Measurement, Structure, and Trends." Working Paper Series, SAN01-25. Terry Sanford Institute of Public Policy, Duke University, Durham, NC.

Bailey, James E., Arthur L. Kellerman, and Grant W. Somes, et al. 1997. "Risk Factors for Violent Death of Women in the Home." *Archives of Internal Medicine* 157(April 14):777–82.

Baker, S. P. 1985. "Without Guns, Do People Kill People?" *American Journal of Public Health* 75:587–88.

Bandura, Albert. 1983. "Psychological Mechanisms of Aggression." In *Aggression: Theoretical and Empirical Reviews, Vol. 1,* edited by R. G. Green and E. I. Donnerstein, 1–40. New York: Academic Press.

Barclay, Gordon, Cynthia Tavares, and Arsalaan Siddique. 2001. *International Comparisons of Criminal Justice Statistics.* Home Office Statistical Bulletin, Issue 6/01. London: Home Office. Available at www.homeoffice.gov.uk/rds/hosbpubs1.html.

Barry, D. S. 1993. "Growing up Violent: Decades of Research Link Screen Mayhem with Increase in Aggressive Behavior." *Media and Values* 6:8–11.

Bebber, Charles. 1994. "Increases in U.S. Violent Crime During the 1980s Following Four American Military Actions." *Journal of Interpersonal Violence* 9:109–16.

Beeghley, Leonard. 1996. *What Does Your Wife Do? Gender and the Transformation of Family Life.* Boulder, CO: Westview.

———. 1999. *Angles of Vision: How to Understand Social Problems.* Boulder, CO: Westview.

———. 2000. *The Structure of Stratification.* 3d ed. Boston: Allyn & Bacon.

Beeghley, Leonard, John K. Cochran, and E. Wilbur Bock. 1990. "The Religious Switcher and Alcohol Use: An Application of Reference Group Theory." *Sociological Forum* 5:261–78.

Bellesiles, Michael A. 2000. *Arming America: The Origins of a National Gun Culture*. New York: Knopf.

Berger, Peter L. 1977. *Facing up to Modernity*. New York: Basic Books.

———. 1977a. "Sociology and Freedom." In *Facing up to Modernity*, edited by P. L. Berger, ix–x. New York: Basic Books.

———. 1986. *The Capitalist Revolution*. New York: Basic Books.

———. 1992. *A Far Glory: The Quest for Faith in an Age of Credulity*. New York: Free Press.

Berkowitz, Leonard. 1963. *Aggression: A Social-Psychological Analysis*. New York: McGraw-Hill.

———. 1989. "Frustration-Aggression Hypothesis: Examination and Reformulation." *Psychological Bulletin* 106:59–73.

Bjerregaard, Beth, and Alan J. Lizotte. 1995. "Gun Ownership and Gang Membership." *Journal of Criminal Law & Criminology* 86:37–58.

Black, Dan A., and Daniel S. Nagin. 1998. "Do Right-to-Carry Laws Deter Violent Crime?" *Journal of Legal Studies* 27:209–19.

Black, Donald. 1983. "Crime as Social Control." *American Sociological Review* 48: 34–45.

Blackman, Paul H. 1996. "Effectiveness of Legislation Limiting Handgun Purchases" (letter to the editor). *Journal of the American Medical Association* 276:1036–37.

Blair, Jayson, and Sarah Weissman. 2000. "The Biography of a Gun." *New York Times*, National Edition. April 9, A1.

Blau, Judith R., and Peter M. Blau. 1982. "The Cost of Inequality: Metropolitan Structure and Violent Crime." *American Sociological Review* 47:114–29.

Blau, Peter M. 1977. *Inequality and Heterogeneity*. New York: Free Press.

Blau, Peter M., and Otis Dudley Duncan. 1967. *The American Occupational Structure*. New York: Wiley.

Blau, Peter M., and Reid M. Golden. 1986. "Metropolitan Structure and Criminal Violence." *Sociological Quarterly* 27:15–26.

Block, Caroline Rebecca, Antigone Christakos, Ayad Jacob, et al. 1996. *Street Gangs and Crime: Patterns and Trends in Chicago*. Research Bulletin. Chicago: Illinois Criminal Justice Information Authority.

Block, Robert, and Caroline Rebecca Block. 1993. *Street Gang Crime in Chicago*. Research in Brief. Washington, DC: National Institute of Justice.

Blumstein, Alfred. 1993. "Making Rationality Relevant—The American Society of Criminology 1992 Presidential Address." *Criminology* 31:1–16.

———. 1995. "Youth Violence, Guns, and the Illicit-Drug Industry." *Journal of Criminal Law and Criminology* 86:10–36.

———. 1998. "Explaining Recent Trends in U.S. Homicide Rates." *Journal of Criminal Law and Criminology* 88:1175–92.

Blumstein, Alfred, and Daniel Cork. 1996. "Linking Gun Availability to Youth Gun Violence." *Law and Contemporary Problems* 59:5–24.

Blumstein, Alfred, and Joel Wallman (eds.). 2000. *The Crime Drop in America*. New York: Cambridge University Press.

Bogus, Carl (ed.). 2000. *The Second Amendment in Law and History: Historians and Constitutional Scholars on the Right to Bear Arms*. New York: New Press.

Boschi, Daniele. 1998. "Homicide and Knife Fighting in Rome, 1845–1914." In *Men and Violence,* edited by Pieter Spirenburg, 121–43. Columbus: Ohio State University Press.

Bragg, Rick. 1998. "5 Are Killed at School; Boys, 11 and 13, Are Held." *New York Times,* National Edition. March 25, A1.

———. 1998a. "Arkansas Boys Held as Prosecutors Weigh Options." *New York Times,* National Edition. March 26, A1.

———. 1998b. "Determined to Find Healing in a Good and Decent Place." *New York Times,* National Edition. March 27, A1.

Braithwaite, John, and Valerie Braithwaite. 1980. "The Effect of Income Inequality and Social Democracy on Homicide." *British Journal of Criminology* 20:45–53.

Brearley, Huntington C. 1932. *Homicide in the United States.* Chapel Hill, NC: University of North Carolina Press.

Brim, Orville G. 1966. "Socialization through the Life-cycle." In *Socialization after Childhood,* edited by O. G. Brim and S. Wheeler, 1–49. New York: Wiley.

Britt, Chester L., Gary Kleck, and David Bordua. 1996. "Notes on the Use of Interrupted Time Series Designs for Policy Impact Assessment." *Law & Society Review* 30:361–80.

Brown, Richard Maxwell. 1975. *Strain of Violence: Historical Studies of American Violence and Vigilantism.* New York: Oxford University Press.

Browne, Harry. 2000. "Harry Browne's Stand on Gun Control," at www.harrybrowne2000.org.

Brundage, W. Fitzhugh. 1997. "Introduction." In *Under Sentence of Death: Lynching in the South,* edited by W. F. Brundage, 1–23. Chapel Hill, NC: University of North Carolina Press.

Brzezinski, Matthew. 2002. "Re-Engineering the Drug Business." *New York Times Magazine* (June 23):24–29, 46–54.

Buka, Stephen L., Theresa L. Stichick, Isolde Birdthistle, and Felton J. Earls. 2001. "Youth Exposure to Violence." *American Journal of Orthopsychiatry* 71:298–310.

Bureau of Justice Statistics. 2000. *Homicide Trends in the United States,* at www.ojp.usdoj.gov/bjs.

———. 2000a. *Sourcebook of Criminal Justice Statistics 1999.* Washington, DC: Government Printing Office.

———. 2001. *Homicide Trends in the United States,* at www.ojp.usdoj.gov/bjs.

———. 2001a. *Sourcebook of Criminal Justice Statistics 2000.* Washington, DC: Government Printing Office.

———. 2001b. "National Correctional Population Reaches a New High." Press Release, August 26. Washington, DC: Government Printing Office.

———. 2001c. *Crime and Justice in the United States and in England and Wales, 1981–96.* Washington, DC: Government Printing Office.

———. 2001d. *Drugs and Crime Facts,* at www.ojp.usdoj.gov/bjs.

———. 2001e. "Prisoners in 2000." *Bureau of Justice Statistics Bulletin* (August). Washington, DC: Government Printing Office.

Bureau of Labor Statistics. 2001. *Employment and Earnings,* at stats.bls.gov/cpsaatab.html.

Bursik, Robert J. 1988. "Social Disorganization and Theories of Crime and Delinquency: Problems and Prospects." *Criminology* 26:519–51.

Bushman, Brad J., and L. Rowell Huesmann. 2001. "Effects of Televised Violence on Aggression." In *Handbook of Children and the Media,* edited by D. G. Singer and J. L. Singer, 223–54. Thousand Oaks, CA: Sage.

Butterfield, Fox. 1996. *All God's Children: The Bosket Family and the American Tradition of Violence.* New York: Avon Books.

———. 1998. "Decline of Violent Crimes Is Linked to Crack Market. Efforts to Seize Guns May Also Be a Factor." *New York Times,* National Edition, December 28, A18.

———. 1999. "Most Crime Guns Are Bought, Not Stolen." *New York Times,* National Edition, April 30, A12.

———. 1999a. "Gun Flow to Criminals Laid to Tiny Fraction of Dealers." *New York Times,* National Edition, July 1, A15.

———. 1999b. "Police Chiefs Shift Strategy, Mounting a War on Weapons." *New York Times,* National Edition, October 7, A1.

———. 2000. "Data Hint Crime Plunge May Be Leveling Off." *New York Times,* National Edition, December 19, A18.

Campbell, Donald T., and Julian C. Stanley. 1963. *Experimental and Quasi-experimental Designs for Research.* Boston: Houghton Mifflin.

Canada, Geoffrey. 1995. *Fist Stick Knife Gun: A Personal History of Violence in America.* Boston: Beacon Press.

Canedy, Dana. 2001. "Boy Who Killed Teacher Gets 28 Years and No Parole." *New York Times,* National Edition, July 28, A7.

Carter, Gregg Lee. 1997. *The Gun Control Movement.* New York: Twayne Publishers.

Center for Media and Public Affairs. 1999. "Merchandising Mayhem: Violence in Popular Entertainment 1998–99." *Media Monitor* 13(September/October):1–8.

Centers for Disease Control. 1991. *Position Papers from the Third National Injury Conference: Setting the National Agenda for Injury Control in the 1990s.* Washington, DC: U.S. Dept. of Health & Human Services.

———. 2000. "Youth Risk Behavior Surveillance—United States, 1999." *Morbidity & Mortality Weekly Report,* June 9: 1–96.

Chamlin, Mitchell, and John K. Cochran. 1995. "Assessing Messner and Rosenfeld's Institutional Anomie Theory: A Partial Test." *Criminology* 33:411–29.

Chen, David W. 1998. "4 Young Lives End Amid the Trivia of Being Young." *New York Times,* National Edition. March 26, A20.

Chicago Police Department. 1999. *Annual Report, 1998.* Chicago: Chicago Police Department.

Cochran, John K., and Leonard Beeghley. 1996. "Religious Stability, Endogamy, and the Effects of Personal Religiosity on Attitudes Toward Abortion." *Sociology of Religion* 57:291–311.

Cochran, John K., Mitchell B. Chamlin, and Mark Seth. 1994. "Deterrence or Brutalization? An Impact Assessment of Oklahoma's Return to Capital Punishment." *Criminology* 32:107–33.

Cockburn, J. S. 1977. *Crime in England, 1550–1800.* Princeton, NJ: Princeton University Press.

Cohen, Esther. 1996. "The Hundred Years' War and Crime in Paris, 1332–1488." In *The Civilization of Crime: Violence in Town and Country since the Middle Ages,* edited by E. A. Johnson and E. H. Monkkonen, 109–24. Urbana, IL: University of Illinois Press.

Collins, Randal. 1986. *Max Weber: A Skeleton Key.* Beverly Hills, CA: Sage.

Cook, Philip J. 1979. "The Effects of Gun Availability on Robbery and Robbery Murder: A Cross-Section Study of Fifty Cities." In *Policy Studies Review Annual, Vol. 3,* edited by Robert H. Haveman and B. Bruce Zellner, 743–81. Beverly Hills, CA: Sage.

———. 1981. "Guns and Crime: The Perils of Long Division." *Journal of Policy Analysis and Management* 1:120–25.

———. 1991. "The Technology of Personal Violence." In *Crime and Justice, Vol. 14,* Michael Tonry, 1–67. Chicago: University of Chicago Press.

Cook, Philip J., Lawrence A. Bruce, Jens Ludwig, et al. 1999. "The Medical Costs of Gunshot Injuries in the United States." *Journal of the American Medical Association* 282:447–54.

Cook, Philip J., and James A. Leitzel. 2002. "'Smart' Guns: A Technological Fix Regulating the Secondary Market." *Contemporary Economic Policy* 20:38–50.

Cook, Philip J., and Jens Ludwig. 1997. *Guns in America: National Survey on Private Ownership and Use of Firearms.* Research in Brief. Washington, DC: National Institute of Justice.

Cook, Philip J., Jens Ludwig, and David Hemenway. 1997. "The Gun Debate's New Mythical Number: How Many Defensive Uses per Year?" *Journal of Policy Analysis & Management* 16:463–70.

Cooney, Mark. 1997. "The Decline of Elite Homicide." *Criminology* 35:381–407.

———. 1998. *Warriors and Peacemakers: How Third Parties Shape Violence.* New York: New York University Press.

Copeland, Monica, William Rectenwald, and Sharman Stein. 1991. "Englewood Longs for the Safe Old Days." *Chicago Tribune,* December 29, Section 2, 1–3.

Corzine, Jay, Lynn Huff-Corzine, and Hugh P. Whitt. 1999. "Cultural and Subcultural Theories of Homicide." In *Homicide: A Sourcebook of Social Research,* edited by M. D. Smith and M. A. Zahn, 42–57. Thousand Oaks, CA: Sage.

Crandall, Cameron, Lenora M. Olson, and David P. Sklar. 2001. "Mortality Reduction with Air Bag and Seat Belt Use in Head-on Passenger Car Collisions." *American Journal of Epidemiology* 153:219–24.

Curtis, Lynn A. 1974. *Criminal Violence: National Patterns and Behavior.* Lexington, MA: Lexington Books.

Cutright, Phillips, and Carl Briggs. 1995. "Structural and Cultural Determinants of Adult Homicide in Developed Countries: Age and Gender Specific Rates, 1955–1989." *Sociological Focus* 28:221–43.

Decker, Scott H. 1993. "Exploring Victim-Offender Relationships in Homicide: The Role of Individual and Event Characteristics." *Justice Quarterly* 10:585–612.

DePalma, Anthony. 1992. "Questions Outweigh Answers in Shooting Spree at College." *New York Times,* National Edition. December 28, A-1.

Department of Justice. 1995. *The Nation's Two Crime Measures.* Washington, DC: Government Printing Office.

Deutsch, Stephen Jay, and Francis B. Alt. 1977. "The Effect of Massachusetts' Gun Control Law on Gun-Related Crimes in the City of Boston." *Evaluation Quarterly* 1:543–68.

Diaz, Tom. 1999. *Making a Killing: The Business of Guns in America*. New York: The New Press.

Dixon, J., and Alan J. Lizotte. 1987. "Gun Ownership and the Southern Subculture of Violence." *American Journal of Sociology* 93:383–405.

Duggan, Mark. 2000. "More Guns, More Crime." Working Paper 7967. Cambridge, MA: National Bureau of Economic Research.

Durkheim, Emile. 1895. *The Rules of the Sociological Method*. New York: Free Press, 1982.

———. 1897. *Suicide*. New York: Free Press, 1951.

Dykstra, Robert R. 1968. *The Cattle Towns*. New York: Knopf.

Eck, John E., and Edward R. Maguire. 2000. "Have Changes in Policing Reduced Violent Crime? An Assessment of the Evidence." In *The Crime Drop in America*, edited by Alfred Blumstein and Joel Wallman, 207–65. New York: Cambridge University Press.

Eckberg, Douglas Lee. 1995. "Estimates of Early Twentieth-Century U.S. Homicide Rates: An Econometric Forecasting Approach." *Demography* 32:1–16.

Elias, Norbert. 1978. *The Civilizing Process: The Development of Manners; Changes in the Code of Conduct and Feeling in Early Modern Times*. New York: Urizen Books.

———. 1989. *The Germans: Power Struggles and the Development of Habitus in the Nineteenth and Twentieth Centuries*. Cambridge: Polity Press.

Ellis, John. 1975. *The Social History of the Machine Gun*. New York: Pantheon Books.

Ellison, Christopher G. 1991. "An Eye for an Eye? A Note on the Southern Subculture of Violence Thesis." *Social Forces* 69:1223–39.

Emerson, Michael O., George Yancey, and Karen J. Chai. 2001. "Does Race Matter in Residential Segregation? Exploring the Preferences of White Americans." *American Sociological Review* 66:922–35.

Erwin, Brigette A., Elana Newman, Robert A. McMackin, Carlo Morrissey, and Danny G. Kaloupek. 2000. "PTSD, Malevolent Environment, and Criminality among Criminally Involved Male Adolescents." *Criminal Justice and Behavior* 27:196–216.

Esping-Anderson, Gosta. 1990. *The Three Worlds of Welfare Capitalism*. Princeton, NJ: Princeton University Press.

Etzioni, Amitai, and Richard Remp. 1973. *Technological Shortcuts to Social Change*. New York: Russell Sage.

Fagan, Jeffrey, and Ko-lin Chin. 1990. "Violence as Regulation and Social Control in the Distribution of Crack." In *Drugs and Violence: Causes, Correlates, and Consequences*, edited by Mario de la Rosa, Elizabeth Y. Lambert, and Bernard Gropper, 8–43. NIDA Research Monograph No. 103. Washington, DC: Government Printing Office.

Fagan, Jeffrey, Franklin E. Zimring, and June Kim. 1998. "Declining Homicide in New York City: A Tale of Two Trends." *Journal of Criminal Law & Criminology* 88:1277–1323.

Fainaru, Steve. 1992. "Barkley Is a Court Jester to the End." *Boston Globe*, August 9:52.

Falco, Mathea. 1994. *The Making of a Drug Free America*. New York: Times Books.

Farley, John E. 1987. "Disproportionate Black and Hispanic Unemployment in U.S. Metropolitan Areas." *American Journal of Economics and Sociology* 46:129–50.

Faupel, Charles. 1991. *Shooting Dope: Career Patterns of Hard Core Heroin Users.* Gainesville: University of Florida Press.

Featherman, David L., and Robert M. Hauser. 1978. *Opportunity and Change.* New York: Academic Press.

Federal Bureau of Investigation. 2001. *Crime in the United States, 1999,* at www.fbi.gov.

Federal Trade Commission. 2000. *Marketing Violent Entertainment to Children,* at www.ftc.gov.

Ferdinand, Theodore. 1967. "The Criminal Patterns of Boston since 1849." *American Journal of Sociology* 73:84–99.

Fiala, Robert, and Gary LaFree. 1988. "Cross-National Determinants of Child Homicide." *American Sociological Review* 53:432–45.

Fischer, David Hackett. 1989. *Albion's Seed: Four British Folkways in America.* New York: Oxford University Press.

Fisher, Joseph. 1976. "Homicide in Detroit: The Role of Firearms." *Criminology* 14:387–400.

Fitzpatrick, Kevin M. 1997. "Exposure to Violence and Presence of Depression among Low-Income African American Youth." *Journal of Consulting and Clinical Psychology* 61:528–31.

Fletcher, Jonathan. 1997. *Violence and Civilization: An Introduction to the Work of Norbert Elias.* Cambridge, England: Polity Press.

Florida Department of Corrections. 2000. *Time Served by Criminals Sentenced to Florida's Prisons: The Impact of Punishment Policies from 1979–1999,* at www.de.state.fl.us/pub/timeserv/annual/indes.

———. 2000a. *Florida Department of Corrections 1998–99 Annual Report: Budget,* at www.de.state.fl.us/pub/annual.

Foner, Eric. 1988. *Reconstruction: America's Unfinished Revolution, 1863–1877.* New York: Harper & Row.

Freedman, Jonathan L. 1988. "Television Violence and Aggression: What the Evidence Shows." In *Applied Social Psychology Annual: Television as a Social Issue, Vol. 8,* edited by S. Oskamp, 144–62. Newbury Park, CA: Sage.

———. 1994. "Viewing Television Violence Does Not Make People Aggressive." *Hofstra Law Review* 22:833–54.

French, Allen. 1925. *The Day of Concord and Lexington, the Nineteenth of April, 1775.* Boston: Little, Brown.

Frye, Northrop. 1986. *Northrop Frye on Shakespeare.* New Haven, CT: Yale University Press.

Fumento, Michael. 1998. "'Road Rage' versus Reality." *Atlantic Monthly,* August 1:1–13.

Garbarino, James. 1992. *Children in Danger: Coping with the Consequences of Community Violence.* New York: Jossey-Bass.

Gartner, Rosemary. 1990. "The Victims of Homicide: A Temporal and Cross-National Comparison." *American Sociological Review* 55:92–106.

Gastil, Raymond D. 1971. "Homicide and a Regional Culture of Violence." *American Sociological Review* 36:412–27.

Gatrell, V. A. C. 1994. *The Hanging Tree: Executions and the English People, 1770–1868.* New York: Oxford University Press.

Gelles, Richard J. 1997. *Intimate Violence in Families.* Thousand Oaks, CA: Sage.

Gibbons, Brian. 1980. "Introduction." In *The Arden Edition of the Works of William Shakespeare: Romeo and Juliet,* edited by B. Gibbons, 1–79. London: Methuen.

Gibson, Gregory. 1999. *Goneboy: A Walkabout.* New York: Kodansha International.

Given, Brian J. 1994. *A Most Pernicious Thing: Gun Trading and Native Warfare in the Early Contact Period.* Ottawa, Canada: Carleton University Press.

Givens, James B. 1977. *Society and Homicide in Thirteenth-Century England.* Stanford, CA: Stanford University Press.

Glassner, Barry. 1999. *The Culture of Fear.* New York: Basic Books.

Goldberg, Carey. 2000. "7 Die in Rampage at Company; Co-Worker of Victims Arrested." *New York Times,* National Edition, December 27, 1.

Goldstein, Paul J. 1985. "The Drugs/Violence Nexus: A Tripartite Conceptual Framework." *Journal of Drug Issues* 14:493–506.

Goldstein, Paul J., Henry H. Brownstein, Patrick J. Ryan, et al. 1989. "Crack and Homicide in New York City, 1988: A Conceptually Based Event Analysis." *Contemporary Drug Problems* 16:651–87.

Goldstein, Paul J., D. S. Lipton, E. Preble, et al. 1984. "The Marketing of Street Heroin in New York." *Journal of Drug Issues* 14:553–66.

Goode, Erich. 1989. *Drugs in American Society.* 3d ed. New York: Knopf.

Goode, William J. 1963. *World Revolution in Divorce Patterns.* New Haven, CT: Yale University Press.

———. 1993. *World Changes in Divorce Patterns.* New Haven, CT: Yale University Press.

Gorn, Elliott J. 1987. " 'Good-Bye Boys, I Die a True American': Homicide, Nativism, and Working Class Culture in Antebellum New York City." *Journal of American History* 74:388–410.

Gottschalk, Peter, Björn Gustafsson, and Edward Palmer. 1997. "What's Behind the Increase in Inequality? In *Changing Patterns in the Distribution of Economic Welfare,* edited by P. Gottschalk, B. Gustafsson, and E. Palmer, 1–11. Cambridge: Cambridge University Press.

Gray, James P. 2001. *Why Our Drug Laws Have Failed and What We Can Do About It.* Philadephia: Temple University Press.

Green, Edward, and Russell P. Wakefield. 1979. "Patterns of Middle and Upper Class Homicide." *Journal of Criminal Law and Criminology* 70:172–81.

Grogger, Jeff, and Michael Willis. 2000. "The Emergence of Crack Cocaine and the Rise in Urban Crime Rates." *Review of Economics and Statistics* 82:519–29.

Grossman, Dave. 1996. *On Killing: The Psychological Cost of Learning to Kill in War and Society.* New York: Little, Brown.

Grossman, Dave, and Bruce K. Siddle. 1999. "Psychological Effects of Combat." In *Encyclopedia of Violence, Peace, and Conflict, Vol. 3,* edited by L. Kurtz, 139–49. San Diego: Academic Press.

Groves, Betsy McAlister. 1997. "Growing up in a Violent World: The Impact of Family and Community Violence on Young Children and their Families." *Topics in Early Childhood Special Education* 17:74–101.

Guest, Avery M., Nancy S. Landale, and James C. McCann. 1989. "Intergenerational Occupational Mobility in the Late 19th Century United States." *Social Forces* 68:351–78.

Gurr, Ted Robert. 1989. "Historical Trends in Violent Crime: Europe and the United States." In *Violence in America, Vol. I,* edited by T. R. Gurr, 21–54. Newbury Park, CA: Sage.

Hackney, Sheldon. 1969. "Southern Violence." *American Historical Review* 74:906–25.

Hagedorn, John. 1998. *The Business of Drug Dealing in Milwaukee.* Titusville, WI: Wisconsin Policy Research Institute.

Hansmann, Henry B., and John M. Quigley. 1982. "Population Heterogeneity and the Suogenesis of Homicide." *Social Forces* 61:206–24.

Hargarten, S., T. A. Karlson, M. O'Brien, J. Hancock, and E. Quebbeman. 1996. "Characteristics of Firearms Involved in Fatalities." *Journal of the American Medical Association* 275:42–45.

Harris, Anthony R., Stephen H. Thomas, Gene A. Fisher, and David J. Hirsch. 2002. "Murder and Medicine: The Lethality of Criminal Assault 1960–1999." *Homicide Studies* 6:128–66.

Hawkins, Darnell F. 1999. "What Can We Learn from Data Disaggregation? The Case of Homicide and African Americans." In *Homicide: A Sourcebook of Social Research,* edited by M. D. Smith and M. A. Zahn, 195–210. Thousand Oaks, CA: Sage.

Hay, Richard, and Richard McCleary. 1979. "Box-Tiao Series Models for Impact Assessment." *Evaluation Quarterly* 3:277–314.

Heller, Joseph. 1961. *Catch-22: A Novel.* New York: Simon & Schuster.

Hemenway, David. 1997. "Survey Research and Self-Defense Gun Use: An Explanation of Extreme Overestimates." *Journal of Criminal Law and Criminology* 86:1430–45.

Hemenway, David, and Deborah Azrael. 2000. "The Relative Frequency of Offensive and Defensive Gun Uses: Results from a National Survey." *Violence and Victims* 15:257–72.

Hemenway, David, Tomoko Shinoda-Tagawa, and Mathew Miller. 2002. "Firearm Availability and Female Homicide Victimization Rates among 25 Populous High-Income Countries." *Journal of the American Medical Women's Association* 57:100–104.

Henry, Andrew F., and James F. Short. 1954. *Suicide and Homicide: Some Economic, Sociological, and Psychological Aspects of Aggression.* Glencoe, IL: Free Press.

Herbert, Bob. 2001. "Addicted to Guns." *New York Times,* National Edition, January 1, A19.

Himmelfarb, Gertrude. 1995. *The De-Moralization of Society.* New York: Knopf.

Hindus, Michael Stephen. 1980. *Prison and Plantation: Crime, Justice, and Authority in Massachusetts and South Carolina.* Chapel Hill: University of North Carolina Press.

Hoffman, Frederick L. 1925. *The Homicide Problem.* Newark, NJ: Prudential Press.

Hofstadter, Richard. 1970. "America as a Gun Culture." *American Heritage Magazine* 21:3–10, 82–85.

Holmes, William F. 1969. "Whitecapping: Agrarian Violence in Mississippi, 1902–1906." *Journal of Southern History* 35:165–85.

———. 1973. "Whitecapping in Mississippi: Agrarian Violence in the Populist Era." *Mid-America* 55:134–48.

Home Office. 2001. *Criminal Statistics, England and Wales 1999*, at www.official-documents.co.uk.

Huesmann, Rowell, Jessic Moise, Cheryl-Lynn Podolski, and Leonard Eron. 1998. "Longitudinal Relations between Children's Exposure to Television Violence and Their Later Aggressive and Violent Behavior in Young Adulthood, 1977–1992." Paper presented to the International Society for Research on Aggression.

Hutson, H. R., D. Anglin, D. N. Kyriacou, J. Hart, and K. Spears. 1995. "The Epidemic of Gang-Related Homicides in Los Angeles County from 1979 through 1994." *Journal of the American Medical Association* 274:1031–36.

Ianni, F. A. J. 1974. *Black Mafia: Ethnic Succession in Organized Crime*. New York: Simon & Schuster.

Inglehart, Ronald, and Wayne E. Baker. 2000. "Modernization, Cultural Change, and the Persistence of Traditional Values." *American Sociological Review* 65:19–51.

Intelligence and Security Committee. 2001. *Criminal Statistics in England and Wales, 1999*, at www.official-documents.co.uk.

Jacobs, Bruce. 2000. *Robbing Drug Dealers: Violence Beyond the Law*. Hawthorne, NY: Aldine de Gruyter.

Jacobs, David, and Katherine Wood. 1999. "Interracial Conflict and Interracial Homicide: Do Political and Economic Rivalries Explain White Killings of Blacks or Black Killings of Whites?" *American Journal of Sociology* 105:157–90.

James, Leon, and Diane Nahl. 2000. *Road Rage and Aggressive Driving: Steering Clear of Highway Warfare*. Amherst, NY: Prometheus Books.

Jankowski, Martín Sánchez. 1991. *Islands in the Street: Gangs and American Urban Society*. Berkeley: University of California Press.

Janoff-Bulman, Ronnie. 1992. *Shattered Assumptions: Toward a New Psychology of Trauma*. New York: Free Press.

———. 1997. "Understanding Reactions to Traumatic Events." *Harvard Mental Health Newsletter* 14(October):8.

Johnson, Bruce D., Paul J. Goldstein, Edward Preble, et al. 1985. *Taking Care of Business: The Economics of Crime by Heroin Abusers*. Lexington, MA: Lexington Books.

Johnson, Eric A., and Eric H. Monkkonen. 1996. "Introduction." In *The Civilization of Crime: Violence in Town and Country since the Middle Ages*, edited by E. A. Johnson and E. H. Monkkonen, 1–13. Urbana, IL: University of Illinois Press.

Johnson, Jeffrey G., Patricia Cohen, Elizabeth M. Smailes, et al. 2002. "Television Viewing and Aggressive Behavior During Adolescence and Adulthood." *Science* 295(March 29):2468–71.

Kandel, Denise B. 1993. "The Social Demography of Drug Use." In *Drug Policy*, edited by R. Bayer and G. M. Oppenheimer, 24–77. Cambridge: Cambridge University Press.

Kasarda, John D. 1988. "Jobs, Migration, and Emerging Urban Mismatches." In *Urban Change and Poverty*, edited by M. G. H. McGeary and L. E. Lynn, 148–98. Washington, DC: National Academy Press.

———. 1989. "Urban Industrial Transition and the Underclass." *Annals of the American Academy of Political and Social Science* 501:26–47.

————. 1995. "Industrial Restructuring and the Changing Location of Jobs." In *State of the Union: America in the 1990s, Vol. I,* edited by Reynolds Farley, 215–67. New York: Russell Sage Foundation.

Kates, Don, and Daniel D. Polsby. 2000. "The Long-Term Nonrelationship of Widespread and Increasing Firearm Availability to Homicide in the United States." *Homicide Studies* 4:185–201.

Kaye, J. M. 1967. "The Early History of Murder and Manslaughter." *Law Quarterly Review* 83:365–95.

Kellermann, Arther L., Frederick P. Rivara, Norman B. Rushford, et al. 1993. "Gun Ownership as a Risk Factor for Homicide in the Home." *New England Journal of Medicine* 329:1084–91.

Kennedy, Stetson. 1995. *After Appomattox: How the South Won the War.* Gainesville: University of Florida Press.

Kennett, Lee, and James LaVerne Anderson. 1975. *The Gun in America: The Origins of a National Dilemma.* Westport, CT: Greenwood Press.

Kifner, John. 1998. "From Wild Talk and Friendship to Five Deaths in a Schoolyard." *New York Times,* National Edition. March 29, p. A1.

Killias, Martin. 1993a. "Gun Ownership, Suicide, and Homicide: An International Perspective." In *Understanding Crime: Experiences of Crime and Crime Control,* edited by Anna A. del Frate, Ugljesa Zvekic, and Jan J. M. van Dijk, 289–302. Rome: United Nations Interregional Crime and Justice Research Institute.

————. 1993b. "International Correlations between Gun Ownership and Rates of Homicide and Suicide." *Canadian Medical Association Journal* 148:1721–26.

Kleck, Gary. 1991. *Point Blank: Guns and Violence in America.* New York: Aldine de Gruyter.

————. 1995. "Using Speculation to Meet Evidence: Reply to Alba and Messner." *Journal of Quantitative Criminology* 11:411–24.

————. 1997. *Targeting Guns: Firearms and Their Control.* New York: Aldine de Gruyter.

————. 1997a. "The Illegitimacy of One-Sided Speculation: Getting the Defensive Gun Use Estimate Down." *Journal of Criminal Law and Criminology* 87:1446–61.

Kohn, Melvin L. 1989. "Cross-National Research as an Analytic Strategy." In *Cross-National Research in Sociology,* edited by M. L. Kohn, 77–103. Newbury Park, CA: Sage.

Kopel, David B. 1992. *The Samurai, the Mountie, and the Cowboy: Should America Adopt the Gun Controls of Other Democracies?* New York: Prometheus Books.

Kotlowitz, Alex. 1991. *There Are No Children Here.* New York: Doubleday.

Kovandzic, Tomislav V., Lynn M. Vieraitis, and Mark R. Yeisley. 1998. "The Structural Covariates of Urban Homicide: Reassessing the Impact of Income Inequality and Poverty in the Post-Reagan Era." *Criminology* 36:569–99.

Kposowa, Augustine, and Kevin Breault. 1993. "Reassessing the Structural Covariates of U.S. Homicide Rates: A County Level Study." *Sociological Focus* 26:27–46.

Krahn, Harvey, Timothy F. Hartnagel, and John W. Gartrell. 1986. "Income Inequality and Homicide Rates: Cross-National Data and Criminological Theories." *Criminology* 24:269–95.

Krug, E. G., K. E. Powell, and L. I. Dahlberg. 1997. "Firearm-Related Deaths in the United States and 35 Other High- and Upper-Middle-Income Countries." *International Journal of Epidemiology* 27:214–21.

Kurtz, Demi. 1993. "Social Sciences Perspectives on Wife Abuse: Current Debates and Future Directions." In *Violence Against Women: The Bloody Footprints,* edited by P. Bart and E. G. Moran, 252–69. Newbury Park, CA: Sage.

Kuznets, Simon. 1985. *Modern Economic Growth.* Washington, DC: Brookings Institution.

Labi, Nadya. 2001. "Portrait of a Killer." *Time Magazine* 157(January 8):3–4.

LaFree, Gary. 1999. "A Summary and Review of Cross-National Comparative Studies of Homicide." In *Homicide: A Sourcebook of Social Research,* edited by M. D. Smith and M. A. Zahn, 125–45. Thousand Oaks, CA: Sage.

———. 1999a. "Declining Violent Crime Rates in the 1990s: Predicting Crime Booms and Busts." *Annual Review of Sociology* 25:145–68.

Lamm, Ruediger, Basil Psarianos, and Theodor Mailaender. 1999. *Highway Design and Traffic Safety Engineering Handbook.* New York: McGraw-Hill.

Land, Kenneth C., Patricia L. McCall, and Lawrence E. Cohen. 1990. "Structural Covariates of Homicide Rates: Are There Any Invariates across Time and Space?" *American Journal of Sociology* 95:922–63.

Lane, Roger. 1979. *Violent Death in the City: Suicide, Death, and Murder in Nineteenth Century Philadelphia.* Cambridge, MA: Harvard University Press.

———. 1997. *Murder in America: A History.* Columbus: Ohio State University Press.

Larson, Eric. 1993. "The Story of a Gun." *The Atlantic Monthly* (January):48–78.

———. 1994. *Lethal Passage: How the Travels of a Single Handgun Expose the Roots of America's Gun Crisis.* New York: Crown.

Lay, M. G. 1992. *Ways of the World: A History of the World's Roads and the Vehicles That Used Them.* New Brunswick, NJ: Rutgers University Press.

Lenski, Gerhard. 1966. *Power and Privilege.* New York: McGraw-Hill.

Lester, David. 1991. "Crime as Opportunity: A Test of the Hypothesis with European Homicide Rates." *British Journal of Criminology* 31:186–88.

Lester, David (ed.). 1994. *Emile Durkheim: Le Suicide One Hundred Years Later.* Philadelphia: Charles Press.

Lester, David, and Gene Lester. 1995. *Crime of Passion: Murder and the Murderer.* Chicago: Nelson-Hall.

Levitt, Steven D. 1996. "The Effect of Prison Population Size on Crime Rates: Evidence from Prison Overcrowding Litigation." *Quarterly Journal of Economics* 111:319–51.

Levitt, Steven D., and Sudhir Alladi Venkatesh. 2000. "An Economic Analysis of a Drug-Selling Gang's Finances." *Quarterly Journal of Economics* 115:755–75.

Lewis, Tom. 1997. *Divided Highways: Building the Interstate Highways, Transforming American Life.* New York: Viking.

Lewis Mumford Center. 2001. *Ethnic Diversity Grows, Neighborhood Integration Lags Behind.* Albany: Lewis Mumford Center at State University of New York.

Lindgren, James, and Justin Lee Heather. 2002. "Counting Guns in Early America." *William and Mary Law Review* 43:1777–1842.

Lipset, Seymour Martin. 1968. "History and Sociology: Some Methodological Considerations." In *Sociology and History: Methods,* edited by S. M. Lipset and R. Hofstadter, 20–58. New York: Basic Books.

———. 1990. *Continental Divide: The Values and Institutions of the United States and Canada.* New York: Routledge.

Lizotte, A. J., J. M. Tesoriero, T. P. Thornberry, and M. D. Krohn. 1994. "Patterns of Adolescent Firearms Ownership and Use." *Justice Quarterly* 16:51–73.

Loftin, Colin, and Robert H. Hill. 1974. "Regional Subculture and Homicide: An Examination of the Gastil-Hackney Thesis." *American Sociological Review* 39:714–24.

Loftin, Colin, David McDowall, and James Boudouris. 1989. "Economic Change and Homicide in Detroit, 1926–1979." In *Violence in America, Vol. I,* edited by T. R. Gurr, 163–77. Newbury Park, CA: Sage.

Loftin, Colin, David McDowall, Brian Wiersema, et al. 1991. "Effects of Restrictive Licensing of Handguns on Homicide and Suicide in the District of Columbia." *New England Journal of Medicine* 325(December 5):1615–20.

Lott, John, and David B. Mustard. 1997. "Crime, Deterrence, and Right-to-Carry Concealed Handguns." *Journal of Legal Studies* 26:1–68.

Lott, John R., Jr. 1998. *More Guns, Less Crime.* Chicago: University of Chicago Press.

———. 1998a. "The Concealed-Handgun Debate." *Journal of Legal Studies* 27:221–43.

———. 2000. "What Can We Do After Wakefield." *Boston Globe,* December 28, A15.

Lottier, Stuart. 1938. "Distribution of Criminal Offenses in Sectional Regions." *Journal of Criminal Law and Criminology* 39:329–44.

Ludwig, Jens. 1997. "Do Carry-Concealed Weapons Laws Deter Crime? No." *Spectrum: The Journal of State Government* 70:29–31.

———. 1998. "Concealed-Gun-Carrying Laws and Violent Crime: Evidence from State Panel Data." *International Review of Law and Economics* 18:239–54.

———. 1998a. "More Guns, Less Crime: Understanding Crime and Gun Control Laws (book review)." *Washington Monthly* 30(June):50–52.

Lyotard, François. 1984. *The Postmodern Condition.* Minneapolis: University of Minnesota Press.

Machlis, Joseph. 1955. *The Enjoyment of Music.* New York: Norton.

Mann, Charles C. 2002. "1491." *The Atlantic* (March):41–53.

Marshall, S. L. A. 1978. *Men Against Fire.* Gloucester, MA: Peter Smith.

Martin, Doug. 1999. "Teen Grieves for His Slain Uncle; Friend Accused in Nightclub Death." *Gainesville Sun,* January 9, B1.

Martinez, Ramiro, Jr., and Mathew T. Lee. 1999. "Extending Ethnicity in Homicide Research: The Case of Latinos." In *Homicide: A Sourcebook of Social Research,* edited by M. D. Smith and M. A. Zahn, 211–20. Thousand Oaks, CA: Sage.

Marvel, James E. 2000. "Would Prevention of Gun Carrying Reduce U.S. Homicide Rates?" (letter to the editor). *Journal of the American Medical Association* 284:1788.

Marvell, Thomas B., and Carlisle E. Moody. 1997. "The Impact of Prison Growth on Homicide." *Homicide Studies* 1:205–33.

Marx, Karl, and Friedrich Engels. 1848. *The Communist Manifesto*. London: Verso, 1998.

Massey, Douglas S. 1995. "Getting Away with Murder: Segregation and Violent Crime in Urban America." *University of Pennsylvania Law Review* 143:1203–32.

Massey, Douglas S., and Nancy A. Denton. 1993. *American Apartheid: Segregation and the Making of the Underclass*. Cambridge, MA: Harvard University Press.

Massey, Douglas S., and Mary J. Fischer. 2000. "How Segregation Concentrates Poverty." *Ethnic and Racial Studies* 23:670–91.

Mauer, Marc. 1997. *Americans Behind Bars: U.S. and International Use of Incarceration*. Washington, DC: The Sentencing Project.

Maxson, Cheryl L. 1999. "Gang Homicide: A Review and Extension of the Literature." In *Homicide: A Sourcebook of Social Research*, edited by M. D. Smith and M. A. Zahn, 239–54. Thousand Oaks, CA: Sage.

McBride, D. C. 1981. "Drugs and Violence." In *The Drug-Crime Connection*, edited by J. A. Inciardi, 105–24. Beverly Hills, CA: Sage.

McDowall, David. 1986. "Gun Availability and Robbery Rates: A Panel Study of Large U.S. Cities, 1974–1978." *Law and Policy* 8:135–48.

McDowall, David, Alan J. Lizotte, and Brian Wiersema. 1991. "General Deterrence through Civilian Gun Ownership: An Evaluation of the Quasi-experimental Evidence." *Criminology* 29:541–55.

McDowall, David, Colin Loftin, and Brian Wiersema. 1992. "A Comparative Study of the Preventive Effects of Mandatory Sentencing Laws for Gun Crimes." *Journal of Criminal Law & Criminology* 83:378–94.

———. 1995. "Easing Concealed Firearms Laws: Effects on Homicide in Three States." *Journal of Criminal Law & Criminology* 86:193–206.

———. 1996. "Comment on Britt et al.'s Reassessment of the D.C. Gun Law." *Law & Society Review* 30:381–91.

McGowen, Randall. 1991. "Firearm Availability and Homicide Rates in Detroit, 1951–1986." *Social Forces* 69:1085–1101.

———. 2000. "Revisiting the Hanging Tree: Gatrell on Emotion and History." *British Journal of Criminology* 40:1–13.

McGrath, Roger. 1989. "Violence and Lawlessness on the Western Frontier." In *Violence in America, Vol. I*, edited by T. R. Gurr, 122–45. Newbury Park, CA: Sage.

McKanna, Clare V. 1997. *Homicide, Race, and Justice in the American West, 1880–1920*. Tucson: University of Arizona Press.

McKeown, Thomas. 1976. *The Modern Rise of Population*. New York: Academic Press.

McPheters, Lee R., Robert Mann, and Don Schlagenfauf. 1984. "Economic Response to a Crime Deterrence Program." *Economic Inquiry* 22:550–70.

McWhorter, Diane. 2001. "The Way We Live Now." *New York Times Magazine*, July 29, p. 11.

Mendelsohn, Robert, William D. Nordhaus, and Daigee Shaw. 1994. "The Impact of Global Warming on Agriculture: A Ricardian Analysis." *American Economic Review* 84:753–71.

Merton, Robert K. 1968. *Social Theory and Social Structure*. New York: Free Press.

———. 1968a. "Social Structure and Anomie." In *Social Theory and Social Structure*, by R. K. Merton, 185–214. New York: Free Press.

————. 1973. "Structural Analysis in Sociology." In *Sociological Ambivalence and Other Essays,* by R. K. Merton, 109–44. New York: Free Press.

Messner, Steven F. 1980. "Income Inequality and Murder Rates: Some Cross-National Findings." *Comparative Social Research* 3:185–98.

————. 1986. "Poverty and Homicide in Detroit, 1926–1978." *Victims and Violence* 1:23–34.

————. 1989. "Economic Discrimination and Societal Homicide Rates: Further Evidence on the Cost of Inequality." *American Sociological Review* 54:597–611.

Messner, Steven F., and Richard Rosenfeld. 1991. *Crime and the American Dream.* Belmont, CA: Wadsworth.

————. 1997. *Crime and the American Dream.* 2d ed. Belmont, CA: Wadsworth.

————. 1997a. "Political Restraint of the Market and Levels of Criminal Homicide: A Cross-National Application of Institutional-Anomie Theory." *Social Forces* 75:1393–1416.

————. 2001. *Crime and the American Dream.* 3d ed. Belmont, CA: Wadsworth.

————. 2001a. "An Institutional-Anomie Theory of Crime." In *Explaining Criminals and Crime,* edited by Raymond Paternoster and Renet Bachman, 151–60. Los Angeles: Roxbury.

Miller, Mathew, Deborah Azrael, and David Hemenway. 2002. "Firearm Availability and Unintentional Firearm Deaths, Suicide, and Homicide among 1–14 Year Olds." *Journal of Trauma, Injury, Infection, and Critical Care* 52:267–75.

Miller, Ted R., and Mark A. Cohen. 1996. "Costs." In *The Textbook of Penetrating Trauma,* edited by Rao R. Ivatury and C. Gene Cayten. Baltimore, MD: Williams & Wilkins.

Mohr, James C. 1978. *Abortion in America: The Origins and Evolution of National Policy.* New York: Oxford University Press.

Monkkonen, Eric. 1981. *Police in Urban America, 1860–1920.* Cambridge, MA: Cambridge University Press.

————. 1989. "Diverging Homicide Rates: England and the United States, 1850–1875." In *Violence in America, Vol. I,* edited by T. R. Gurr, 80–101. Newbury Park, CA: Sage.

————. 2001. *Murder in New York City.* Berkeley, CA: University of California Press.

Muccigrosso, Robert. 1993. *Celebrating the New World: Chicago's Columbian Exposition of 1893.* Chicago: Ivan R. Dee.

Nadelman, Ethan. 1988. "The Case for Legalization." *The Public Interest* 92(Summer):3–31.

Nader, Ralph. 1965. *Unsafe at Any Speed: The Designed-in Dangers of the American Automobile.* New York: Grossman.

National Center for Health Statistics. 2000. *Deaths: Final Data for 1998.* National Vital Statistics Reports 48(no. 11). Washington, DC: U.S. Dept. of Health & Human Services.

————. 2000a. *Health, United States, 2000.* Washington, DC: U.S. Dept. of Health & Human Services.

————. 2001. *United States Life Tables, 1998.* National Vital Statistics Reports 48(no. 18). Washington, DC: U.S. Dept. of Health & Human Services.

National Injury Surveillance Unit. 1998. *Australian Injury Prevention Bulletin,* Issue 17, at www.flinders.edu.au.

National Institute of Justice. 1995. *Research Preview: Youth Violence, Guns, and Illicit Drug Markets*. Washington, DC: Government Printing Office.

———. 1996. *Victim Costs and Consequences: A New Look*. Washington, DC: Government Printing Office.

———. 2000. *Extent, Nature, and Consequences of Intimate Partner Violence*. Washington, DC: Government Printing Office.

———. 2001. *Reducing Gun Violence: The Boston Gun Project's Operation Ceasefire*. Washington, DC: Government Printing Office.

National Television Violence Study. 1996. *National Television Violence Study, Volume I*. Thousand Oaks, CA: Sage.

———. 1997. *National Television Violence Study, Volume II*. Studio City, CA: Mediascope.

———. 1998. *National Television Violence Study, Volume III*. Santa Barbara: University of California, Santa Barbara, Center for Communication and Social Policy.

Nisbett, Richard E., and Dov Cohen. 1996. *Culture of Honor: The Psychology of Violence in the South*. Boulder, CO: Westview.

O'Carroll, Patrick W., Colin Loftin, John B. Waller, et al. 1992. "Preventing Homicide: An Evaluation of the Efficacy of a Detroit Gun Ordinance." *American Journal of Public Health* 81:576–81.

Office of Juvenile Justice and Delinquency Prevention. 1999. *Promising Strategies to Reduce Gun Violence*. Washington, DC: Government Printing Office.

Office of National Drug Control Policy. 1994. *National Drug Control Strategy: Reclaiming Our Communities from Drugs and Violence*. Washington, DC: Government Printing Office.

Orr, Daniel. 1997. "Regulating Firearm Advertisements" (letter to the editor). *Journal of the American Medical Association* 278:701.

Ostrowski, James. 1989. *Thinking about Drug Legalization*. Washington, DC: Cato Institute.

Paik, Haejung, and George Comstock. 1994. "The Effects of Television Violence on Antisocial Behavior: A Meta-analysis." *Communication Research* 21:516–46.

Pampel, Fred, and Rosemary Gartner. 1995. "Age Structure, Socio-political Institutions, and National Homicide Rates." *European Sociological Review* 11:243–60.

Parker, Karen F., and Patricia L. McCall. 1999. "Structural Conditions and Racial Homicide Patterns: A Look at the Multiple Disadvantages in Urban Areas." *Criminology* 37:447–77.

Parker, Robert Nash. 1995. *Alcohol and Homicide*. Albany: State University of New York Press.

Patterson, Orlando, and Christopher Winship. 1999. "Boston's Police Solution." *New York Times*, National Edition. March 3, A23.

Petersilia, Joan. 2000. *When Prisoners Return to the Community: Political, Economic, and Social Consequences*. Washington, DC: National Institute of Justice.

Peterson, Ruth D., and William C. Bailey. 1991. "Felony Murder and Capital Punishment: An Examination of the Deterrence Question." *Criminology* 29:367–95.

Peterson, Ruth D., and Lauren J. Krivo. 1993. "Racial Segregation and Black Urban Homicide." *Social Forces* 71:1001–26.

Physician Leadership on National Drug Policy. 2000. *Position Paper on Drug Policy*. Providence, RI: Center for Alcohol and Addictions Studies, Brown University.

Pierce, Glenn L., and William J. Bowers. 1981. "The Bartley-Fox Gun Law's Short-Term Impact on Crime in Boston." *Annals of the American Academy of Political and Social Science* 455:120–45.

Piquero, Alex, and Nicole Leeper Piquero. 1998. "On Testing Institutional Anomie Theory with Varying Specifications." *Studies on Crime and Crime Prevention* 7:61–84.

Pollan, Michael. 1995. "How Pot Has Grown." *New York Times Magazine* (February 19):31–38.

Preble, Edward, and John J. Casey Jr. 1969. "Taking Care of Business: The Heroin Addict's Life on the Street." *International Journal of the Addictions* 4:145–69.

Reagan, Leslie. 1997. *When Abortion Was a Crime: Women, Medicine and the Law in the United States.* Berkeley: University of California Press.

Redfield, Horace V. 1880. *Homicide, North and South.* Philadelphia: J. B. Lippincott.

Redmond, Lynn. 1989. *Surviving: When Someone You Love Was Murdered.* Clearwater, FL: Psychological Consultation and Education Services.

Reed, John Shelton. 1993. *My Tears Spoiled My Aim, and Other Reflections on Southern Culture.* Columbia: University of Missouri Press.

Reidel, Marc. 1998. "Counting Homicides: A Case of Statistical Prestidigitation." *Homicide Studies* 2:206–19.

———. 1999. "Sources of Homicide Data: A Review and Comparison." In *Homicide: A Sourcebook of Social Research,* edited by M. D. Smith and M. A. Zahn, 78–95. Thousand Oaks, CA: Sage.

Reiss, Albert J., Jr., and Jeffrey A. Roth. 1993. *Understanding and Preventing Violence.* Washington, DC: National Academy Press.

Reuter, Peter. 1991. "On the Consequences of Toughness." In *Searching for Alternatives: Drug Control Policies in the United States,* edited by M. B. Krauss and E. Lazear, 138–65. Stanford, CA: Hoover Institution Press.

Reuter, Peter, Robert MacCoun, and Patrick Murphy. 1990. *Money from Crime: A Study of the Economics of Drug Dealing in Washington, D.C.* Santa Monica, CA: Rand Corporation.

Rhodes, Richard. 1999. *Why They Kill: The Discoveries of a Maverick Criminologist.* New York: Knopf.

Riddle, Amanda. 2001. "Brazill Convicted of Second-Degree Murder, Assault in Teacher Slaying." *South Florida Sun-Sentinel,* May 16, 1.

Ritakallio, Veli-Matti. 2001. "Trends in Poverty and Income Inequality in Cross-National Comparison." Luxembourg Income Study Working Paper No. 272, at lisweb.ceps.lu/publications/wpapers.htm.

Robertson, Leon S. 1981. "Automobile Safety Regulations and Death Reductions in the United States." *American Journal of Public Health* 71:818–22.

Robinson, Thomas N., Marta L. Wilde, Lisa Navracruz, et al. 2001. "Effects of Reducing Children's Television and Video Game Use on Aggressive Behavior." *Archives of Pediatrics and Adolescent Medicine* 155:17–23.

Rose, Harold M., and Paula D. McClain. 1990. *Race, Place, and Risk: Black Homicide in Urban America.* Albany: State University of New York Press.

———. 1998. "Race, Place, and Risk Revisited." *Homicide Studies* 2:101–29.

Rosenberg, Nathan, and L. E. Birdsell, Jr. 1990. "Science, Technology, and the Western Miracle." *Scientific American* 263(November):42–54.

Rosenfeld, Richard. 2000. "Patterns in Adult Homicide: 1980–1995." In *The Crime Drop in America,* edited by A. Blumstein and J. Wallman, 130–64. New York: Cambridge University Press.

Roth, Randolph. 2001. "Homicide in Early Modern England, 1549–1800." *Crime, History, and Societies* 5:33–68.

———. 2002. "Guns, Gun Culture, and Homicide: The Relationship between Firearms, the Uses of Firearms, and Interpersonal Violence." *The William and Mary Quarterly* 59:223–40.

Rule, James B. 1978. *Insight and Social Betterment.* New York: Oxford University Press.

Russell, Carl P. 1975. *Guns on the Early Frontiers.* Berkeley: University of California Press.

Sagan, Carl. 1983. "Nuclear War and Climatic Catastrophe: Some Policy Implications." *Foreign Affairs* 62:257–95.

Saltzman, Linda E., James A. Mercy, Patrick W. O'Carroll, et al. 1992. "Weapon Involvement and Injury Outcomes in Family and Intimate Assaults." *Journal of the American Medical Association* 267:3043–48.

Sanders, William. 1994. *Gangbangs and Drive-Bys: Grounded Culture and Juvenile Gang Violence.* New York: Aldine de Gruyter.

Sarvesvaran, R., and C. H. S. Jaywardene. 1995. "The Role of the Weapon in the Homicide Drama." *Medicine and Law* 4:315–26.

Sassen-Koob, Saskia. 1989. "New York's Informal Economy." In *The Informal Economy: Studies in Advanced and Less Advanced Countries,* edited by A. Portes, M. Castells, and L. A. Benton, 60–77. Baltimore, MD: Johns Hopkins Press.

Savolainen, Jukka. 2000. "Inequality, Welfare State, and Homicide: Further Support for the Institutional Anomie Theory." *Criminology* 38:1021–42.

Schiraldi, Vincent, Jason Ziedenberg, and John Irwin. 1999. *America's One Million Nonviolent Prisoners.* Washington, DC: Justice Policy Institute.

Schumpeter, Joseph A. 1954. *A History of Economic Analysis.* New York: Oxford University Press.

Shannon, Lyle. 1954. "The Spatial Distribution of Criminal Offenses by States." *Journal of Criminal Law and Criminology* 45:264–73.

Sharpe, James A. 1996. "Crime in England: Long-term Trends and the Problem of Modernization." In *The Civilization of Crime: Violence in Town and Country since the Middle Ages,* edited by E. A. Johnson and E. H. Monkkonen, 17–34. Urbana: University of Illinois Press.

Shaw, Clifford R., and Henry D. McKay. 1942. *Juvenile Delinquency and Urban Areas.* Chicago: University of Chicago Press.

Shenk, Joshua Wolf. 1995. "Why You Can Hate Drugs and Still Want to Legalize Them." *The Washington Monthly* 27(October): 32–40.

Sherman, Lawrence W., and Dennis P. Rogan. 1995. "The Effect of Gun Seizures on Gun Violence: Hot Spot Patrol in Kansas City." *Justice Quarterly* 12:673–94.

Sherman, Lawrence W., James W. Shaw, and Dennis P. Rogan. 1995. *The Kansas City Gun Experiment.* Research in Brief. Washington, DC: National Institute of Justice.

Shihadeh, Edward S., and Nicole Flynn. 1996. "Segregation and Crime: The Effect of Black Social Isolation on the Rates of Black Urban Homicide." *Social Forces* 74:1325–52.

Shihadeh, Edward S., and Michael O. Maume. 1997. "Segregation and Crime: The Relationship between Black Centralization and Urban Black Homicide." *Homicide Studies* 1:254–80.

Sieber, Sam. 1981. *Fatal Remedies: The Ironies of Social Intervention.* New York: Plenum Press.

Simon, David. 1991. *Homicide: A Year on the Killing Streets.* New York: Ballantine.

Simon, David, and Edward Burns. 1997. *The Corner: A Year in the Life of an Inner-City Neighborhood.* New York: Broadway Books.

Sloan, Henry D., Arthur Kellerman, Donald T. Reav, et al. 1988. "Handgun Regulations, Crime, Assaults, and Homicide: A Tale of Two Cities." *New England Journal of Medicine* 319:1256–62.

Smith, Charles, and Terrence P. Thornberry. 1995. "The Relationship between Childhood Maltreatment and Adolescent Involvement in Delinquency." *Criminology* 33:451–81.

Soll, Rick. 1993. "The Killing Fields." *Chicago Magazine* (March):54–59, 97–99.

Soltow, Lee. 1975. *Men and Wealth in the United States, 1850–1975.* New Haven, CT: Yale University Press.

Sorenson, Susan B., Julie G. Peterson Manz, and Richard A. Berk. 1998. "News Media Coverage and the Epidemiology of Homicide." *American Journal of Public Health* 88:1510–14.

Spellman, William. 2000. "The Limited Importance of Prison Expansion." In *The Crime Drop in America,* edited by A. Blumstein and J. Wallman, 97–129. New York: Cambridge University Press.

Spitzer, Robert J. 1998. *The Politics of Gun Control.* 2d ed. New York: Chatham House.

Stinchcombe, Arthur. 1975. "Merton's Theory of Social Structure." In *The Idea of Social Structure,* edited by Lewis Coser, 11–34. New York: Free Press.

Stone, J. L., T. Lichtor, L. F. Fitzgerald, J. A. Barnett, H. M. Reyes. 1995. "Demographics of Civilian Cranial Gunshot Wounds: Devastation Related to Escalating Semiautomatic Usage." *Journal of Trauma* 38:851–54.

Stone, Lawrence. 1965. *The Crisis of the Aristocracy, 1558–1641.* Oxford: Clarendon Press.

———. 1983. "Interpersonal Violence in English Society 1300–1980." *Past and Present* 101:22–33.

Straus, Murray A., Richard Gelles, and Susanne Steinmetz. 1980. *Behind Closed Doors.* Garden City, NY: Doubleday Anchor.

Sullivan, Mercer L. 1989. *Getting Paid: Youth, Crime, and Work in the Inner City.* Ithaca, NY: Cornell University Press.

Swidler, Ann. 1986. "Culture in Action." *American Sociological Review* 51:273–86.

Swirko, Cindy. 1999. "Homicides Soaring." *Gainesville Sun,* August 5, B1.

Tenner, Edward. 1996. *Why Things Bite Back: Technology and the Revenge of Unintended Consequences.* New York: Knopf.

Teret, Stephen P., Susan DeFrancesco, Stephen W. Hargarten, and Krista D. Robinson. 1998. "Making Guns Safer." *Issues in Science and Technology* 14:37–41.

Teret, Stephen P., Daniel W. Webster, Jon S. Vernick, et al. 1998a. "Support for New Policies to Regulate Firearms." *New England Journal of Medicine* 339:813–18.

Thomas, William I., and Dorothy Swaine Thomas. 1928. *The Child in America.* New York: Knopf.

Thompson, Starley L., and Stephen H. Schneider. 1986. "Nuclear Winter Reappraised." *Foreign Affairs* 64:981–1006.

Thornton, Russell. 1987. *American Indian Holocaust and Survival: A Population History since 1492.* Norman: University of Oklahoma Press.

———. 2001. "Trends among American Indians in the United States." In *America Becoming: Racial Trends and Their Consequences, Vol. I,* edited by Neil Smelser, William Julius Wilson, and Faith Mitchell, 135–69. Washington, DC: National Academy Press.

Tiende, Marta. 1989. "Puerto Ricans and the Underclass Debate." *Annals of the American Academy of Political and Social Science* 501:105–19.

Tolnay, Stewart E., and E. M. Beck. 1995. *A Festival of Violence: An Analysis of Southern Lynchings, 1882–1930.* Urbana: University of Illinois Press.

Tolnay, Stewart E., E. M. Beck, and James L. Massey. 1992. "Black Competition and White Vengeance: Legal Execution of Blacks as Social Control in the American South." *Social Science Quarterly* 73:627–44.

Transportation Research Board. 1987. *Relationship between Safety and Key Highway Features.* Washington, DC: National Research Council.

Trelease, Allen W. 1971. *White Terror: The Ku Klux Klan Conspiracy and Southern Reconstruction.* New York: Harper & Row.

Tucher, Andie. 1994. *Froth & Scum: Truth, Beauty, and the Ax Murder in America's First Mass Medium.* Chapel Hill: University of North Carolina Press.

Turner, Frederick Jackson. 1920. *The Significance of the Frontier in American History.* New York: Henry Holt.

Turner, Jonathan H. 1997. *The Institutional Order.* New York: Addison Wesley Longman.

Turner, Jonathan H., Leonard Beeghley, and Charles Powers. 2002. *The Emergence of Sociological Theory.* 5th ed. Belmont, CA: Wadsworth.

Turner, Jonathan H., and David W. Musick. 1985. *American Dilemmas: Sociological Interpretations of Enduring Social Issues.* New York: Columbia University Press.

United Nations. 1998. *International Study on Firearm Regulation.* New York: United Nations.

———. 2000. United Nations Crime and Justice Information Network, at www.uncjin.org.

United States Bureau of the Census. 1975. *Historical Statistics of the United States.* Washington, DC: Government Printing Office.

———. 1980. *The Social and Economic Status of the Black Population in the United States: An Historical View.* Current Population Reports, Series P-23, No. 80. Washington, DC: Government Printing Office.

United States Department of Health & Human Services. 2001. *Summary of Findings from the 2000 National Household Survey on Drug Abuse.* Washington, DC: Government Printing Office.

———. 2001a. *Child Maltreatment, 1999.* Washington, DC: Government Printing Office.

United States Department of Transportation. 1985. *National Traffic and Motor Vehicle Safety Act of 1966: Legislative History.* Washington, DC: Government Printing Office.

United States Sentencing Commission. 1995. *Special Report to the Congress: Cocaine and Federal Sentencing Policy.* Washington, DC: Government Printing Office.

Unnithan, N. Prabda, Lynn Huff-Corzine, Jay Corzine, and Hugh P. Whitt. 1994. *The Currents of Lethal Violence.* Albany: State University of New York Press.

van der Kolk, Bessel A., Alexander C. McFarlane, and Lars Weisaeth (eds.). 1996. *Traumatic Stress: The Effects of Overwhelming Experience on Mind, Body, and Society.* New York: Guilford Press.

van Dijk, Jan J. M., Pat Mayhew, and Martin Killias. 1990. *Experiences of Crime Across the World: Key Findings from the 1989 International Crime Survey.* Boston: Kluwer Law and Taxation Publishers.

Vandal, Gilles. 2000. *Rethinking Southern Violence: Homicide in Post–Civil War Louisiana, 1866–1884.* Columbus: Ohio State University Press.

Venkatesh, Sudhir Alladi. 1996. "The Gang and the Community." In *Gangs in America,* 2d ed., edited by C. Ronald Huff, 241–56. Thousand Oaks, CA: Sage.

Verhovek, Sam Howe. 1998. "A Grieving, Shattered Town Asks, Who Are These Boys?" *New York Times,* National Edition. March 26, A1.

———. 1998a. "In Arkansas Jail, One Boy Cries and the Other Studies the Bible." *New York Times,* National Edition. March 27, A1.

Vernick, Jon S., and Stephen P. Teret. 2000. "A Public Health Approach to Regulating Firearms as Consumer Products." *University of Pennsylvania Law Review* 148:1993–2008.

Vernick, Jon S., Stephen P. Teret, and Daniel W. Webster. 1997. "Regulating Firearm Advertisements That Promise Home Protection: A Public Health Intervention." *Journal of the American Medical Association* 277:1391–98.

Vinson, T. 1974. "Gun and Knife Attacks." *Australian Journal of Forensic Science* 7:76–83.

Violence Policy Center. 2000. *When Men Murder Women: An Analysis of 1998 Homicide Data,* at www.vpc.org.

Voyles, Karen. 1999. "First Homicide of '99 Occurs Outside Club." *Gainesville Sun,* January 2, A1.

Waller, Patricia. 2002. "Challenges in Motor Vehicle Safety." *Annual Review of Public Health* 23:93–113.

Weber, Max. 1904. "'Objectivity' in Social Science and Social Policy." In *The Methodology of the Social Sciences,* by M. Weber, 49–112. New York: Free Press, 1949.

———. 1905. *The Protestant Ethic and the Spirit of Capitalism.* 3d Roxbury ed. Los Angeles: Roxbury, 1998.

———. 1913. *Religion of China.* New York: Free Press, 1951.

———. 1917. *Religion of India.* New York: Free Press, 1952.

———. 1918. "Science as a Vocation." In *From Max Weber: Essays in Sociology,* edited by Hans Gerth and C. Wright Mills, 129–58. New York: Oxford University Press, 1947.

———. 1920. *General Economic History.* Glencoe, IL: Free Press, 1950.

Webster, Daniel, Jon S. Vernick, and Lisa M. Hepburn. 2002. "Effects of Maryland's

Law Banning 'Saturday Night Special' Handguns on Homicides." *American Journal of Epidemiology* 155:406–12.

Weil, Douglas S. 1996. "Effectiveness of Legislation Limiting Handgun Purchases" (reply to letter to the editor). *Journal of the American Medical Association* 276:1036–37.

Weil, Douglas S., and Rebecca C. Knox. 1996. "Effects of Limiting Handgun Purchases on Interstate Transfer of Firearms." *Journal of the American Medical Association* 275:1759–62.

Weller, S. C. 1993. "A Meta-analysis of Condom Effectiveness in Reducing Sexually Transmitted HIV." *Social Science and Medicine* 36:1635–44.

Welsh-Ovcharov, Bogomila. 1974. *Van Gogh in Perspective.* Englewood Cliffs, NJ: Prentice-Hall.

Welten, D. C., H. C. G. Kemper, G. B. Post, and W. A. van Staveren. 1995. "A Meta-Analysis of the Effect of Calcium Intake on Bone Mass in Young and Middle Aged Females and Males." *Journal of Nutrition* 125:2802–13.

Widon, Cathy S. 1992. *The Cycle of Violence.* Research in Brief. Washington, DC: U.S. Department of Justice.

Widon, Cathy S., and Michael G. Maxfield. 2001. *An Update on the "Cycle of Violence."* Research in Brief. Washington, DC: U.S. Department of Justice.

Williams, Lou Falkner. 1996. *The Great South Carolina Ku Klux Klan Trials, 1871–1872.* Athens: University of Georgia Press.

Williams, Terry M. 1990. *The Cocaine Kids: The Inside Story of a Teenage Drug Ring.* Reading, MA: Addison Wesley.

Wilson, William Julius. 1996. *When Work Disappears.* New York: Random House.

Winship, Christopher, and Jenny Berrien. 1999. "Boston Cops and Black Churches." *The Public Interest* 136(Summer):52–68.

Wintemute, Garen J. 1987. "Firearms as a Cause of Death in the United States, 1920–1982." *Journal of Trauma* 27:532–36.

———. 1994. *Ring of Fire: The Handgun Makers of Southern California.* Sacramento, CA: Violence Prevention Research Program.

———. 1996. "The Relationship Between Firearm Design and Firearm Violence." *Journal of the American Medical Association* 275:1749–53.

Wintemute, Garen J., Carrie J. Parham, Mona A. Wright, et al. 1998. "Weapons of Choice: Previous Criminal History, Later Criminal Activity, and Firearms Preference among Legally Authorized Young Adult Purchasers of Handguns." *Journal of Trauma* 44:155–60.

Wolfe, Thomas. 1936. *The Story of a Novel.* New York: Charles Scribner's Sons.

Wolff, Edward N. 2001. *Top Heavy: The Increasing Inequality of Wealth in America and What Can Be Done about It.* New York: New Press.

Wolfgang, Marvin E., and Franco Ferracuti. 1967. *The Subculture of Violence.* New York: Tavistock Publications.

Worden, J. William. 1991. *Grief Counseling and Grief Therapy.* New York: Springer.

World Almanac Books. 2000. *World Almanac and Book of Facts, 2000.* New York: Primedia Reference.

World Health Organization. 2000. *1997–1999 World Health Statistics Annual,* at www.who.int/whosis.

Yeats, William Butler. 1933. *Collected Poems*. New York: Macmillan.

Zahn, Margaret A. 1989. "Homicide in the Twentieth Century: Trends, Types, and Causes." In *Violence in America, Vol. I*, edited by T. R. Gurr, 216–34. Newbury Park, CA: Sage.

Zahn, Margaret A., and Patricia I. McCall. 1999. "Trends and Patterns of Homicide in the 20th-Century United States." In *Homicide: A Sourcebook of Social Research*, edited by M. D. Smith and M. A. Zahn, 9–26. Thousand Oaks, CA: Sage.

Zangrando, Robert L. 1980. *The NAACP Crusade Against Lynching, 1909–1950*. Philadelphia: Temple University Press.

Zillman, Dolf, and James B. Weaver III. 1999. "Effects of Prolonged Exposure to Gratuitous Media Violence on Provoked and Unprovoked Hostile Behavior." *Journal of Applied Social Psychology* 29:145–65.

Zimring, Franklin E. 1972. "The Medium Is the Message: Firearms Caliber as a Determinant of Death from Assault." *Journal of Legal Studies* 1:97–123.

Zimring, Franklin E., and Gordon Hawkins. 1997. *Crime Is Not the Problem: Lethal Violence in America*. New York: Oxford University Press.

Zingraff, Mathew T., Jeffrey Leiter, Kristen A. Myers, et al. 1993. "Child Maltreatment and Youthful Problem Behavior." *Criminology* 31:173–202.

# Index

215

# About the Author

Leonard Beeghley is professor of sociology at the University of Florida. He is the author of six previous books, among them *Living Poorly in America* (1983), *What Does Your Wife Do? Gender and the Transformation of Family Life* (1996), *The Structure of Stratification in the United States* (3rd edition, 2000), and *The Emergence of Sociological Theory*, with Jonathan H. Turner and Charles Powers (5th edition, 2002).